THE SECRET
MAGISTRATE

HAWKSMOOR
PUBLISHING

First published 2020 by Hawksmoor Publishing

Kemp House, 152-160 City Rd, London, EC1V 2NX

www.hawksmoorpublishing.com

ISBN: 978-1-8380990-0-8

This book is dedicated to my partner, the rest of my family,
both two- and four-legged, and to everyone –
district judges, lawyers, legal advisers, list callers, defendants,
witnesses and fellow magistrates – who has provided
the inspiration for this book.

CONTENTS

FOREWORD

The volunteer magistrate, unpaid and not legally qualified, represents the community in the justice system. They represent a commitment to public service that is a very British value. That service has been offered for over 650 years and their courts were until recently a very visible sign of an accessible, public, open justice system through local courthouses.

Magistrates don't hide their job away; they are proud of the role they perform and their communities know who they are and what they do. Or do they?

I was a magistrate for 30 years until 2018 and never ceased to be surprised by the lack of understanding of their appointment process, role, responsibilities, powers and constraints. Most perceive them only vaguely through the reporting in the tabloids of either an allegedly lax sentence (almost certainly without the reporter being anywhere near the relevant courtroom, or perhaps any other, and who certainly hasn't bothered to understand the circumstances of the case), or a high-profile case that has been heard by a District Judge, mistakenly called "the magistrate". Sadly, successive governments of all colours and persuasions have used this to attack, undermine, devalue and demoralise the institution.

This fascinating and highly readable book gives unique insight into all aspects of the work of criminal magistrates and their court and the satisfaction and frustration derived from working in it. To my knowledge, it is unprecedented in its range and detail. To the lay reader (and many who appear professionally in a magistrates' court), it will demonstrate the breadth of matters that come before the entry tier of the criminal court system and how they are handled. These may only fleetingly include alleged murders, rapists and robbers – but the pages can definitely still claim "all human life is here". Readers will see why justice must always have a human face, and how much care, concern and dedication is expended in trying to do the right thing by society when dealing with increasing numbers from whom most in that society would prefer to turn away and see them as someone else's problem.

If it causes some readers to inquire more about the magistracy and even consider applying to join its ranks then that is all to the good. One of the principal claims to an ongoing central role in the justice system is that the magistracy must be able to demonstrate that it is indeed representative of the communities it serves – age, gender, ethnicity, sexual orientation, socio-economic group, educational achievement – all must be included in the search for the best people to do the job. That's not to say that a defendant, witness or victim should expect to see someone like them on the bench in front of them – that's neither possible nor desirable. All members of the judiciary must be scrupulously fair and even-handed in their administration of the law, and continually trained to ensure they keep that perspective. It is all of society's job to ensure that everyone feels they will be fairly treated in any court in England and Wales they are called before, irrelevant of the make-up of the particular tribunal. The magistracy, unique in its size, powers and unparalleled history will only deserve to survive if it has the authority and public confidence that comes from that diversity.

Perhaps, having read this book, more people will feel it right to ask the Ministry of Justice why they allowed the defenestration of such a great institution to occur. There is still time to rebuild it, though in the aftermath of the pandemic (assuming we can even be confident we have now reached the aftermath), there will be all too many excuses to duck the challenge.

Malcolm Richardson OBE

Chair, Magistrates Association, 2015-17

INTRODUCTION

I have been a magistrate for several years now, and sit regularly in an inner-city courthouse. Every criminal prosecution – large or small – starts its journey in a magistrates' court, and the overwhelming majority end there too. In 2019, my 14,000 or so colleagues and I dealt with almost 1.4 million cases. We are truly at the coalface of English justice. It is a role that I take great pride in, and enormously seriously, and I work as hard as I can to improve my overall knowledge and competence.

As a result, I always take a keen interest in articles, blogs, and books on our Criminal Justice System. When, in early 2018, I heard on the grapevine about the imminent publication of a book by a renowned legal blogger – The Secret Barrister – who was telling it 'as it is' about the law and how it is broken, I was one of the first in line to buy a copy.

As I turned the pages of this coruscating, witty, and forensically researched polemic – spellbound and increasingly bemused and angry as more and more desperate stories unfolded about the iniquities and unfairness of the system, the drastic and draconian cuts to the Ministry of Justice budgets, court closures, and the decimation of the right to legal aid, amongst many others – I found myself simultaneously nodding in agreement and shaking my head in anger and disbelief at the carnage that was being unveiled.

To a degree, I had already seen some evidence of the decay even when sitting in a magistrates' court: the ever-increasing number of litigants in person deprived of legal aid and professional assistance, the number of cases delayed by court papers not being emailed to lawyers in advance, the late or total non-disclosure of evidence to the defence, behind the scenes foul-ups, lack of court staff, and even the broken down and unrepaired lifts, but nothing really prepared me for the devastating level of detail and vituperative attack that emerged in that book.

I came to Chapter 2, intriguingly titled "The Wild West: The Magistrates' Court", and so engrossed was I at the prospect of discovering so many new things that I decided to leave reading this until the end; after all, I thought I had a pretty good handle on magistrates and the job that we do, after the years of service that I had already put in.

By the time that I was ready to return to that chapter, my knowledge and level of understanding of the Criminal Justice System, and its alleged shortcomings, were significantly greater than when I began. I was enormously grateful to whoever The Secret Barrister is for lifting the lid on so many issues that – in his or her opinion – predicated against a smooth running and in some cases, perhaps even fair, courts system.

The Secret Barrister writes beautifully, and I was soon drawn into the stories recounted from his or her own dreadfully frustrating experiences in the magistrates' courts, and I quickly found myself recoiling and questioning myself. Did I recognise the litany of incompetence, ignorance, and sheer pig-headedness outlined within this chapter, which contained a forensic and detailed (albeit often hilarious) attack on every aspect of our being? Attention was drawn in particular to our apparent age, lack of diversity, lack of formal legal qualifications, our slowness, and amateurism.

Wait, there's more.

We were also seen as unrepresentative of those we judge,

naïve, poorly recruited, inadequately trained, out of touch, and unable to grasp or interpret much of the evidence presented before us. We also didn't understand fundamental legal points, judgments, and principles. Our very purpose and existence were put under the microscope and into serious question.

The attitude towards us and our capabilities was perhaps best summed up by The Secret Barrister's description of a bench's impartiality and judgement as, "You're normally facing a combination of General Melchett starting Captain Blackadder's trial by commanding, 'Pass me the black cap, I'll be needing that,' and Alan Partridge suggesting to a lawyer interviewee that 'with the greatest respect, the police are hardly likely to arrest a man if he's innocent, are they?'"

I finished the chapter with my head reeling and blood boiling, and I threw the book down with some force, feeling that I had been subjected to a succession of body blows – some decidedly below the belt. My first reactions were anger, frustration, and disbelief at how inaccurate, out-dated and indeed, patronising I found some of the accusations and generalisations, given how dedicated, hard-working, experienced, sensitive, skilful and prepared so many of my JP colleagues are. I could barely prevent myself from biting back.

When I eventually calmed down and thought about matters more rationally, and less emotively, I realised that I found it ever so strange and hard to reconcile that the author could be so devastatingly accurate about much of the Criminal Justice System... with the sole exception of the magistracy. How could he or she have got it so wrong about us?

Then it finally struck me; perhaps The Secret Barrister is correct about us after all? I wondered what other evidence I would find about the value and future of the magistracy.

It did not take me long to find more criticism, when in a blog post from the 19th of August 2015 The Secret Barrister proposed – as the adopted motto of much magistrates' court justice – the decree of the Queen of Hearts when presiding over the trial involving the stolen tarts, "Sentence first – verdict afterwards".

I discovered much vitriol elsewhere on the Internet with magistrates widely described as a "waste of space" and the "three wise monkeys" or worse. In turn, please forgive me if I did not laugh when I read that hoary old chestnut of the collective name for a bench of magistrates – *a miscarriage of justices*.

Thankfully, there were far more serious information and insights to be gleaned from reports such as Sir Robin Auld's *Review of the Criminal Courts of England and Wales* in 2001, the Ministry of Justice's 2013 research on *The Strengths and Skills of the Judiciary in the Magistrates' Court*, and the Leveson *Review of Efficiency in Criminal Proceedings* in 2015 which provided a far more balanced view of the magistracy and its benefits – and its shortcomings too.

I thought about the best way to proceed, and decided to just let the public, and indeed myself, make up their minds for themselves. I would simply record a year or so in the life of an ordinary inner-city magistrate and describe exactly what we do and how we do it. I'd discuss our recruitment, training, and assessment, and also outline all the obstacles, dilemmas, problems, and issues that we face, and have to deal with every day in the courtroom.

I would be entirely open, truthful and honest and not gild the lily or gloss over difficult subjects, although in order to protect both the innocent and the guilty, I would need to change all names and places as well as any facts that would help to identify court users on both sides of the bench. All opinions expressed in what follows are, of course, mine and mine alone, and do not represent those of anybody else within or outside the system.

The final chapter of the book attempts to sum up my, perhaps changed, views of the magistracy and its future and to what extent I agree with some of the criticism I have outlined previously. Hopefully, I might even persuade some of those reading this book to consider becoming magistrates themselves.

So, here we go, come and read about justice at the sharp end – arise *The Secret Magistrate*.

1. YOU F***ER

Today is breach court day when the probation service prosecutes defendants charged with failing to comply with the requirements of their community or suspended sentence orders.

There is always a packed court list, and today is no exception with 28 cases down for us to deal with. The reality, however, is generally not so daunting.

By their very nature, we are dealing with people who are accused of disregarding court orders, so for defendants to get to court by 9.30 am for a 10 o'clock start is far beyond the wit, capacity, organisational ability and sometimes even desire of many of them, who straggle in throughout the day, or simply fail to turn up at all. Their absence or tardiness is eventually recognised with a warrant without bail being issued against them, which means that they will be arrested and kept in custody until their next court appearance. Last year, 70,000 such warrants were issued across England and Wales.

I am the bench chair – or presiding justice as we were recently renamed – a pompous and clunky, albeit gender-neutral, title that neither resonates with me, nor trips easily off the tongue. That means that I sit in the middle and play a speaking role in court, but I am not in charge, as we are all equal and every decision is made after consultation with my colleagues.

It is a bench of only two magistrates today rather than the customary three, something that happens far too frequently nowadays with the ongoing problems of magistrate recruitment and availability, subjects that we will return to later. That means that the two of us ideally need to be singing

11

from the same song sheet, as we will obviously be unable to come to a majority decision.

My colleague, Fran, is a newly-appointed magistrate who, on meeting for the first time, surprises and disconcerts me by mentioning that she saw me in action when she was doing her court observations recently, and that she considers me to have been "soft" in my sentencing.

I grit my teeth and smile warmly and welcomingly at her, whilst hiding and controlling my true feelings, which are far less charitable. I mention that every case is different and that there are very often mitigating factors to take into account which mean that the most severe sentences available to us need not necessarily be applied.

We discuss the mechanics of the breach court where the prosecutor outlines specifically what it is alleged the defendant has failed to do. This typically takes the form of not turning up for probation supervision appointments or unpaid work, or failing to keep to the terms and constraints of their daily tagged curfew.

If the breach is denied by the defendant, then the case has to be put to the test by means of a trial. But most breaches are admitted, even if reluctantly, and it is then a case of seeing if there is a reasonable excuse before deciding upon a suitable punishment.

Given that so many offenders have chaotic, disorganised, and feckless lifestyles, and all too often suffer from mental health problems or addictions to alcohol or drugs that make it next to impossible for them to follow instructions to the letter, should they turn up we are likely to hear a succession of explanations, justifications, and excuses – some more credible than others – as to how and why they were unable to get out of bed or leave their home in time to attend their appointment.

We must remember, and take into account, that many have no home to go to, or struggle to find the necessary bus or train fare. We will have to sort out the wheat from the chaff and decide whether their explanations are plausible and acceptable.

We are magistrates and not social workers – although all too often it is hard to tell the difference – and day after day we see situations that leave us in anger, despair (or a combination of the two), and wonder, as to why so many desperate people in desperate circumstances are put into the Criminal Justice System (CJS). They are left to flounder when they really need understanding, plus help and support from social services that are oversubscribed, underfunded, or no longer exist. It is a vicious circle, and we are often left to pick up the pieces.

*

We go into court at 10 am and see, to my relief, that we have been blessed with an excellent breach prosecutor who, from past experience, I know will be fully prepared and have actually read her case files beforehand, unlike some of her colleagues who sometimes appear to be making it up as they go along. The legal adviser, a qualified lawyer who is there to assist and keep an eye on us and ensure that our judgments and decisions are lawful, is also experienced and battle-hardened.

All augurs well although, as feared if not unexpected, nothing is ready for us given the late arrival of those who have actually managed to turn up. Far more worrying is the fact that more and more defendants are litigants in person, unable to afford a lawyer, or unable to obtain legal aid because of the reduction in the threshold for legal aid eligibility. They either defend themselves, which further slows down proceedings as everything must be carefully explained to them, or have to rely upon the assistance of the overworked and overstretched court-appointed duty solicitors who provide an exceptional service, although there are firm rules about whom they can and cannot represent.

So, almost as fast as we descend a few steep flights of stairs – the lift being out of order, as it has been for many months now – it is now time to plod back upstairs to the retiring room, a draughty and starkly unwelcoming anteroom, full of contemporary furniture – contemporary if it was still 1965 – and munch some unappetising Ministry of Justice (MoJ) issue biscuits. They're a brand that exists nowhere else on this planet.

Apparently, though, we should be grateful for small mercies as I discover we are currently one of the few remaining courthouses where the magistrates still receive free biscuits! Way back in 2013, the courts were told to stop purchasing biscuits for magistrates as an austerity measure. It's good to know we are so valued, although I understand that there has recently been a change of heart and policy, and all courthouses will now continue to receive their biscuit allocation! A triumph for common sense, if not for our stomachs and taste buds.

I notice, in passing, that HM Courts & Tribunal Service (HMCTS) is proudly trumpeting the appointment of a new caterer and the imminent opening of a new café at Croydon magistrates' court. I await a similar announcement at our court, but hardly with anticipation and bated breath. Some of my older colleagues still reminisce fondly about the days when a tea lady wheeled her trolley and serviced the retiring room. Those times are long over, and austerity rules.

As an aside, I remember being advised by a judge at my swearing-in ceremony (when I officially became a magistrate) to tuck into the free biscuits provided, as they would be the only perk ever offered to us magistrates. How right she was!

It is hard to overstate the amount of time lost and wasted almost every day as we wait for something to happen and for court proceedings to commence. The late or non-arrival of defendants, complainants, interpreters and witnesses, court papers not being emailed in advance to lawyers, the refusal of prisoners to leave their cells, the regular and unforgiveable failure by the overstretched Crown Prosecution Service (CPS) to disclose necessary evidence and information to the defence until the day of trial, the lack of court staff, over-running or late starting conferences between defendants and their lawyers, the need to view CCTV or, more often nowadays, body-worn camera footage, all contribute to a seemingly never-ending series of frustrating and largely avoidable delays. Magistrates often seem to spend more time hanging around in the retiring room, trying to keep warm, or cool in the summer months, than doing their duty in court.

This is really frustrating for us as we are all volunteers, giving up our time to help administer local justice for local people; we would much rather sit in court than the retiring room. It often appears that we are almost the last people whose needs are taken into account... treated as unpaid employees who are simply instructed to put up with the gradual disintegration of the court system, and get on with it, as best we can.

And that is just what we do. Almost without exception, magistrates have a well-developed sense of duty and responsibility, and whilst we might not be very happy about some of our working conditions, our lack of voice, and the endemic problems we see every day in court, we simply concentrate on doing our job to the best of our ability and without complaint.

Most of us magistrates also enjoy what we do despite the problems we face. According to a survey carried out in December 2017, 80% of respondents said they had a strong feeling of satisfaction with their role, 89% said they had a strong personal attachment to the role, and 91% said they would recommend the role to friends or colleagues. I am not so sure that an identical study conducted now would come up with similar answers.

*

Eventually, we are ready to begin, and the morning starts to develop a rhythm as we dispose of a number of cases where the breaches are admitted. We mark them by adding extra hours of unpaid work or curfew to the existing community order. We make it clear to offenders that subsequent breaches will most likely result in the current order being revoked and their being resentenced for the original offence. This will inevitably result in a more severe punishment being handed out.

Then… a familiar figure enters the courtroom.

Ms T is a stooped and haggard woman of late middle age, but who looks far, far older; her body and mind desiccated and demonstrating clear evidence of decades of alcohol and drug abuse.

If we ran a frequent flyer programme in our magistrates'

court, she would be a founder member of the platinum club. Over the years, she has amassed well over 100 – in fact closer to 200 convictions – mainly for being drunk and disorderly, assaulting policemen, shoplifting to feed her habit, and abusing innocent passers-by in the street. In short, she is a total nuisance, but despite that, there is a certain charm and dignity about her and – at times – you can still see the woman she must have been before she was ravaged by her demons.

She has recently been given new housing of which she is extremely proud, and she vehemently denies not being at home when Serco staff, who administer the scheme, allegedly came (on two occasions) to fit her monitoring tag, "I was waiting in for them and they didn't come", and she is totally correct as they had gone to the wrong address. This is not a rare occurrence.

Vindicated, she looks triumphantly around the courtroom, espies me – well, she could hardly miss me sitting on a raised dais – and says in passing, "I know you don't I?"

"Yes, Ms T, we have met a few times before."

She gives a faraway smile, comments on her latest haircut, "'Orrible isn't it?" and leaves the courtroom, hopefully to stay out of trouble, but probably not for too long.

Our last encounter, which thankfully she had not fully remembered, occurred a couple of years ago when she came up in front of a bench chaired by me for the third time in only a couple of weeks. Twice she had been sentenced to a fine, which we let her off, on account of her having spent a short amount of time in custody waiting to sober up and for her case to be called on, meaning that she had nothing to pay. Now, we decided to fine her for real. This did not go down well.

A couple of hours later, I left the courthouse at lunchtime and she was hovering on the court steps, probably by now the worse for wear. Her eyes narrowed as she peered malevolently at me and shouted, "Are you the fucker who just fined me?"

"Yes, I'm the fucker who just fined you", I replied, as I hurried on my way.

*

The clock slowly and inexorably moves on its journey towards our lunch break at 1 pm when, without thinking, I instinctively make a cardinal error and stupidly accede at 12.55 pm to the entreaty from a defence lawyer that all presiding justices agree to at their peril, "Please can you fit my case in before lunch? It's really straightforward and will only take a couple of moments."

Beware the siren song of an advocate who is eager and determined to complete his workload before lunch in order to free him to move onto another courthouse. I have been bitten on so many occasions, and now keep a mental checklist of those miscreant lawyers who have kept us back the longest.

Today was no exception as the so-called "simple" case develops a life and unforeseen complications of its own and we finally escape at 1.20 pm, which necessitates a shortened lunch for all court users given that we have to start again at 2 pm. "Never again", I vow, as yet another name is added to my growing blacklist.

*

I come back after lunch giving an extremely wide berth to an exceptionally tall and fit-looking middle-aged man stripped to his T-shirt despite the bitter cold, muscles rippling, taking up martial art poses and stances, and screaming abuse into the ears of startled passers-by on the main road. I am not totally surprised when, a few minutes later, he is standing in front of us to answer for his alleged breach.

Jack has apparently breached his curfew on two separate occasions by stepping outside his hostel late at night to the adjacent dustbin area. There can only be one explanation for his behaviour. His lawyer and I exchange furtive glances and simultaneously mouth the word "smoking" at each other. He goes outside to smoke a cigarette and triggers the alarm. We wonder why the seemingly obvious solution of simply extending the boundary for his curfew has not been taken but, unfortunately, he has now been deemed as *unsuitable* for a curfew owing to his mental health problems.

We learn that Jack is otherwise complying perfectly with all his other appointments and interventions, and I congratulate him for that, but commit the cardinal sin of mentioning this current breach.

This arouses his ire and the courtroom shakes as he roars, "I did NOT breach my curfew, I WAS at home!"

Given his issues, we think it wise to allow him to vent for a few more seconds before he calms down, emotions spent. We substitute extra hours of supervision appointments, where Jack can receive help from probation services for his problems, for his unworkable curfew and, satisfied, he shoots me a gap-toothed smile, calls me an indecipherable name (which I judicially decide to take as a compliment), and leaves the court a happy man. Honours even, and crucially for his self-respect, in control of his own destiny.

*

Another teenager, Miles, denies breaching his order by missing the first two of his 12 pre-ordered sessions at an attendance centre, where groups of young offenders aged under-25 are ordered to go for three hours on alternate Saturday afternoons to receive help and advice about how best to stop re-offending, and guidance on developing life skills.

Without providing any evidence to back up his case, Miles is adamant that a previous bench of magistrates ruled that he did not have to attend these appointments, and he is eager to go to trial to prove his innocence.

Unfortunately for him, the breach prosecutor's records indicate otherwise, and the duty solicitor painstakingly takes time and trouble to explain to his angry and frustrated young client – who is barely holding it together in court – that going to trial is a pointless exercise. Even if he wins the case, he would still need to serve his outstanding 36-hour sentence, and if he loses, he will probably also end up being lumbered with trial costs of around £300, on top of having to complete his original attendance centre order.

After much muttering and wrangling, Miles agrees and admits the breach, which we mark with a fine deemed served so he has nothing to pay, and leaves still mouthing imprecations. We get to the right place in the end, but it isn't a very satisfactory encounter.

*

Next comes Mike, who admits breaching his suspended sentence order by failing to attend his supervision appointments. The starting point for such a breach is to activate the prison sentence in full, or in part, unless it is deemed unjust to do so.

Normally, it is the defence lawyer who urges us to stay our hand and spare his client prison, but today – rarely and extremely surprisingly – it is the prosecutor who gives us a highly positive and in-depth update on the defendant's progress and potential. He then states that probation services are totally unsupportive of the suspended sentence being activated at all. This is a turn-up for the books.

We turn towards the defence lawyer who, despite his best efforts, is unable to hide the look of delight on his face. We ask him to provide his mitigation for his client, but I can't resist adding, "Although it would appear that the prosecution has already done your job for you."

It is, of course, up to the bench to decide how best to proceed and whether or not to send Mike to prison, but given the sheer weight of the evidence presented jointly by both normally opposing parties, we decide in these exceptional circumstances not to do so. We make his existing order more onerous, whilst reminding him in no uncertain terms that he has been given an opportunity that he should take, and that he is still subject to his suspended sentence order.

*

It is now 5.30 pm and the pace is finally lagging as it has been a full-on afternoon and we are down to our last case which, of course, turns out to be complex and fiddly and takes the best part of an hour to unravel.

Frank has not been attending his unpaid work sessions and, in this instance, our options are to add extra hours, consider replacing the existing unpaid work order with a curfew, fine him, or revoke his existing sentence and resentence him for his original offence.

He is a long-distance lorry driver now working six days and often nights per week, who has not been attending his unpaid work given his actual work commitments. Adding extra hours to his sentence is, therefore, not practical. We then discuss a curfew, but he often drives through the night so that would also be unworkable, and a daytime curfew is fairly pointless.

Before considering a fine – and he earns around £350 per week – we listen to the facts of the case for which he received a community order with a requirement of 150 hours of unpaid work.

We are disturbed to hear that it is a particularly nasty, serious, and sustained domestic assault on his ex-partner, causing her some injuries, which takes place in her home and in front of her young daughter, which aggravate the offence further. Marking the breach with a fine would, therefore, seem totally inadequate; resentencing him seems to be the best option.

On reading the outline facts from the police report, it appears to us that – on the face of it – the custody threshold has been well and truly passed for his original offence, and we wonder why he was only given a community order.

But it is not quite so simple. The assault took place in a different part of the country, and we do not possess all the information that might well explain why the original sentence appears to have been extremely lenient after he was found guilty after trial.

Frank's lawyer has not represented him before and possesses no knowledge of the offence, and we need to read the sentencing remarks of the original bench which will explain how they came to their verdict, as well as the level of seriousness of the offence, and perhaps why they gave the sentence that they did.

We also need sight of the pre-sentence report produced soon afterwards by probation services. Only then would we be in full possession of the facts and be in a position to resentence him from a position of knowledge.

It is now almost 6.15 pm and we are not going to get any further today. We are forced to adjourn matters for a fortnight to give time for all the necessary information to be provided, before a different bench decides how best to deal with this matter.

A frustrating way to end a long, varied, and sometimes difficult day, and we are left to wonder why a case like this was left until so late in the day to be called on; if we had heard it earlier, then it is likely that it could have been concluded there and then.

So much for speedy justice!

We thank the court staff for their help, have a brief post-court review meeting with the legal adviser who still has work to do in terms of entering the outcomes of the final cases onto his computer system (an extra and unwelcome task for legal advisers), and Fran and I trudge back upstairs (have I mentioned the lift?).

We discuss the day's work and feel that we have worked well together. In passing, I ask my new colleague from the morning if, having seen me in action all day, she still feels that I am soft on sentencing, "No, you dealt with everyone totally fairly."

Neither a zealot nor a wimp – that's a relief!

2. ON REMAND

The queue of Serco prisoner escort vans stretching around the corner of the building is a reminder that today is Monday, the busiest day of the week in magistrates' courts. This is the day of reckoning for those who misbehave or perhaps over-celebrate over the weekend and end up sleeping it off in a police cell. Their next port of call is invariably the remand court, which is where everybody accused of a criminal offence makes their first court appearance.

There are generally two types of remand court. They operate in tandem each Monday to deal with the crush, in order to streamline matters. One is reserved for those expected to plead guilty (guilty anticipated plea – GAP court), and the other for those predicted to plead not guilty and who elect to go to trial (not guilty anticipated plea – NGAP court).

It is all very good in theory, and generally the system works pretty well in practice, but defendants are fully entitled to change their mind about their plea after consulting a lawyer before entering court, so invariably each remand court deals with a combination of guilty and not guilty pleas which slows things down.

Those pleading guilty are either sentenced there and then, if matters are straightforward (with the carrot of a discount of a third off their sentence for making an immediate guilty plea), but if they are more serious, then they can be committed to the Crown Court for sentence. If there are perhaps offender issues identified relating to mental health, drugs, or alcohol then probation services are generally asked to interview the defendant and prepare either an oral or written report to help the bench in their sentencing decision. If a not guilty plea is entered, then it is our job to make all the preparations for their eventual trial.

As happens more often than not, despite the fact that we are expecting a busy and varied day, no cases are ready for us to hear when we enter court at 10 am and we, therefore, make a quick exit back to the retiring room and resign ourselves to a long wait.

The court papers have not yet been provided electronically for the prosecutor to study, and there is also a long queue of defendants in the cells who do not have lawyers; they are waiting to see the duty solicitor to consider their options before they are ready to enter a plea.

All of this means a frustrating and unwanted delay of around 45 minutes before we can get started. Ours is nominally a GAP court where we are anticipating guilty pleas but, as mentioned, who knows what we will find.

That is one of the chief joys and attractions of being a magistrate; no sitting is quite the same. You sit in a variety of types of court and nothing is ever quite what you anticipate or expect; you never stop learning and seeing new things.

*

Finally, we are ready to start, and we soon get into a smooth tempo aided, as we are, by an excellent prosecutor in Mr W who, despite the late arrival of the electronic files, has quickly grasped the key facts and nuances of each case.

We are also blessed with an experienced legal adviser who calls on each case as swiftly and efficiently as she can, given the need for her to handle the dreaded digital mark up (DMU). The DMU system allows legal advisers at the conclusion of each case to enter the outcome directly onto their computer in court, rather than writing longhand into a paper file in court. We are in the 21st century after all.

It's an excellent idea, in theory, as it eliminates the need for another layer of administrative support, but it totally backfires in practice, as ideally remand courts should be relatively fast-paced, given the number of cases that have to be dealt with on most days. DMU slows down the court proceedings interminably, with delays of up to ten minutes between cases whilst some legal advisers struggle to handle the additional task now demanded of them – some with far better grace than others. There is often some interesting *sotto voce* language flying around, which we do our best to rise above and ignore!

If a defendant pleads not guilty, we first have to decide where the trial will take place. The least serious cases (*Summary*) can only be heard in a magistrates' court, and make up about 80% of all prosecutions. Others, such as possession of drugs, burglary, and assault occasioning actual bodily harm, are called *Either Way* offences and can be heard either in a magistrates' or Crown Court. The most serious, such as murder, rape, perjury and robbery (*Indictable only*), have to be sent to the Crown Court.

In 2019, 1.37 million defendants were prosecuted at magistrates' courts and 71% of all Either Way offences were also heard in a magistrates' court rather than the Crown Court. In all, 83% of all defendants had their cases concluded at magistrates' courts. Given that all criminal cases start in a magistrates' court, these figures just emphasise the crucial role that magistrates' courts play in the overall administration of justice.

*

Magistrates go through what is called an allocation process, first hearing submissions from both lawyers as to where they think the case should be tried, and it is then up to us to decide if we will keep an Either Way offence in a magistrates' court. We base our decision on the level of seriousness of the alleged crime and what sentence it is likely to attract should the defendant plead or be found guilty. Even if we decide to keep it, though, the defendant has the final say and can choose, or elect, the court in which his trial will be held.

Very often you see, and try to cast a blind eye to, some wild gesticulating, whispering, and semaphoring going on between the defence lawyer and his client – separated from him in the dock – getting their wires crossed as they try to come to a consensus.

The latest CPS figures confirm that you are more likely to be convicted in a magistrates' court than the Crown Court, but only by a pretty narrow margin – 84.8% to 78.9%. It should be noted, however, that the figures are skewed by the fact that 78% of defendants plead guilty straight away in a magistrates' court and thus benefit from the one-third discount offered off their sentence.

Some critics feel that magistrates are far more likely to take the side of authority and believe a police officer's evidence against that of a civilian witness or defendant simply because of his or her uniform. I can honestly say that I have never seen that happen and, in my experience, we always scrutinise each witness's evidence equally rigorously and totally on its merits, and afford it the credence that it deserves.

Many defendants prefer to take their chance in the Crown Court where their ultimate fate lies in the hands of 12 jurors, who almost invariably take their duties conscientiously and seriously. The fundamental principle is the same wherever a trial is held – nobody in England or Wales can be convicted except on the say-so of lay people – whether it be 12 jurors or three magistrates, and hopefully this will never change. So, why do some defendants choose to have their trial in a magistrates' court instead of the Crown Court? Perhaps, because if convicted in a magistrates' court, you can always appeal and have another crack at it in the Crown Court, as there is an unfettered right to an appeal. Summary trials are also generally cheaper and heard far quicker than those in the Crown Court, which can take many months or even years to be held. This can reduce the stress for both the innocent – and guilty – of waiting for the trial to take place, and means less time on bail with the restrictions on liberty that can bring.

I recently heard of a case of mobile phone theft, which took place way back in 2018, being listed for a one-day Crown Court trial in April 2021. How can this be right, particularly when so many courts lie empty and unused? The ever-increasing backlog of unheard cases in the Crown Court is a national scandal and disgrace, and is purely due to penny pinching and the refusal to allocate sufficient funds to a creaking and overstretched Criminal Justice System.

*

One of our first cases today concerns David, a smartly-dressed man in his late twenties, with several previous convictions for both drug possession and supply. He pleads guilty to a raft of similar offences and it is now up to us to decide how best to sentence him. We consult our Sentencing Guidelines and, without taking into consideration the aggravating factor of his previous convictions, the starting point for his crime of street dealing is one year in prison with a range of between 26 weeks' to three years' custody.

The highest sentence we, as magistrates, can impose is six

months' imprisonment – or 12, if there are two separate Either Way offences for us to deal with – so in this instance we decide to commit him to the Crown Court as we believe he needs greater punishment than we can give him.

Yes, we magistrates are all bound by very thorough and detailed Sentencing Guidelines, which are designed to ensure fairness and uniformity in sentencing no matter which magistrates' court you are sentenced in. Hopefully, the days of "local rules and practices", where the severity of your sentence often depended upon where the case was heard, or the whim of the bench, are long since gone. We are not left to our own devices and can't, as I am sure many suspect, make things up on the hoof according to how we feel about the offender or indeed the offence. Sentencing is based on the nature and seriousness of the offence, the defendant's previous record, and level of compliance with previous court orders.

The latest Ministry of Justice figures show that 78% of all offenders in 2019 received fines, easily the most common punishment.

There is a highly structured approach to sentencing that we are all trained to follow, and follow it we must, unless we can demonstrate (and then clearly articulate and give reasons in open court) why in a specific instance we do not think it appropriate to follow the guidelines that we have been given. They are guidelines rather than tramlines, and there are times when it is appropriate to go outside them, given the particular circumstances of the offender or the offence.

*

Next up is Jo, a 19-year-old woman, who pleads guilty to possession of cannabis, a Class B drug. It is not her first conviction for doing this and she receives a fine of £120, reduced from £180 because of her discount for an early guilty plea. But that is not the end of it, as she has to pay a victim surcharge of £32 as well as costs of £85. That makes for a very expensive joint, which will set her back a total of £237 that she has to pay at a rate of £10 every fortnight.

She has represented herself and tells us that she is trying to get into college. When advised of the size of the fine, she shudders and states emphatically, "It won't happen again!" Let's hope that she keeps her word.

*

Then comes Mark, yet another 19-year-old, who pleads guilty to possession of cannabis, but his case is different as this is his first offence and a disturbing story emerges of him claiming to be coerced and groomed into holding the drugs by another gang member. He has been kept in custody overnight and says that he fears for his safety. Given these circumstances, we are very surprised by his guilty plea and say so to the duty solicitor representing him. We also consider whether he may have been acting under duress, in which case we can decide not to accept his guilty plea. His lawyer confirms that he advised Mark that he has a potential defence in law but that even when this is explained to him, Mark insists on pleading guilty, getting the matter dealt with immediately and saving himself from having to face a trial.

We express our concern for his welfare but are told that the young man intends to leave town straight away and go and stay with relatives far from his current haunts, so we give him a small fine which we deem to have been served given the night he has spent in the cells, and silently wish him luck as he leaves the court for what seems an uncertain future.

Today's prosecutor, Mr W, has a justly earned reputation for efficiency and fairness given his skill in swiftly reading and assimilating the relevant information on each case. He is a formidable advocate.

I totally respect his competence and skill and have never known him to make even a minor mistake before in court, but today it finally happens.

Contact between magistrates and lawyers outside the court is strictly frowned upon in order to ensure that there can be no accusations of impropriety, favouritism, or bias, and it is also entirely proper that we scrutinise everything that is said to us in court and don't necessarily take it at face value. However, we see each other at work on a regular basis and we all know our runners and riders as well as their respective idiosyncrasies, strengths, and weaknesses.

A few years ago, I was eating lunch on my own in a nearby restaurant when three lawyers who are regulars at our courthouse walked in, saw me, and given that there were no free tables, immediately joined me. I was slightly nonplussed but could not see a polite or practical way of asking them to move. After a somewhat faltering start, we ended up having a fascinating conversation about the magistracy. Despite their long-term experience of working in magistrates' courts, they had no real idea about how we work or even get to sit on the bench. They actually thought we were paid for doing what we do, and were staggered when I disabused them of their misconception. "We're volunteers", I explained. Probably feeling sorry for me, they tried to pay for my lunch, but I made it clear that this was a step far too far, and we parted hopefully having a much better understanding of our respective roles.

As a quick digression, magistrates are unpaid volunteers, many of whom do not even claim expenses. Mileage is paid at a rate of up to 58 pence per mile, depending upon the engine size of the motor vehicle, and there is also a daily subsistence allowance of £10.38 towards food if the magistrate is away from home for between eight and twelve hours. Magistrates who suffer a loss of earnings as a result of their duties can also claim a loss allowance. We are certainly not doing this for the money!

I hate to think, although I can surely guess, what the lawyers think of me and the way in which I chair the court, but from past experience Mr W knows that I always want the prosecutor to indicate the level of seriousness of each charge; in other words, whether the Crown places it in, say, Category 1 – the highest, or perhaps Category 3 – the lowest. This has a massive effect upon where the case might be heard if it goes to trial, or the level of sentence that we will give if there is a guilty plea. In the end, though, despite the indication given, it is up to the bench to decide how serious they think it is.

In this case, we are deciding upon the venue for a trial for an accusation of assault occasioning actual bodily harm (ABH). This is a serious assault, which results in some injury to the victim, such as a broken tooth or extensive cuts and bruising.

In order to decide upon the category, we have to consider the level of culpability and harm for each offence. If an allegation of ABH is considered to be in Category 1, then the trial must take place in the Crown Court. If Category 2 or 3, the bench is far more likely to retain jurisdiction and decide, subject to the whim of the defendant, that the trial should be held in a magistrates' court.

In this instance, Mr W advises us that he places this allegation of ABH into Category 2 and that the trial can, therefore, be heard in a magistrates' court. The defence then makes no comment on the matter, perhaps for a reason that becomes apparent shortly afterwards.

We have a quick and muffled conversation on the bench, but we disagree with the prosecutor as we can see that not only is there greater harm, because this is allegedly a sustained and lengthy assault, but there is also higher culpability because apparently a 'shod foot' which is designated as a weapon, is used to kick the complainant. This makes it a more serious Category 1 offence, rather than Category 2, which we decide to send to the Crown Court.

Mr W is human after all(!) and has the grace to nod his apology towards us.

Deciding whether or not to grant bail to a defendant is one of the hardest things a bench has to do. If you remand someone into custody, you are depriving them of their liberty at a time when they have not been convicted of the crime with which they have been charged. It might also, in practical terms, mean that they are in custody for longer *before their trial* than the actual sentence they might receive if eventually found guilty of the offence. They might well not receive a custodial sentence at all or even be found innocent after trial. Last year, magistrates remanded only 4% of all defendants in custody.

It is always a big decision to make, and I am sure we take more time and care over bail decisions than for almost anything else that we do. Our task is to make a risk assessment about the defendant and whether, if granted bail, he or she can be relied upon to turn up for their next court date, not to commit offences whilst on bail, nor to attempt to influence or intimidate witnesses.

The Crown needs to outline its specific objections to bail under one or more of these three headings, and provide detailed representations to back up its judgement. This could relate to facts surrounding the current case or even how the defendant has behaved when granted bail in the past. The defence lawyer will then attempt to allay our concerns and propose a package of conditions that, if put into place, would make it safe for us to grant bail. Generally, they have thought the situation through and their suggestions are sensible, but sometimes they over-egg the pudding and suggest so many conditions that bail seems hardly worth granting. Occasionally, they have their head in the sand and seem to ignore all the concerns expressed by the prosecutor, and propose that we grant their client unconditional bail.

These conditions could include an order of non-contact with the complainant, particularly so in cases involving domestic abuse, not allowing them to go to a certain address or area where the complainant or witnesses might live or work, ensuring they live and sleep at their home address (perhaps also with the addition of a tagged curfew each night as a direct alternative to custody), and reporting regularly to a nearby police station – if, of course, one can be found that still remains open and allows reporting.

The starting point for the bench when making its decision is that everyone is entitled to be granted unconditional bail – unless there are substantial grounds not to do so.

Sometimes, the bench is absolutely certain what its bail decision is going to be, but they will still almost always retire, even briefly, to discuss the matter properly and in a structured manner, and to give it the care and attention that it merits.

That being said, I do recall several years ago one of the more autocratic and old-school chairmen – now thankfully long since retired – who, without even looking at his two wingers, told the defendant in the dock to stand up as soon as both lawyers had finished making their representations on bail. Hail Caesar! Our self-appointed leader was about to pronounce HIS rather than OUR bail decision without bothering to consult us.

Gratifyingly, he eventually, if reluctantly, acknowledged the angry hissing coming from both sides of him, caved in, and unconvincingly announced that he was, in fact, telling the defendant to stand up so that he could inform him that we were about to rise to deliberate – a likely story!

This was the same chair who, immediately prior to my first ever sitting with him, told me that if I had any questions or anything that I wished to say to him in court, then I was to write him a note on the bench, otherwise I was to keep quiet and let him get on with HIS job – so much for teamwork. A dying breed, thankfully!

One of my first ever sittings as a naïve and wet behind the ears winger, who had absolutely no idea about what was going on around me, saw two alleged bank robbers brought into a courthouse that was surrounded by a phalanx of Darth Vader helmeted police marksmen outside on the street and on neighbouring rooftops wearing bulletproof vests and flourishing machine pistols. I really should have grasped that this was not a normal first appearance. Bail was opposed, but their lawyers went through the motions and made a token bail application on their behalf to which the experienced chair and his other less callow winger smiled knowingly at each other. Knowing no better, I audibly expressed the view that perhaps we should retire to discuss this at more length, at which point the smug legal adviser (no, I never did forgive or forget her) said to me patronisingly, "Don't worry, most new magistrates are totally useless at first."

Thanks Monica! Let's just say that I bit my tongue, never forgot what she said to me, and used it as motivation to ensure that I never repeated this *faux pas* and improved and learned as much as possible as quickly as I could. Finally, two long years later, she had the grace to apologise.

We aim to be entirely fair and objective when deciding upon bail and we look carefully at whether the defendant has previously committed offences whilst on bail or failed to turn up to court. Quite frankly, if more than three of the possible bail conditions are considered to be necessary then the bench might well feel that bail should not be granted.

Perhaps we can sometimes err on the side of caution as nobody wants to see themselves pilloried on the front pages of the national press for bailing somebody who immediately goes out on the rampage and commits a serious or violent crime… perhaps against the original complainant. But you can only go on what the respective lawyers tell you in court and a defendant's previous record.

As always, we have to announce in open court our detailed reasons for not granting bail, which again helps to concentrate our minds.

Today, we grant bail to Joe, a middle-aged man accused of assaulting his partner, whilst issuing a bail condition of non-contact with her and I hear somebody in court state that, "any way that you can think of contacting her, such as telephone, email, social media or fax is forbidden."

Fax?

Who outside a football club trying to complete a last-minute deal on transfer deadline day still uses a fax nowadays?

Who even knows or remembers what a fax machine is?

Who is this stupid old fart babbling on and spouting such nonsense from the bench?

That stupid old fart is me.

3. TRAFFIC COURT

It is always a good idea to check your online rota the day before you are due to sit in court. The system has recently been revamped, and the software upgraded, and for the most part, it works remarkably well and efficiently. Quite often, though, you find that the court in which you are due to sit has been changed at the last minute, and it is always helpful to know this in advance of arriving in court, so that you have a pretty good idea of what awaits you.

Very occasionally, the system goes on the blink and you find that two presiding justices have been double-booked to appear in the same court and have to negotiate their way to a satisfactory solution. Or, worst of all, a magistrate arrives in court, keen and eager to do his or her bit, scans the list carefully, does a double take, and then finds that they have been left off the rota completely. Unless somebody else has failed to turn up, they have had a wasted journey, which is a poor show indeed.

Today, I see that I have been switched into the DVLA court that deals with the failure of motorists to properly tax, take off the road (SORN), or insure their vehicles, and where registered keepers have ignored or failed to respond to reminder letters. They are then summonsed to appear in court and given one more opportunity to either pay the outstanding arrears, provide a satisfactory explanation as to why matters have been allowed to get this far, or ask for a hearing to try to rebut the accusation.

This is generally a last resort and pretty much a forlorn hope, as failure to tax or insure a vehicle are what are called *strict liability* offences, in which responsibility for breaking the law is enforced without the need to prove intent. In other words, quite simply, if you do not obtain the necessary cover – you are guilty in law.

This court is the personal fiefdom of the DVLA prosecutor, the formidable and redoubtable Ms B who bestrides it like a colossus, as she has done for many years now. She is a kindly but authoritative lady of certain years, who is the resident encyclopaedic expert and authority on motoring law. She certainly knows more about this specialist and arcane area of the law than any magistrate or legal adviser.

Thankfully, she is a benevolent and sympathetic despot and, as normal, spends the first part of the morning on her own, without the presence of the magistrates, dealing personally with everyone who has turned up and doing her utmost to persuade them to come to an agreement with her about paying the outstanding arrears without the need for the magistrates to get involved, and then almost certainly having to levy a fine for non-payment.

Court is supposed to start promptly at 10 am, although this is often a convention more honoured in the breach than in the observance for a number of reasons covered previously. When it comes to the DVLA court, you know that – depending upon the number of people who have attended – you are highly unlikely to be needed much before 11 o'clock at the earliest. Hopefully, by that stage, most of the cases will have already been settled by agreement or negotiation.

Thankfully, I am prepared for this delay and have armed myself with a book, which if not quite "War and Peace" in length, is a long and stimulating read. I sit down and start reading, knowing that I should have at least an hour or so to myself before we are called upon.

How do magistrates occupy themselves during these long periods of inactivity? Some, perhaps braver than others, relax in the retiring room, chewing and struggling to swallow the dry and unappetising court issue biscuits, searching desperately, and generally in vain, for the last custard cream. By the way, it is considered extremely bad form to be the person who tears open the silver foil covering up a new layer of biscuits. Resist the temptation and let someone else do it!

The hot drinks machine also has its devotees. I suppose we should be grateful that we still receive free drinks, although any resemblance to real tea and coffee is entirely accidental.

Others concentrate on filling out the new style expenses form, patiently working out the exact time they left and returned home on each sitting day, and the size of their car's engine.

Some exchange grumbles, war stories, and small talk with other colleagues similarly waiting for court to start or recommence. My rules of engagement in the retiring room are NEVER to discuss anything that could potentially be perceived as either controversial, in bad taste, or political. Keep the subject matter light, innocuous, uncontentious, and humorous, but be careful… is your sense of humour going to be understood and appreciated by your listeners? Do not openly discuss the case that you are currently hearing or pass opinions upon the likely guilt or innocence of defendants, and – most importantly – avoid the slightest possibility of giving offence, real or imagined.

The majority of my colleagues are pleasant and interesting company with fascinating tales to tell of their varied life experiences, past and present, and I delight in hearing them and hopefully sharing some of my own. That being said, it has been known for the odd apparently innocent or maybe even slightly injudicious comment to be taken the wrong way by some of our more sanctimonious and politically correct colleagues who might then grass you up.

To avoid running the risk of finding yourself up before the beaks, my advice is never to provide anyone with the slightest piece of ammunition that can later be used against you.

That is not to say that a flagrantly racist or unacceptable comment should be allowed to pass unchecked without being challenged and then taken further. Unfortunately, one of my colleagues did not heed this advice one day when he was looking at his court list for the morning. A defendant charged with a particularly unpleasant armed robbery had an obviously foreign name. He said that he thought this was a Somali name and then added in full hearing of a number of his fellow magistrates in the retiring room, "That's typical of the Somali community – they're all thieves, aren't they?"

Oh dear!

Such a biased, racist, and prejudicial remark could not be allowed to pass unchallenged. He was reported to the Bench Chair and ended up receiving a severe reprimand, as well as being ordered to attend equality and diversity training. He was lucky. I would have advocated zero tolerance for such an offence. He could – and perhaps should – have been thrown off the bench for his behaviour.

Recently, a comments book has been left on the table for us to fill in with our thoughts and suggestions. An excellent and long overdue idea, it is already bursting with a combination of magistrates' moans and a litany of woes relating to the lack of basic staples such as: milk and expense forms, non-functioning toilets, lifts, clocks, iPads, heating and air conditioning, flickering migraine-inducing lights in courtrooms, as well as any number of constructive suggestions relating to rota issues, car parking and best practice in terms of how we are asked to do our job.

Our patient and hard-working Bench Chairman and his deputy take the time and trouble to listen to our comments, follow up individually with us, and sort out as many of our problems as they can, although sometimes it seems as if they are pushing water uphill. It's really good to be heard!

*

Finally, the call comes at 11.15 am, and we are ushered back into court. The silver-tongued Ms B has once again worked her magic. There were almost 30 cases on our morning list but the overwhelming majority have now been disposed of.

There are a few non-appearances, and in each instance, we agree to proceed in the defendant's absence, listen to Ms B outline the facts, query and then clarify them mainly for our own self-respect (and so that we do not appear to be a mere rubber stamp), and – where we deem it appropriate – issue the relevant fine.

By not appearing and pleading guilty in person, defendants lose the one-third discount they would otherwise have received off their fine, which is set according to a defendant's means and ability to pay, ideally within a 12-month period.

If somebody is unemployed, a student, or on benefits, their relevant weekly income is set as £120 per week. However, if they do not appear in court and we do not possess any information about their means or personal circumstances, then the starting point when assessing fine levels is an assumption of a much steeper weekly income of £440.

This means that when fines are combined with court costs and any victim surcharge (which is a general fund used for victim services), it can make for an extremely costly day – and a very unpleasant surprise – when they eventually discover that they have been sentenced in their absence.

There are also two contested cases for us to deal with. In the first, Glen does not accept that his car is not properly taxed, but is unable to provide any evidence that he has informed the DVLA that he has sorted the matter. The prosecutor is sympathetic and helpful, as we and the legal adviser are, to an unrepresented defendant who initially does not really understand the proceedings, but when we inform him that he is going to be fined, he bursts into an uncontrollable bout of tears. Between halting sobs, Glen blurts out that he has no money, does not receive any benefits, and used his last cash to get to court.

Given the circumstances, we pass him a box of court issue tissues (which must have slipped through the net as they are still provided in all courtrooms despite the budget cuts), allow him time to recover, set the fine at the lowest possible level, make no award for costs against him, and allow him 12 months to pay, pointing him in the direction of the court helpdesk where he can hopefully get some assistance in terms of applying for benefits. Glen's initial reaction was also a salutary reminder to us magistrates of the impact that we have on peoples' lives and the responsibility that we bear.

*

After lunch, Mandy, our final defendant, claims that she has registered her car as being off the road (SORN) and denies leaving it on a public rather than private road, which would invalidate her SORN declaration and render her liable for excise duty. She is carefully cross-examined by Ms B and admits that she has no evidence to prove that where she parks her car – adjacent to a block of flats – is indeed private land. Mandy does not know who maintains it, nor is she aware of any signs indicating that the land is privately owned.

That is all very well, but whilst she demonstrates and highlights the clear gaps in the defendant's evidence, Ms B – in her turn – surprisingly does not provide us with any information that proves that the *road is indeed public*. We are well aware that the defence does not have to prove anything, it is for the prosecution to prove its case beyond reasonable doubt – or so that we are sure – and in this instance, Ms B has singularly failed to do so. After a brief discussion, we acquit Mandy, who lets loose a barely muffled whoop of delight, and looks ready to embark on a lap of honour.

The day ends early at about 3.30 pm, and despite all the frustration of sitting around and twiddling our thumbs waiting for something to happen in the morning, it has been a curiously fulfilling and interesting day. DVLA court can be fascinating; you learn something new every sitting. On my way home, I take extra care to keep to the speed limit and not stray into a bus lane.

4. TAKING THE CHAIR

Being a magistrate is generally very fulfilling, but there are several pinpricks which continually annoy and frustrate us all. The worst of which, at the moment, is the infuriating Multi-Factor Authentication (MFA) system – a security nightmare introduced several months ago.

MFA is an authorisation tool that we have to use practically every time we want to access our emails, rota, and all other important information relating to the magistracy. We have to choose a password (which has to be updated with monotonous regularity) and then – every three days – we receive a notification, not just on our computers or laptop, but individually on every device that we use to access our emails and rota. It tells us to sign in with our password and we then immediately receive a validation telephone call or text, which we again have to respond to correctly before we are finally and grudgingly allowed access to our eJudiciary accounts. It is an endurance test, and a total pain. There is also no escape as you have to comply whenever Big Brother tells you, or else you risk being locked out of all your accounts.

I fully appreciate and accept that as officers of the court we are potentially vulnerable and susceptible to cyber-attack by criminals, and need to take reasonable precautions, but this relentless, clunky, and intrusive system that requires us to jump through so many unnecessary hoops does seem like a case of overkill. An atom bomb to kill an ant.

I know in reality it is far less often, but it almost feels that pretty much every day I receive yet another reminder on my computer, iPhone, laptop or iPad – or all four – requiring me to drop everything and sign in and then waste time waiting for, and responding to, the follow-up phone call before being granted access to my account. A recent holiday was interrupted by constant requests to authenticate my account.

Talking to my colleagues, it seems that they are all as fed up with this system as I am, and I understand that the patient and long-suffering staff on the eJudiciary helpdesk have also been inundated with calls and subjected to a litany of complaints from members of the judiciary far higher up the food chain than us mere magistrates.

Finally though, and long overdue, just as I write this, some element of sanity seems to have prevailed and from now on I understand that we are only going to be required to sign in every fortnight – progress and small mercy indeed.

So why am I mentioning this now? It is just that when hurrying out of the house this morning, in order to get to court in good time, I am asked to sign in and authorise my email account on my home computer. This I do – several times, in fact – each time with less grace and worse language than before, as the computer-generated voice on the telephone calls me three times in less than five minutes to inform me that my sign-in has been successfully verified. Despite this, my email account stubbornly refuses to open and allow me access, necessitating a long and fruitless call to a member of the helpdesk who eventually informs me that there is an on-going problem with my Safari browser that they are working to resolve.

The time expended in trying to sort this problem out is enough to put me behind schedule and means that I get to court later than normal and have to forgo my customary and much-anticipated tea and toast, and leisurely perusal of the newspaper, at a nearby café, if I am going to have sufficient time to prepare for my sitting.

I am lucky in that I only have a short and easy commute from home to my local courthouse, which has so far survived the cull and recent drastic cuts to the court estate.

Many of my colleagues are far less fortunate. Over the last decade more than half of the magistrates' courts – 164 out of 320 – have been shut down and sold off with their sale raising at least £223 million, earmarked to help fund some of the much-needed planned improvements to the court system, such as new digital systems and a move towards virtual courts. The culling is not finished yet, as the government plans to close another 77 courthouses by 2025/26.

This rationalisation has resulted in a centralisation of administration, which was previously handled locally, and an amalgamation of many benches.

The South East has seen the most closures (25), closely followed by Wales and the North West.

Horseferry Road magistrates' court fetched £20m, Greenwich was sold for over £12 million, and Haringey raised over £10 million (it is now an exceptionally smart and expensive apartment block aptly called "Highgate Court"). At the other end of the spectrum, Rochdale Magistrates' Court fetched a mere £6,316 at auction.

Magistrates' courts have traditionally provided local justice, for local people, by local people, but that mantra is now no longer the case; the spate of closures, over the past decade, has resulted in many people no longer having easy access to a local court.

It is now harder and more expensive than ever to get access to justice, particularly for people from low-income households, or those with children, disabilities, vulnerabilities, or mobility issues. The required travel times and distances have increased, and examples abound of complainants, witnesses, and defendants, alike, now facing the prospect of an exhausting round-trip of several hours to reach their nearest court. Perish the thought – they also run the risk of bumping into each other on public transport!

It has always been difficult to persuade defendants to arrive at court in good time, and now, with the increasing need for them to rely on patchy and irregular bus and train services – particularly from rural areas and outside the main conurbations – there is another good reason or excuse for them not to do so, thus causing further delays to an already overstretched Criminal Justice System. The closures are yet another blow for local businesses, many of which relied upon the custom from their local courthouse.

Magistrates traditionally prided themselves on their local knowledge, which often came in useful when hearing a case. When I started out, one of our most experienced magistrates, now sadly deceased, was a walking, talking A-Z who boasted a comprehensive and exhaustive knowledge of nearly every road and business in his local area; something that is rarely the case nowadays, as we have to cover a much greater area.

John Bache, the Chair of the Magistrates Association, is one of many commentators and interested parties who expressed concern that so many courts are now, "worryingly remote from the communities that they serve" – a view with which I heartily concur. Should the mooted and much heralded improvements and updates to the courts system finally be completed, and result in a leaner and more efficient and effective service being provided, then – and only then – might I change my mind and see the court closures slightly more positively.

*

I am chairing a remand court today and sitting with a highly experienced presiding justice who is acting as a winger. It is a long time since I sat with him; in fact, it was one of my last appraised sittings when I was still training to become a chair. He was extremely helpful and supportive on that occasion, and I'm sure he will be the same today.

However, after a few minutes, and haltingly dealing with the first couple of cases, I can tell that I am not as relaxed and confident as usual, and far more stilted and hesitant in my pronouncements. I recognise signs of nerves and stage fright and realise that, for some reason, I feel intimidated by having such an experienced and august presiding justice looking over my shoulder.

I immediately think back a few years to when, after sitting as a winger for four years, it just seemed a natural progression to apply to become a chair, as I wanted to develop my skills and experience and relished the prospect of the additional workload and responsibility. I suppose it was also the thwarted and frustrated performer and barrister in me.

It is not quite so simple as just waking up one morning and deciding that you want to become a presiding justice. Before I could even apply, I needed to have had two satisfactory winger appraisals, formally observed another chair in action, and also completed a shedload of specific online training modules, including sessions on diversity and unconscious bias, and a comprehensive and challenging series of exercises in the *Becoming a Presiding Justice* Workbook.

I then filled in the application form and after an initial interview, which was by no means a forgone conclusion either, commenced what is quite rightly a taxing, lengthy, and convoluted process that takes well over a year to complete.

My two-day training course was both exhaustive and exhausting as a myriad of information was drummed into me. It was followed by six formal appraisals (now trainee chairs can be confirmed in position after just four successful appraisals). I also had a large number of supported sittings with a more experienced colleague sitting alongside me as co-pilot offering me advice when necessary – or even when it wasn't – and then giving me feedback about my performance.

Not everybody makes it. Some candidates fall by the wayside and withdraw during the process, as they find it too difficult to take on the extra pressure and responsibility of controlling the court, saying the right thing at the right time, and grasping all the necessary additional information. Others are found wanting, and the series of appraisals sort the wheat from the chaff.

Chairs need to be able to juggle several balls in the air simultaneously and, crucially, leave their ego by the door – it isn't about you, you are just a minor cog in the wheel who is only there as part of a team to help matters go smoothly, do justice, and treat people fairly and properly. Chairs must never be afraid to ask for advice but at the same time must give off the air and impression that they actually know what they are saying and doing even if – in reality – they have not really grasped everything that is going on. It really is not an easy job and is incredibly daunting, if not terrifying at first.

Each candidate is certainly given a lot of support and feedback, as well as an interim report that indicates where improvements are necessary if they are to succeed. Indeed, I remember saying at the beginning of my training process that

I would quite understand if I was ultimately deemed not to be up to the job; however, I would be extremely unhappy if that verdict came as a shock to me.

I had role-played acting as a chair during my training, but that was make-believe as absolutely nothing prepares you for the real thing and the feeling of abject terror as, dragging your feet behind you, you reluctantly enter the courtroom for the first time as a trainee chair.

This is not a dummy run, this is for real, and you can almost see the L Plates on your arms and feel the eyes of everyone in court boring into you, followed by an expectant and eerie silence as they wait for you to do or say something – anything! Your mouth goes dry; your whole life flashes before you as you desperately try to think of a way to get the show on the road. What on earth should I say? Eventually, after what seems like hours, but is probably only about 20 seconds, inspiration strikes: "Good morning, please sit down", I hear myself say. Everyone breathes an audible sigh of relief and relaxes as we finally get on with our day's work.

Some chairs, when sitting on the wing in a supporting role, find it extremely hard, if not impossible, to give the trainee chair the breathing space he or she needs to perform, or even, at worst, enough rope to hang themselves. They subject the chair to a whispered running commentary throughout the day along the lines of, "Don't forget to mention victim surcharge and costs/make a collection order/thank the interpreter/tell the defendant to sit down/etc./etc." (Delete where applicable).

This barrage and litany of well-meant advice went on so relentlessly during one of my early supported sittings – when I had the singular misfortune to have not one, but two chairs bookending me and subjecting me to a seemingly non-stop synchronized Greek chorus of instructions, advice and reminders – that after putting up with it for an interminable half hour I informed a surprised court that the bench needed to rise for a moment. I took my two equally perplexed colleagues outside the court and plaintively said, "I know you are both doing your best to help me, and thank you, but your constant reminders and interruptions are having totally the opposite effect. I would be really grateful if you could try to allow me the freedom and space to make my own mistakes before you correct me and tell me what I should have done instead." That seemed to have the desired effect and things got much easier after that.

I have always tried to learn from that example when supporting a trainee chair myself.

Less is sometimes more.

*

Today turns out just fine. In a quiet moment between cases, I mention my trainee chair story to my colleague who laughs and takes the hint; after that, we get on famously. I regain my poise and composure as a chair, he and the other winger do their jobs well, and we gel into an effective team.

We deal with a not guilty plea for an allegation of assault by beating. It is a domestic abuse case where David is accused of pushing Fiona, his partner, several times after an argument.

It might be worthwhile, at this point (given how frequently magistrates hear such cases), to explain the difference between the various types of assault offence, as well as discuss domestic abuse.

A person is guilty of *common assault* if they intend to use violence against someone else, or make them feel that they are about to be attacked. Actual physical violence is not necessary and an aimed punch that fails to connect, threatening words, or a raised fist would constitute an assault; the offence covers both intentional and reckless acts.

If there is actual violence or direct physical contact, it is called a *battery* and the offender would be charged with *assault by beating*.

This is a slightly confusing title for many defendants, as it does not necessarily mean that the victim was actually battered, beaten up, or even hit or kicked. It could be that they were pushed, grabbed, or spat at. David is no exception; when he hears the charge described in court as *assault by beating*, he grimaces and shouts, "I didn't hurt her."

The victim may not, therefore, have suffered any injury, and if any were incurred, it would need to be quite minor to fall under common assault

The maximum sentence for common assault is six months' in prison, and these cases can only be heard in a magistrates' court. We have to increase the sentence to take into account a racially or religiously aggravated assault, where the maximum sentence is two years' imprisonment, and these cases can be heard in the Crown Court as well.

An assault occasioning *actual bodily harm* (ABH) is where some physical harm has been caused to the victim which is more than "transient or trifling" – apologies for the jargon and legalese – but that does not cause any permanent damage.

Some cases of ABH are heard in a magistrates' court, but the most serious are dealt with in the Crown Court, as the maximum sentence is five years' custody.

The most serious assault charge is *unlawful wounding* or inflicting *grievous bodily harm* (GBH). This means causing really serious physical harm, which is severely detrimental to the victim's health. Such cases are almost invariably heard in the Crown Court.

We now refer to "domestic abuse" rather than just "domestic violence" as it relates to any incident of controlling, coercive, or threatening behaviour, violence, or abuse between intimate partners or family members.

Domestic abuse encompasses far more than physical violence as it also covers psychological, physical, sexual, emotional, or financial abuse.

There is no specific offence of domestic abuse, but it can be prosecuted under a range of offences depending upon the particular circumstances.

In a magistrates' court, we mostly see accusations of domestic abuse prosecuted as common assault or assault by beating where the fact that the assault is domestic in nature is an aggravating factor because of the abuse of trust involved.

There is also the relatively new charge of controlling and coercive behaviour in an intimate or family relationship that we are beginning to see more regularly in court.

We are also commonly asked to hear applications by the police for domestic violence protection orders (DVPO), which act like a restraining order in allowing some temporary breathing space for up to 28 days between a couple when problems arise, but before an actual offence is committed.

We set a trial date for David and, much to our surprise, the prosecutor suggests that the defendant should be granted unconditional bail, which is highly unusual in such cases. We decide that a bail condition forbidding any contact with the complainant is necessary to help ensure that there are no further problems.

There is a similar situation later that morning with a father accused of child cruelty, and we again impose a non-contact requirement with the child when the prosecution was happy with unconditional bail.

Perhaps we are being overly cautious, and unnecessary bail conditions are rightly frowned upon; given the circumstances, it just seems common sense for us to do so.

The tragic suicide of Caroline Flack whilst awaiting her trial has caused me to give further thought to this situation. She was accused of assaulting her boyfriend, Lewis Burton, by beating, in December 2019 after she was alleged to have attacked him with a lamp. At the preliminary hearing, Mr Burton, who had called the police on the night in question, told prosecution lawyers that he neither supported the case nor considered himself a victim. Ms Flack was bailed with a condition forbidding her from having any contact with Mr Burton or from attending his address. This, as I have said, is the normal practice when dealing with this type of domestic abuse case when it is felt that keeping the defendant and complainant apart until after the trial is the most sensible option. Here, we have a situation where the alleged victim has withdrawn his complaint. Again, this is something that is a fairly common occurrence, which can take place for any number of reasons that I do not think I need to spell out.

Should this, plus the fact that the defendant is in a fragile mental state, cause the magistrates or District Judge to grant unconditional bail or not prevent the couple from being in contact with each other? Ms Flack's lawyers did, in fact, apply for the bail conditions to be amended once it was clear that Mr Burton was not supporting the prosecution. The application was refused.

A human rights barrister who specialises in cases involving violence against females stated at the time that the strict bail condition that banned the couple from contacting one another was unusual and "paternalistic". I can well understand the anger and emotion that possibly lay behind that comment given the tragedy that arose, but I cannot agree with it.

I conducted my own straw poll amongst several magistrates from my bench, and we all agreed that you cannot, and must not, generalise (as every case must be judged on its own merits, and that might well take into account the mental state of either party), but none of my colleagues – on the basis of what has been made public – would have permitted any contact between the two of them before the conclusion of the trial.

As to whether the CPS made the right decision in intending to proceed with the trial, they have stringent guidelines and, at the time of writing, it appears that they were simply following them. The fact that any alleged victim withdraws his or her complaint should not, on its own, be a decisive factor in deciding whether there is either a realistic chance of conviction, or if it is in the public interest to proceed with the case.

Figures from Her Majesty's Inspectorate of Constabulary show that no less than 11% of all crimes committed in this country are related to domestic violence and abuse. A report by the London Assembly found that domestic abuse offences in London nearly doubled from 46,000 in 2011 to 89,000 in 2019. They now account for 10% of all offences in the capital. Less than 15% resulted in a prosecution as many alleged victims do not proceed with a complaint, and only 6,896 domestic abuse-related convictions in London were recorded in 2019/20.

According to the Office for National Statistics, the number of such offences reported to police throughout the country in 2019 rose by 24% on the previous year to a record 746,219.

Those figures, alarming as they are, are probably only a drop in the ocean as it is estimated that almost two million people suffer domestic abuse each year, 1.3 million of whom are women.

Given the problems and pressures caused by couples forced to spend so much time together throughout the Coronavirus lockdown, one can only guess at how much those figures will increase over the next year.

*

Back in court, and as is almost invariably the case, the morning is punctuated with a series of delays, one of almost 40 minutes, whilst missing case files are located, and defendants talk to their solicitors. Interpreters – sometimes actually even speaking the same language as the defendant – finally grace us with their presence, and the legal adviser struggles through muffled imprecations to laboriously enter case details into the dreaded DMU system.

When we eventually get started again, we have another domestic abuse case and given that the defendant is likely to be self-representing, and won't have a lawyer when the case comes to court, we make an order forbidding him from cross-examining, or asking his former partner (the complainant in this matter) any questions; something that would be deeply inappropriate and unfair. We tell him that the court will appoint a lawyer who will do this on his behalf. Sometimes, this lawyer (called a Section 38 lawyer) will also decide to assist the defendant throughout the remainder of the trial on a *pro bono* basis, a worthy and generous act, although under no obligation to do so.

Stephen, a 20-year-old, pleads guilty to possession of cannabis – an awful lot of cannabis too – 16 self-seal bags in total, for his own personal use, as his lawyer assures us. Sometimes, on the bench, you wonder why the much more serious charge of possession of drugs with intent to supply has not been laid. Perhaps it is to encourage an early guilty plea by pleading to a lesser charge, to save the time and expense of a trial, but we can only sentence on the facts in front of us, not on what we might suspect has occurred.

In this case, this is Stephen's fourth identical conviction, and instead of fining him, we decide that given his previous record, his latest offence is serious enough for us to impose a community order. Given that he is under 25 years of age, we order him to attend an attendance centre for a total of 36 hours over 12 sessions, which will certainly keep him occupied and out of mischief every other weekend for the foreseeable future. We also order the forfeiture and destruction of the drugs, which is something that we always do in cases involving drugs and offensive weapons such as knives.

Separately, I remember a case where someone V-signed and swore at a passing police car, which screeched to a halt, reversed back, and then stopped the man. When searched, he was found to be in possession of a couple of mobile phones, and several wraps of Class A drugs – which were secreted somewhere unmentionable on his person. I don't envy the police officer who had to conduct the search.

*

In 2018/19, there were 151,000 drug offences recorded in

England and Wales, over 80% of which were for possession rather than the supply of drugs. The latest figures from the Ministry of Justice show that more than one in every hundred people imprisoned in Britain over the past five years were convicted of a cannabis offence. Five years ago, there were 1,393 people in prison for cannabis-related offences, a figure that has more than halved now to 682.

Leaving aside the rights or wrongs of legalising or decriminalising cannabis – a subject that is way above my pay grade – these figures imply that some police forces are perhaps turning more of a blind eye to cannabis offences.

We are there to implement the law as it presently stands, and the Sentencing Guidelines currently allow for a range of punishments for possession of Class B drugs, according to the circumstances, from a fine to six months' custody for serious repeat offenders. However, a fine or even a conditional discharge plus forfeiture and destruction of the drugs is the most likely penalty for a first offender.

It is only when someone comes back to court more often for possession of cannabis, or they are arrested whilst in possession of an exorbitant amount of drugs, that a more serious penalty will probably be imposed. This could well be a community order incorporating a requirement for unpaid work, a curfew, or an attendance centre order, but custody is also an option. Being convicted of either possession with intent to supply or production of cannabis is far more likely to bring about a custodial sentence.

*

Next, comes an application by the Crown for bad character evidence to be admitted in a forthcoming trial. Justin faces charges of dangerous driving and aggravated vehicle taking, and the Crown wants the court to allow evidence to be heard in his trial of his propensity for committing similar offences in the past.

Normally, a bench of magistrates, or a jury in a Crown Court trial, is not allowed to hear any evidence relating to a defendant's previous criminal record as it could well be prejudicial to his prospects of being found not guilty of the current charge.

Now, whether we think it fair or not, the Crown can apply for a bad character direction if they can show that a defendant has a recent proclivity or disposition to commit offences of the kind with which he is currently being charged.

We have to scrutinize these applications rigorously, given the likely effect they will have on the outcome of any trial. In this instance, Justin does indeed have five previous convictions for taking a vehicle without consent but, crucially, the last of them occurred over 15 years ago, far too long in the past for us to feel that a predilection to commit similar crimes has been established. We have also not been provided with specific details of the circumstances of these convictions; they might have helped us to consider whether or not they were relevant.

We, therefore, reject the application and rule that it would be fundamentally unfair and not in the interests of justice to adduce bad character in this instance, and that evidence of his previous convictions should be excluded from his trial.

The Crown normally has 28 days after the defendant's initial not guilty plea at his first appearance in the magistrates' court to make the bad character application, which means that, like today, we have heard the application well in advance of the trial date.

On occasions, though, the bench has to decide on the day of the trial whether a bad character application can be made late, and out of time, which means that even if they reject the application – perhaps for similar reasons that we did today – then the bench trying the case will still have been made aware of the defendant's previous record (even if bad character was not eventually adduced).

The defence lawyer will almost certainly make his displeasure at this situation known, but will hopefully be reassured, and his concerns assuaged, by the assertion that this is "an experienced bench" which will be able to disregard, or put out of our mind, this knowledge when coming to a decision, and you know what – we do!

The antithesis of bad character is good character, and if a defendant in a trial has no previous convictions or cautions, we will be given what is called a good character direction by the legal adviser just before we rise to consider our verdict. This confirms that the defendant has no previous convictions or cautions and therefore supports his overall credibility; it may also mean that he is less likely to have committed the offence with which he is charged. It is up to us in our deliberations to decide how much weight to give to this direction.

*

We finish our work at about 4 pm and the list caller checks to see whether we can assist another court. Just when it looks as if we can sneak off home, we are assigned a sentencing decision for what turns out to be a highly unusual case.

When a defendant pleads or is found guilty in a magistrates' court, in the interests of speedy justice he or she is generally sentenced immediately. However, if the matter is serious or there are potential issues relating to the offender, then the probation services are asked to interview him and put together a pre-sentence report which is subsequently considered by another sentencing bench, as is the case today.

Generally, we ask for a fast delivery or oral report which, workload permitting, can generally be put together by the probation services within an hour or two. If, however, probation need to consider potential addiction or safeguarding issues, or make external enquiries, then the report will generally take up to three weeks to complete, and a decision will need to be made by the bench regarding whether to bail the offender or remand him in custody in the meantime.

Owen has recently been found guilty of possession of both an axe and a knife in a public place and has come back today for sentencing. He is in his late forties, tall, thin as a rake, pale and wan with long, lank, greasy hair, and a distant, faraway, dreamy expression on his face. He seems nervous and restless in the dock and is supported by a large group of friends who pack the public gallery.

He lives on a houseboat, and on the day of the offence sees someone nearby driving on the towpath in what he considers to be a dangerous manner. Owen comes outside and remonstrates loudly with the driver from a distance before the man drives off. Unfortunately for Owen, he is holding the axe when he does so and when the police arrive, called by a passer-by, they also find a knife in his pocket. His defence at trial is one of having a reasonable excuse for possession of both items as he states that he uses the axe to chop wood to heat his houseboat, and the knife for cutting down branches. The bench does not accept his explanation, and he is convicted.

In mitigation, his lawyer says that Owen does not realise that he is actually carrying the axe when he goes outside, or how threatening he must appear. The man's poor driving annoys him, and he rushes outside without thinking. Owen also has serious mental health issues, suffers from PTSD and depression, is on strong medication, and has certainly not had the easiest of lives given some difficult and, quite frankly, disturbing family circumstances. His doctor and several friends also provide letters of support for him.

The probation report states that Owen does not pose a high risk of reoffending, that he could be managed within the community, and would benefit from some concerted help in developing better thinking skills.

That is all very well, but what is equally important for us to consider is that he is in possession of not one but two offensive weapons in a public place, even if neither is brandished or used to threaten anybody.

We then go outside to deliberate together, consider the facts and the mitigation we have heard, and then decide how best to sentence Owen. This is not going to be a quick or easy decision, given everything we have to take into consideration.

There are several factors that we have to consider when sentencing Owen. The five specific purposes of sentencing are:

1. Punishment
2. Rehabilitation
3. Reparation
4. Protection of the public
5. Reduction of crime

We must consider which of the above we are seeking to achieve through the sentence we are about to impose. It is quite possible that more than one purpose might be relevant, and we must weigh the importance of each against the particular offence – and Owen's specific background and circumstances – when determining our sentence.

Owen has not been in trouble for many years and has no similar convictions. There was no specific victim to consider as the driver did not stop, made no complaint, and according to witnesses was also verbally abusive towards Owen, so there was also some element of provocation involved.

The use or even carrying of knives (and axes too!) in a public place is abhorrent, and also requires a deterrent sentence given the current atmosphere.

Looking at our Sentencing Guidelines, these offences more than cross the custody threshold. Possession of a knife is an extremely serious matter, particularly in the times in which we find ourselves when stabbings are an almost daily occurrence.

Having decided that the offences cross the custody threshold and that there is no alternative to a custodial sentence, we have to decide whether it can be suspended.

In making that decision, we consider what his lawyer told us about Owen, his troubled and difficult background, and his current frail mental and physical state. We have to consider the effect that prison would have on what is clearly a vulnerable individual who has led a fairly sheltered life; someone who was perhaps not totally aware of the potential impact and repercussions of his behaviour. We also have to decide whether there is a realistic prospect of rehabilitation and if immediate custody would have a significant impact on others.

It is a difficult decision and the three of us take around 20 minutes to discuss all our sentencing options, and the pros and cons and appropriateness of each one in terms of all the facts that have been outlined to us.

Hopefully, I never lose sight of the responsibilities that we always face and just how seriously we must take our role as magistrates, and it is at times like this that you become even more acutely aware of how we can affect peoples' lives by taking away their liberty, plus also not forgetting the impact on their immediate family.

Before making a tough sentencing decision that could conceivably end up with different outcomes, I find it extremely helpful to imagine that I have to explain our decision to the victim, or concerned members of the public. Will they consider the sentence to be appropriate and fair?

After much discussion, we are eventually in total agreement and decide that the prison sentence can be suspended in this instance given the particular circumstances of this case, Owen's own vulnerabilities, and the unlikelihood of his re-offending.

We come back into court, and it is my task as presiding justice to announce our decision.

Owen receives two concurrent suspended sentences for possession of both the axe and the knife, which are both to be forfeited and destroyed, as well as 25 days of rehabilitation activity in which he will receive help from the probation services in terms of improving his thinking skills and decision-making.

I make it clear just how serious his offences are, how close he came to receiving an immediate custodial sentence, and why – given his own situation – we barely decided not to impose it. Should he re-offend within the next 12 months, then he can fully expect to serve this prison sentence.

There is an audible gasp of relief from the public gallery followed by some applause, and Owen and his lawyer thank us for making the decision we did.

We conduct a post-court review and rehash our thinking and decision-making processes. We are all still happy with our sentence and the structured way in which we arrived at it.

Were we correct not to send Owen to prison today? We believe so, but it was a close-run thing.

5. ON TRIAL

I receive a reminder that Christmas is almost upon us when I arrive at court this morning. I enter the retiring room and join a rapidly growing group of magistrates surrounding and eyeing up a large, mouth-watering gift box of Quality Street chocolates which has kindly been left for us by Mr D, one of the regular group of defence lawyers who practice at our courthouse. Everybody is waiting for someone else to be the first to dive in, so I happily oblige.

"Does he really think that we can be bought so cheaply?" is the unexpressed thought going through my head, my mouth full of Caramel Swirl. Of course not, but I make a mental note not to be seen stuffing my face with a chocolate next time I see Mr D in court.

It is a most generous gesture by him, and one genuinely appreciated by all of us who take it in the spirit that was intended.

Today, I am sitting in a trial court along with two experienced and highly competent wingers, Joan and Patrick. Looking at our list, I see we have two morning trials, and one in the afternoon, and we scour our iPads to see if any information has been downloaded for us.

When defendants come to court and plead not guilty at their first appearance, both sets of lawyers then have to fill in a detailed form (called a Preparation For Effective Trial – PET – form), which ideally contains all the information required to ensure that the actual trial can go ahead efficiently and effectively.

The legal adviser and the presiding justice both check and add to it to make sure that everything has been included and all necessary directions made. They work together to ensure that it has been fully completed, but I believe that it is the chair's responsibility to take charge and ask all the necessary questions in court, to ensure that this has been done, with nothing omitted.

The defendant's details must be taken in full, particularly a mobile telephone number, should, for some reason, he or she decide not to turn up on the day of trial. It is quite remarkable how few of them can remember their number when asked by the bench without first being prompted.

The PET form lays out all the agreed facts of the case and the specific issue that is in dispute; in other words, why the defendant asserts that he/she is not guilty as charged – for example, a claim of self-defence in response to an assault charge. This information must be disclosed in advance to ensure that there are no surprises or ambushes on the day of trial.

The form lists all the witnesses required to attend by both the prosecution and defence, what evidence they will provide, and how long is needed for them to give their evidence both in chief and in cross-examination.

It is the chair's job to probe and clarify and ensure that there is no overkill and all the proposed witnesses are necessary and bringing something different to the party. The chair also makes sure that the correct timings have been agreed, without any slack, bearing in mind that allowances have to be made for interpreters or the playing of CCTV or body-worn camera footage.

The prosecutor can also apply for a witness summons to be granted for any witnesses whom they feel might be unwilling to attend. The general rule of thumb is that even if one is not requested, most benches grant one for the complainant and key witnesses in domestic abuse cases. How many of them are actually served by the prosecution is another matter.

The prosecutor can also ask for special measures, which are a series of provisions – such as screens or giving evidence via a live link – that help vulnerable and intimidated witnesses give their best evidence in court and are aimed at relieving some of the stress involved. The test we apply is whether the quality of their evidence is likely to be enhanced if the application is approved. Often, there seems to be a choreographed dance routine going on as defendants are moved out of eye view as a vulnerable witness comes into court and sits behind a carefully positioned screen. We watch like hawks to ensure that there is no intimidation going on, and I once gave a very stern and final warning to a defendant who was blatantly mouthing threats aimed at his former partner as she came into court to give evidence against him. Intermediaries and interpreters can also be provided to help witnesses with special needs or who speak different languages.

If the defendant is not legally represented, then the prosecutor can, in some circumstances, also ask the court to prohibit cross-examination of a witness by the defendant and a lawyer to be provided for this purpose. This too must be noted on the PET form.

Most importantly, the date (28 days hence) by which the prosecutor must provide initial disclosure and serve any further evidence to the defence also has to be confirmed on the form.

Whilst this is all going on, the legal adviser is searching for the first available trial date based on its length, and if it is high or low priority in terms of its level of seriousness.

A high priority trial is any case where:

- The defendant is being held in custody for the matter for which he is to be tried
- The trial has previously been vacated or ineffective
- There is a vulnerable witness
- There is an allegation of domestic abuse
- There is a prosecution for a sexual offence

A medium priority trial is any case where:

- There is an expert witness
- A witness or other party has a disability or special need
- It is expected to last longer than one day
- There are witnesses who have travelled a significant distance

A low priority trial is one that does not fall into either of the other two categories.

We try to reduce the waiting time for a trial as much as possible, recognising just how nerve-wracking these proceedings are for defendants, complainants, and witnesses alike. Thankfully, most trials can be fixed within a couple of months in a magistrates' court unlike the situation in the Crown Court where the unconscionable reduction in court sitting days has resulted in a massive backlog of cases, currently standing at well over 40,000 and certain to increase given the effects of Coronavirus, which has certainly worsened, but is NOT the initial cause of the backlog.

Careful and effective case management at the first hearing, which correctly identifies all the key issues that are likely to arise during the trial, is essential; if properly completed, the PET form is an invaluable tool that provides a timesaving and accurate blueprint and framework for the management of the actual trial.

Luckily, the legal adviser has already downloaded both morning PET forms onto our iPads, and we can see that whilst both cases are allegations of common assault by beating, one is a domestic incident, which means that it takes priority and should be the first one that we hear.

*

We arrive in court to an eerie silence and, apart from the legal adviser and list caller, a deserted room. Eventually, the prosecutor and defence lawyer come into court late, having earned a black mark from us for lack of courtesy. It is simple good manners and customary for them both to be in place at 10 am, when the bench arrives to update us on the status of the impending trials, and ask for more time to be granted if necessary.

They explain that they are both chasing around the building searching in vain for their clients and witnesses who were all meant to arrive at 9.30 am and have no idea where any of them are, or even when they or their colleagues were last in contact with them. We give them 30 minutes to try to sort out the mess, trace the missing defendant, complainant, and witnesses, and see if we can have an effective trial. Just the customary frustrating start to the day in the trial court!

The only change when we return, stuffed full of Quality Street, is that the defendant is now in court, but there is still no sign of either the complainant or chief prosecution witness.

It is now gone 10.30 am, and we cannot afford any more delays and need to make a decision on how best to proceed. It is time to ask the prosecutor some pointed questions.

We ask when the CPS last had contact with their witnesses and if he can explain their absence. With a resigned shrug of his shoulders, and a worryingly blank look on his face, he gives a vague explanation that he thinks the complainant has gone away but is not sure where to, or even when he might return. The security guard who apparently witnessed the alleged assault has also since left his job without leaving a forwarding address, and has seemingly disappeared off the face of the earth. He can provide us with no comfort or guarantee that they will ever attend court should the matter be adjourned today.

We then ask him to provide us with some background about the case, which apparently concerns an argument between two cousins who both work in a street market. The defendant claims that he was attacked first and was simply using reasonable force to defend himself, that there was already bad blood between them, and that his cousin has made several spurious complaints against him in the past.

Given that there is now no possibility of us having a trial today, we also learn that whilst the defendant is of good character, the complainant has several convictions for violence.

The prosecutor confirms that he cannot proceed with the case without the presence of his two key witnesses – the complainant and the security guard, and asks for an adjournment.

The defendant's lawyer vehemently opposes this application, and states that his client, who is of good character, has attended court today (albeit late) and has been waiting for several months since the alleged incident for the opportunity to clear his name and should, therefore, not be forced to endure any further delay. The prosecution has also given the court no real explanation for the absence of their key witnesses and cannot guarantee their appearance at any time soon should be trial be adjourned.

What now comes into play is the *Criminal Practice Direction Number 8*, which was introduced on April Fools' Day 2019. This deals with adjournments in a magistrates' court and ensures that they are not lightly or easily granted, particularly when applications to adjourn are made on the day of trial.

The previous legal precedent that we had to follow, when deciding upon adjournments, was the case of Picton that stated that delays were "scandalous". They are now described as "inimical to the interests of justice", and yes, I also had to look that word up too!

The starting point is that the trial *should* proceed; however, we now have to consider the following factors:

- Dealing justly with the case
- The need for expedition
- The history of the case
- The public interest in ensuring that criminal charges are adjudicated upon thoroughly
- That more serious charges have a greater public interest in being tried
- Whether a defendant can present their defence fully without the adjournment, and the extent to which the defence will be compromised
- The consequences on witnesses – the longer they have to wait to give evidence, the worse their memory will be

- The impact of an adjournment on other cases, with specific reference to the extent of delay on other cases

We also have to play the blame game. Who is at fault for the delay? We must examine the reason for the adjournment request; if the party applying for it is at fault, then that is a factor against granting it.

We retire to consider our decision, but in this instance it is straightforward. The prosecution is totally at fault owing to the absence of their two key witnesses, for not taking the necessary steps to ensure their presence, and being unable to convince the court that they are likely to attend on a new date anytime soon, if at all, should we agree to adjourn the trial. Having checked with the legal adviser, we learn that there would be a delay of around two months before another suitable trial date becomes available.

The missing witnesses are crucial to the trial and their evidence certainly cannot be agreed as it is totally disputed by the defence.

The alleged offence is not pleasant, but neither is it the most serious of assaults, involving some pushing and shoving, and no injuries arose out of it. We also, in this instance, do not have a complainant in court baying for justice.

We come back into court and refuse the application for an adjournment. As a result, the prosecutor is unable to proceed and offers no evidence. The defendant leaves court without a stain on his character.

This means that the trial goes down as "cracked" which is the term used for a case that closes unexpectedly and is resolved without actually going to trial and requires no further attention. As has been the case today, the non-appearance of a witness is a common reason for a cracked trial, as can be a late guilty plea. The latest MoJ statistics confirm that 39% of all magistrate court trials crack, of which 58% were due to a late acceptable guilty plea being received.

Had the trial been adjourned then it would have been recorded as "ineffective", something that is to be avoided if at all possible given that a further trial listing is required. Currently, around 15% of all trials held in the magistrates' court are ineffective.

We have taken well over an hour to get nowhere and need to get going with our second trial. Fortunately, everyone has turned up and we are quickly underway.

*

Nathan is accused of assaulting an emergency worker; in this case, a policeman. This is a new Either Way offence, only introduced in 2018, which can be heard either in a Crown or magistrates' court that demonstrates just how seriously assaults on the police, prison and custody officers, firefighters, ambulance and health services, and the like, are taken when they are acting in the execution of their duties. The potential punishment is now more severe than it would be for an attack on a member of the public with a maximum penalty of 12 months in custody (six months more than we magistrates are allowed to impose for a single offence).

Recent figures have highlighted that the problem still remains and is, in fact, growing steadily. The CPS prosecuted more than 50 such assaults a day in the first year of the new legislation. Between November 2018 and 2019, almost 20,000 offences were charged under the new offence – three-quarters of which were assault by beating. Nine in ten assaults were against police officers – almost always when the attacker was intoxicated on drink or drugs, and being arrested for an unrelated offence.

Spitting was common but the violence perpetrated was wide-ranging and included kicking, punching, head butting, slapping, and biting. When the figures are tallied for 2020, it is inevitable that there will be a substantial rise as people claiming to have Coronavirus deliberately cough on emergency workers. The seriousness of the health situation combined with the nature of their offence should result in an immediate prison sentence for almost all convicted "Coronavirus Coughers" and the Home Secretary also plans to double the maximum sentence for this offence to two years.

Nathan is a fashion plate, immaculately dressed in a smart, well-cut, three-piece suit and tie and well-shined black shoes. I am well aware of unconscious bias and how we all need to be mindful of the danger of potentially, even if unwittingly, favouring people with whom we can identify, or who perhaps are dressed or look the same as us.

Often, lawyers recommend that their clients dress smartly and appropriately for court in order to demonstrate that they respect the courtroom, and are also taking the matter in hand seriously. Not everybody, however, listens to this advice.

I saw television coverage of a celebrity defendant attending a court hearing recently, dressed as if she was about to go clubbing; appearances are certainly something that the bench takes note of, even as it reminds itself not to be judgemental and jump to any conclusions.

You also have to remember that defendants might not own any clothes other than those that they are wearing, that there might be religious reasons for wearing a cap in court, and that having hands in pockets might mean that they are holding their beltless trousers up rather than showing disrespect. I did read of another defendant who dressed up as Homer Simpson for his recent court appearance. I have no idea what point he was trying to make, or if he had just come from a fancy dress party!

The danger of unconscious bias is something that magistrates are, quite correctly, constantly reminded about, and there is excellent mandatory training on this subject. The Sentencing Council has also published research that identified a small discrepancy where black and ethnic minority defendants in the Crown Court were, between 2012 and 2015, more likely to receive a prison sentence for drug-related offences compared with white defendants. This is deeply disturbing, and whilst there is no reason to suppose that the anomaly is caused by unconscious bias of any sort, constant vigilance and self-monitoring is essential. In that regard, I recently saw a pre-sentence report that also, in passing, highlighted this disparity in sentencing and indirectly encouraged magistrates to think carefully before sentencing.

Initially, I was annoyed that it was felt necessary to make this point to the bench, but I can also understand why it was done.

Nathan is accused of spitting at a police officer who had stopped him for another matter that is not part of this case. That is all very well, but when we view body-worn camera footage of the incident in question, we clearly see it labelled with the words "possession of an offensive weapon".

This is incredibly sloppy, unacceptable, and prejudicial behaviour on the part of the CPS as it provides us with information about the defendant and his alleged behaviour that we should definitely not be in possession of, at this stage in time. We can only assume that nobody bothered to check the footage before playing it in open court.

I immediately stop the proceedings and make the bench's extreme concerns and displeasure eminently clear to an embarrassed and apologetic prosecutor. I also reassure the defence lawyer and his client that the bench will put this unwanted information out of our mind when judging this case.

Three police officers give similar evidence of the defendant being questioned and restrained and then – for several minutes – staring at, and verbally abusing one of the officers standing in front of him, to whom he appears to take an instant dislike. Then, he spat at him, with the spittle landing on his trousers.

The other two officers were close at hand, saw the incident, and decided to put a spit hood on Nathan.

One of the officers tries to give evidence simply by reading his notes aloud in court, so we remind him that he can refresh his memory by looking at his contemporaneous notes, but they should ideally not be read out *verbatim*.

The court needs to be satisfied that the notes record the witness's recollections of the matter at an earlier time, and that their recollection of what happened is likely to have been significantly better at the time of making the notes, than at the time of giving evidence.

Renowned law commentator Professor John Spencer aptly summed up that giving evidence should not become a "memory test" – otherwise courts need to "accept two remarkable principles; first, that memory improves with time; and secondly that stress enhances a person's power of recall."

Sir Robin Auld also pointed out that many police officers have no independent memory of the events they describe and rely totally on their notes. So, it is really up to the bench to decide whether to allow the officer to read out his statement.

That being said, what really frustrates me is how many witnesses – police officers included – waltz into court to give evidence and quite plainly have never bothered to even look at their statements since the day they made them. I appreciate how busy police officers are, and just how nervous witnesses must be at the prospect of giving evidence, but surely they should realise how much easier the ordeal of giving evidence will be if they have some inkling of what they intend to say in court.

What makes matters a little confusing when watching the footage is that the three officers are all tall, well-built, and shaven-headed, and at first glance, it is not easy to differentiate between them. However, the spittle can clearly be seen on the first officer's leg.

In his interview, which took place shortly after the incident, Nathan denies spitting at the officer. He says that he was aiming at the floor and that if he had wanted to spit at him, then he would have aimed directly at him.

He repeats this assertion in court today and says that he suffers from anxiety and depression, and that he spat because was angry, as he had previously been assaulted, and that the police officers had ignored his complaint. He denies being aggressive and says that he spat at the floor as a gesture of contempt and the policeman's foot just happened to be in the way.

We go outside to consider the verdict and decide that even if Nathan had not intended to spit at the policeman, his behaviour was still reckless. He admits to having spat in the direction of the officer who was standing very close to him, and he should have realised the potential consequences of what he had done. We are therefore sure that he is guilty as charged.

We have to write out our reasons for every decision that we make and how we came to our verdict. They are a collaborative effort with all three members of the bench contributing to them. The reasons are read out by the presiding justice in open court and kept on file. They are particularly useful if sentencing is postponed because either the defendant is absent on the day of trial, or a pre-sentence report is required, and a different bench is called upon to make the eventual sentencing decision.

As do all my colleagues, I take detailed notes of all the evidence given throughout the trial and use this as an *aide memoire* when deciding upon the verdict with my colleagues. These notes are then disposed of in a confidential waste bin.

Since the day when I carelessly and stupidly threw away our carefully thought-out and articulated reasons, seconds before I was due to announce them in a packed court – forcing me to rapidly re-write them from memory – I now take particular care that I have disposed of the correct pieces of paper.

We now expect to hear from Nathan's lawyer with his mitigation before we pass sentence. Spitting is deeply unpleasant, should be condemned, and has potential health risks for the victim too; however, in isolation, it is still not considered a particularly serious assault, and it can often (pre-Coronavirus) be punished with a fine depending upon the defendant's previous record.

We don't get to sentence him, as given what we had learned

earlier about Nathan – when viewing the body-worn footage – we are not too surprised to discover that he has other outstanding matters that require sentencing, and he is now also in breach of a Crown Court issued suspended sentence.

As such, we bail him and send everything to the Crown Court where Nathan will eventually be sentenced.

*

After a break for lunch, in which there was great excitement and commotion when a court employee was assaulted just outside the courthouse by a desperate man – perhaps just looking to book himself a warm prison cell to stay in over the Christmas period – we return to court for our third trial of the day.

This is another accusation of assault by beating in a domestic context, which allegedly took place in a hotel room when the couple were on a romantic weekend break that went badly wrong. Angela, the complainant, has asked for screens when giving her evidence, but this will now not be necessary as Max, her former partner, has not turned up to court.

The prosecutor applies for the trial to proceed and for us to attempt to prove the case in absence. We confirm that Max was aware of the date of the trial and that there has been no acceptable reason given for his absence.

His lawyer has no idea where his client is and has not taken any specific instructions from him regarding his defence, which is one of factual denial – in other words claiming that the assault never happened.

The default position in these circumstances is that the trial proceeds, and we, therefore, decide to do so. The defence lawyer withdraws and the prosecutor basically now has an open goal to shoot into, as he can present his evidence without it being challenged by the defence.

Angela gives clear evidence of Max, after a few drinks, becoming upset at a phone call she receives from another friend and then striking her in a fit of anger and jealousy, causing visible bruising, of which we see photographic evidence. A police officer who was called to the scene tells of arresting the man as he attempted to leave the hotel and of seeing her facial injuries.

Given the lack of evidence to the contrary, this is an open and shut case, and we convict after a brief discussion and issue a warrant for the arrest of the absent defendant.

I did once sit as a winger on a case where a quite obviously unprepared and overconfident prosecutor got himself so flummoxed and confused that he singularly failed to prove his uncontested case! In that instance, we comfortably acquitted a defendant who had failed to appear, but that was certainly the exception rather than the rule!

6. KEEPING UP STANDARDS

It is an important and nerve-wracking day for me today, as I am going to be appraised for the first time as a presiding justice.

The appraisal system was fully reviewed recently by the Judicial College – the organisation responsible for training judges and magistrates – and rightly, it has been made far more robust and challenging.

Whilst it is not necessary for magistrates to have any formal legal knowledge, as we have legal advisers who provide us with all necessary information and ensure that everything we do in court is lawful, we have the power to imprison individuals for up to six months (or 12 if sentencing for two Either Way offences) and – to state the obvious – it is therefore imperative that the highest standards are maintained, and our competence is rigorously and regularly checked.

Most, if not virtually all, magistrates of my acquaintance take their job enormously seriously – and yes to me it IS a job – albeit an unpaid one, and we welcome every opportunity for CPD and on-going learning and development, whether through formal training, extra reading, sharing knowledge and experiences with colleagues, or visits to relevant and related organisations.

Magistrates are assessed against a pre-determined competence framework and the purpose of the appraisal is to ensure that we have reached, or maintained, the necessary levels of expertise, as well as having any training or development needs identified.

A trained and approved appraiser is responsible throughout the sitting for recording evidence of the magistrate's performance against the competence framework. They assess all the tasks and behaviours set out in the appraisal form, and also note any perceived training needs.

It is not the appraiser's job to decide upon the competence or otherwise of the appraisee, or even to try and catch them out, but simply to observe what is said and done on the day, and objectively and thoroughly record evidence whenever specific skills and requirements of the role are demonstrated in court.

A comprehensive, but predominantly tick-box, form is filled in at the conclusion of the appraisal by both parties, together with comments from the legal adviser, and sent for consideration by the Justices' Training, Approvals, Authorisations and Appraisals Committee – known as the JTAAAC (an acronym that trips lightly off the tongue!).

Purely on the basis of the anonymised report, they decide if the magistrate is competent or whether he or she needs some additional support or training on specific aspects of the role. Occasionally, it is decided that a second appraisal is necessary after the completion of the required training.

*

The annual requirement is for magistrates to sit for a minimum of 13 days each year, or 26 half days for those who are unable to sit for the entire day, which might not seem much; the reality is that the minimum requirement is more than doubled in the first year, once all the additional bench meetings and training requirements are also taken into consideration. Many magistrates also sit far more frequently, and can run the risk of being warned that they are sitting too often!

Occasionally, that might be the case, and Janice, a

magistrate who retired recently, would invariably be ensconced in her favourite chair by the door in the retiring room – her second, or maybe even her main home – doing The Times crossword whenever I arrived for my sitting. You could set your watch by her. Janice was simply part of the furniture and her life seemed to revolve around the magistracy. I have no idea how often she sat, but it must have been at least three times a week, if not more. I can see the concerns that might well raise about a "professional" magistracy, but she would simply say that she was helping out and filling gaps in the rota when required. As far as I was concerned, it was just helpful to have someone around who was so knowledgeable, and whose brains I could pick whenever I needed.

The magistracy rightly demands a heavy time commitment and ideally an agreement to serve for a minimum of five years. Why invest resources and valuable training time on somebody who is not going to sit for a reasonable period of time? You need to sit regularly if you are to develop the necessary skills to do the job to the best of your ability and maintain your competences. For many people who work full time, or have family commitments, this is sometimes too much to ask of them, which creates serious problems both in terms of the recruitment and retention of magistrates.

Magistrates, like judges, have a statutory retiring age of 70, and it is also unlikely that a candidate aged 65 or more will be appointed to the bench. It is crucial to keep replenishing and refreshing the crop of magistrates, hopefully ensuring that they are not hidebound, remain contemporary in their outlook, and are able to keep abreast of what is happening in the world around them. Older magistrates also run the risk of being perceived as out of touch, and having little in common with younger defendants. From my experience, we have had to lose some of the sharpest magistrates we possess because of statutory retirement, even though they are still in total control of their faculties, have moved with the times, and possess a wealth of experience to pass onto newcomers to the magistracy. They are generally also available to fill the gaps in the rota by sitting regularly.

That being said, I am sure we all know people aged 50 years or less who are 'old' well before their time. I am very conscious of the on-going shortage of magistrates, particularly younger ones, and the need to tailor our recruitment strategy in such a way as to attract them. However, I would propose that to help address this massive drain of talent and experience that all magistrates approaching enforced retirement are appraised by JTAAAC, if they wish to continue. If found still to be competent, they should be allowed to sit for another year with their progress carefully monitored annually, and with the potential to sit until they reach the age of 75. Jurors can serve until they are 75, so why not magistrates too?

Some magistrates, unfortunately, also need prompting and to be reminded to read their emails regularly to keep up-to-speed with their rota, updates, changes to the law, and revised Sentencing Guidelines. This information needs to be assimilated and taken into account if you are to do your job properly.

By the end of their first year, a new magistrate who sits regularly will undoubtedly have learned and experienced much on the job but, just as importantly, will also have completed their initial three-day induction training (which, from April

2020, has been increased to three-and-a-half days to allow for specific IT training), and then further two-day consolidation training. He or she also has to complete specific modules on domestic abuse, equality, diversity, and unconscious bias, then visit a probation office, attendance centre, and young offenders' and adult prisons. At this point, once they have also completed six formal mentored sittings, they are generally deemed ready for an initial threshold appraisal which usually takes place around 12 to 18 months after appointment.

Once magistrates are found competent at their threshold appraisal, they are further appraised every four years for wingers and two for presiding justices (a winger is eligible to become a presiding justice after four years) to ensure that standards have been maintained.

If – and I know this is a big 'if' – there were sufficient appraisers available, I would like to see all magistrates appraised every two years to ensure standards are maintained, and ideally for more cross-bench appraisals to take place as – generally – members of our own bench appraise us, rather than magistrates who sit elsewhere.

That is not satisfactory in my view as however well-intentioned and objective the appraiser, there is a risk, even if only perceived, of bias or of opinions being clouded, even unconsciously, by previous experiences of sitting together, despite the appraisal being meant only to take account of what is demonstrated and evidence gleaned on the day in question.

Whilst it will always be the case that appraisers appraise each other, I have also heard of situations where two appraisers appraise each other within a short period of time, and this is something that ideally should not occur so as to avoid accusations of mutual backscratching.

In my view, the more thorough training we receive the better; ideally related to situations we will encounter in court, and whilst we are all volunteers, I believe that most magistrates would find the time to attend or complete more training aimed at improving their levels of competence and even legal knowledge.

The current appraisal form does ask for further evidence to be provided if a specific behaviour was not totally demonstrated on the day of observation, and there is a small box for additional comments and ideally positive feedback and examples of good practice. The legal adviser is also asked to provide comments and advice in relation to the management of the court and the content of all the pronouncements made by the presiding justice.

The current appraisal form is much easier and quicker for the appraiser to fill in, whereas the previous version of the form required much more thought, detail, and time to complete.

Apparently, a massive 96% of all appraisals end with the appraisee being deemed competent. This is very encouraging and fully supports my view that the overwhelming majority of magistrates are doing a truly excellent job.

Would reverting to the old-style more detailed appraisal form and employing more cross-bench appraisals result in a lower success rate? Perhaps. Who knows?

*

As soon as I was informed of my appraisal date, I booked myself onto a court skills refresher training day, specifically designed to help magistrates prepare for their imminent appraisal.

It was an eye-opening experience as, given the fact that I sit regularly, I smugly and erroneously assumed that I pretty much knew what I was doing in court, and was *au fait* with most of the tasks and skills required of a presiding justice. I left the training room at the end of an illuminating and exhausting day, and emerged back in the real world humbled and gobsmacked by my rustiness and ignorance. I had been made only too aware of just how much I had forgotten or never even known, and the myriad bad habits I had lazily allowed myself to fall into. Hubris indeed!

For example, when deciding on whether a trial should be heard in a magistrates' court, or sent to the Crown Court, I always thought that your allocation decision was based on how serious the offence was, only taking into account how you are addressed by both prosecution and defence lawyers; however, now I realise that you must drill down much deeper into all the aggravating and mitigating factors related to the offence before coming to a decision and, if necessary, take a more inquisitorial role.

All in all, this was a day well spent and it was also illuminating to share experiences and war stories with my peers from other benches who were also awaiting their own appraisals.

The next step was for me to read and fill in the long and voluminous Preparation for Appraisal Checklist, which I had been sent by Bench Support. This is a new innovation and a good one as it is a self-assessment form that mirrors the actual appraisal form and is intended to help the appraisee reflect upon his or her knowledge and performance in advance of the appraisal. I was required to review all the competences that would be assessed and note any that may require work or attention.

I initially saw this as a formality but, after the training day, which highlighted so many areas where I didn't know as much as I thought I did, I end up ticking several of the boxes!

*

Finally, the dreaded day arrives and – feeling slightly anxious and uneasy – I arrive at court bright and early to meet my appraiser. Dawn is someone who I know from the odd conversation in the retiring room, but given that we are both presiding justices, our paths have rarely crossed in court. We meet to discuss the appraisal and she soon puts me at ease, reassuring me that she is simply there to record evidence and not to judge me or try to find fault.

I contrast this approach with my threshold appraisal from a few years back, which was a total and unmitigated disaster. Trevor, my appraiser, was a difficult, solitary, and abrasive man who thought he knew best, ran the court with a rod of iron, and expected his wingers to bow down and kowtow to his own self-perceived superior knowledge and experience. Collaboration, teamwork, and shared opinions were not high on his list of priorities. Arrogance most certainly was.

Throughout the morning, every time my fellow winger or I wanted to make a point, or clarify a situation, we received a shrug or a peremptory dismissive wave from our chair who would then turn his back, ignore us, and continue to make his own decisions without any hint of consultation. It was a frustrating and humiliating experience.

Even though we tried our best to hide our feelings, it was plainly obvious that we were both distinctly unhappy and angry at the chair's attitude and behaviour; at lunchtime, we quietly spoke to the legal adviser who said that she was aware of our concerns, shared them, and would speak to the chair, and also support us if we took matters further.

It was finally time for me to discuss my now half-forgotten appraisal with Trevor. It felt like I was entering the headmaster's study. What should I do? Should I play the game, smile sweetly, and keep my mouth shut as my partner had wisely advised me only that morning, or let rip and give him a piece of my mind? He was a highly experienced magistrate of long-standing and I was still very new. Who would believe me? I was totally undecided and conflicted.

He made my mind up for me when, straight away, he told me that he thought it had been a straightforward and uneventful morning in court without any issues or problems. This was too much. Was he so lacking in perception – and so stuffed full of his own arrogance and self-importance – that he could not see the car crash he had caused? My first words to him were – and I remember them clearly to this day, "I think you are a total disgrace", and I proceeded to tell him exactly what I thought of him and why. His mouth agape, he replied, "I have no idea what you are talking about", and left the room.

So ended my first appraisal, and I hardly slept for the next week waiting for Armageddon. Finally, an email slithered into my inbox – a completed appraisal form that blandly found no fault with my performance nor identified any training needs.

Back to today's appraisal, and I demonstrate to Dawn that I know my way around the court-issue iPads and can quickly find all the relevant guidelines and downloaded information on each case – a prerequisite for all magistrates. Magistrates used to be given a printed set of Sentencing Guidelines – a gargantuan, back-breaking tome – on appointment, and were issued with regular updates. Those profligate days are long gone and the online version that replaced it has gradually been upgraded, and is now fit for purpose, and pretty user friendly.

Most magistrates can now handle the required technology and the court-issue iPads – even through gritted teeth – but there are still a few Luddites who struggle to cope and require help to even log in and out, let alone access data. Thankfully, from April, they will be offered a new half-day IT training session that will help them address this problem. Let's just hope they are able to find, open, read, and reply to the eJudiciary email inviting them to attend.

I realise that I must not do anything different, and treat today as a normal sitting. I must, with difficulty, put out of my mind faded memories of taking my driving test many decades ago, and of deliberately accentuating the all-important Mirror/Signal/Manoeuvre (MSM) routine to ensure that my examiner took note of what I was doing.

LOOK, I am driving this car carefully and safely.

We hold a quick pre-court review meeting and I allocate roles to the two wingers. Winger 1 – Dawn (who will also be appraising me), and therefore probably needs the use of three hands – will look up the relevant Sentencing Guidelines, and Winger 2 – Brian – will open up each defendant's Police National Computer (PNC) document that lists all of their previous convictions.

We then examine the list of cases and see that we are in an NGAP remand court where it is anticipated (by the police) that defendants will plead not guilty. I remark that, in some cases, they might well change their mind; in which case, there will be a lot of case management to do and Preparation for Effective Trial (PET) forms to fill in.

There are a variety of cases that we will have to deal with, and I hopefully score some brownie points with my appraiser by pointing out that we have a triple-hander with all three defendants facing a charge of harassment without violence; plus a 16-year-old youth accused of robbery along with a 19-year-old co-defendant.

Normally, youths are only tried in the adult court if jointly charged with an adult; however, robbery is an indictable only offence, which will need to be dealt with by the Crown Court.

We also scan the list for any familiar names that might present us with a conflict. Thankfully, there are none today, although I once had to ensure that someone who had attended the same school as my son had his case moved to another court. On a different occasion, I well remember another defendant – about to sit down in the dock – causing much merriment by looking up and greeting the legal adviser with a wave and a cheery cry of, "Hello mate, how are you?" They had been at school together!

Anyone can fall foul of the law. A momentary lapse of concentration and attention when driving can have catastrophic and life-changing consequences. A colleague told me recently of queuing to go through security at her courthouse when she noticed a familiar face also waiting to have his bag checked. It was a friend of hers, an eminent psychologist. She asked him why he was there, expecting to be told he was going to be an expert witness and was taken aback when he proudly declared that he was a defendant, one of the over 1,800 Extinction Rebellion protesters arrested in October. "And I'm not pleading guilty", was his parting shot.

*

We go into court together, and I ensure that I make a deep bow before sitting down. This tradition has a curious origin, due to the presence of the Royal Coat of Arms that sits behind the bench where the magistrates sit. As people enter the room, whether they be magistrates, court officials, lawyers, or members of the public, it is customary to bow to the Royal Coat of Arms — and indirectly those presiding over the case. This is in recognition of the fact that justice stems from the Monarch, and that law courts are part of the Royal Court.

A crusty and anachronistic magistrate with, I believe, a political and military background (now retired), once took me outside the court and gave me a resounding finger-wagging and telling off, as – in his view – I had not bowed in unison with him and had therefore shown deep disrespect to the Monarch.

Unusually, there are no major delays today, and after greeting the prosecutor and list caller, we start dealing with a varied list of cases. The list caller will often try to call on the first case the moment we sit down, but I will make him or her wait until the bench is settled and completely ready for action. I'm not trying to be a tinpot dictator but it is for the bench to run the court and set the pace in conjunction with the legal adviser.

Russell, our first defendant, pays us a fleeting visit as he is accused of possession with intent to supply both heroin and crack cocaine, and we decline jurisdiction on his matters and send him for trial to the Crown Court. He has an aggressive manner and smirks at us throughout the proceedings. Granted unconditional bail, he slouches out of court, and Dawn points out that he has been standing in the dock with his hands in his pocket without my commenting. I reply that she is right, but he has not been causing any problems in court or showing blatant disrespect; given the circumstances, I simply wanted to deal with him as quickly as possible and not seek unnecessary confrontation.

Every presiding justice must develop his or her individual style, remembering that you are simply there to administer justice fairly and efficiently, and not be the star of the show. Some are very authoritarian and rigid in their style and approach. Others let their personality shine through. I prefer to be outwardly more pleasant and outgoing in my manner, and I do my best to run things in an open and collaborative manner, hopefully without showing weakness or losing my sense of authority – or humour.

This is quite deliberate, on my part, as court can be quite daunting, stressful, and intimidating, particularly for those attending for the first time. Frankly, I want to help put everybody at their ease and make their courtroom experience as palatable, inclusive, welcoming, and tension free – or the least unpleasant – as possible. In my experience, the calmer and more relaxed they are, the better people will behave, and it is my job to keep things ticking over smoothly and without fuss.

Throughout the day, I try to remain punctiliously polite, listen hard, and treat everyone in court, whatever their role, with dignity and respect. I also endeavour to explain what is happening to all defendants and court users, ideally using plain English and avoiding jargon and legal language. It must be really frustrating and confusing whenever there is a delay caused by, perhaps, the legal adviser entering the details of the previous case into the system, or the bench retiring to consider a decision. Good communication is key.

Communication works both ways, of course, and it is also important to have some level of understanding of the constantly changing slang, argot, jargon, abbreviations, and acronyms employed by many of our customers – particularly the younger ones and gang members. I am not suggesting that we also use the language of the younger generation – far from it – as that would be false and cringeworthy, just that we are aware of it and have some element of understanding.

For the most part, this policy seems to work well for me, and I try to pick my fights carefully and very, very seldomly. I don't seem to have many issues with defendants' behaviour or problems in court. If anyone does kick off, overstep the mark, or is rude or supercilious towards the bench or a court official (particularly list callers, who are unable to answer back or stand up for themselves), then I am quick to clamp down firmly – but hopefully still politely – and ideally nip trouble in the bud.

One defendant who was denied bail threatened to "get me" on his release, his words accompanied by the appropriate cut-throat gesture; another loudly suggested that I do something particularly vile and disgusting to my mother, but these comments were made over their shoulders as they were already on their way downstairs to the cells. Given their destination, it hardly seemed worth calling them back into court to seek confrontation; putting someone into contempt of court is something to be avoided if at all possible. I contented myself by thinking that at least I was going home that night.

Yes, it does worry me that one day somebody could put their words into action as we enjoy open justice, and the names of all magistrates are easily available to the public, but these are invariably idle threats made in the heat of the moment without any intention of being carried out.

There have also been a few other unruly defendants, previously, who ignore my warnings to 'keep quiet and stop being disruptive' and end up being sent downstairs to cool down in the cells for a while, before being brought back up and invariably apologising for their outburst. Fortunately, I have never been put in the position of having to exclude a defendant from a trial and proceed in absence because of his/her disruptive behaviour.

I was once a winger on a case when one of the defendants was caught red-handed by the list caller surreptitiously taking photographs of prosecution witnesses and even attempting to film a video of the proceedings on her mobile phone. Her efforts were thwarted, her phone was confiscated, and she was given a severe warning by the chair as she could well have faced contempt charges.

Generally, you are addressed as "sir/madam" or "your worship" in court, ("Don't expect that at home", remarked my partner), but the odd defendant has also called me "judge" or even "your highness" to my face – and heaven only knows what to my back.

I do sometimes wish that I was able to see some of our defendants and their demeanour, outside the court as well as in. You know that many of them are "performing" in court and trying to make a good impression. I will never forget an apparently quietly spoken young man who barely opened his mouth throughout his trial for an allegation of domestic assault – a veritable George Washington. But when acquitted, he was clearly heard screaming "Fuck, yeah!" at the top of his voice as he ran out of the building. One can only guess whether he was relieved, or if he knew he had gotten away with it.

A 16-year-old youth faces a robbery charge along with his 19-year-old adult co-defendant. The youth is in court; the adult is nowhere to be seen. They should be tried together in the adult court otherwise complainants and witnesses will need to attend court on separate occasions. The youth is of good character and is alleged to have played a minor role in snatching an iPhone from a customer in a fast-food restaurant.

Thankfully, I remember to make a Section 45 pronouncement before we start. This imposes reporting restrictions for children and young people involved in criminal proceedings and prevents their identity being revealed until they reach adulthood. We then grant a 14-day adjournment in the expectation that the missing adult will be traced within that period, and I explain to the confused young person why he has had a wasted morning in court, and must turn up again in a fortnight.

*

The next case is really weird as Daniel – a middle-aged, longhaired man with a faraway dreamy expression on his face – beams and practically waves at us from the dock. He pleads not guilty to robbery, assault occasioning actual bodily harm, and criminal damage. Daniel is accused of approaching two elderly trainspotters at a local overground station and, for no apparent reason and without provocation, attacking and injuring one of them, and taking the other's expensive camera, which he then destroyed. Daniel, who is of good character, pleads not guilty, so the cases are sent for trial to the Crown Court, he is granted bail, and leaves the court with a beatific smile still on his face.

Magistrates are expected to keep a poker face on the bench but we cannot stop ourselves from exchanging furtive glances and shrugs. What on earth was that all about? Was he drunk? It all sounds totally bonkers. We are in total ignorance given that he gave a "no comment" interview after arrest. Hopefully, all will be revealed when it comes to trial in a few months' time and I will be able to discover the outcome.

*

Jeff is accused of non-domestic burglary, and not for the first time either, and appears to be having problems in deciding how to plead. His lawyer asks for a minute to clarify matters with his client. I suggest that the bench retires but we are told that it is not necessary for us to do so.

Jeff and his lawyer huddle together for a conversation that soon turns into a muffled argument with arms waving and Jeff's voice raised. Despite all our efforts not to earwig, the whole courtroom can clearly hear Jeff stating, "Of course I did it, but I'm going to plead not guilty." This puts his lawyer in an impossible position but he retorts, "Okay, but the CCTV *clearly* shows that it is *you* inside the building." Jeff then says, "I know, but I want to spend a bit more time at home before I go to prison." The soap opera ends, and Jeff finally enters a belated plea of guilty, is remanded in custody, and committed to the Crown Court for sentence.

*

Stephen is next in court, charged with a domestic assault on his partner. He is of good character although social services have previously been involved after earlier incidents in the home. He apparently verbally abuses his partner on a regular basis, threatens and humiliates her, and often shouts at her in front of their two young children. On the night in question, they argue again, matters escalate and get out of hand. He snatches her phone, lunges at her, slaps her hard on the right cheek, and she falls backwards onto the floor, all in the presence of the children. She has suffered bruising to her cheek and has on-going pain in her back.

We listen carefully to the prosecution case and, on the basis of the facts outlined to us, we place this assault in the second category of seriousness. We find that there is greater harm because the victim is particularly vulnerable because of her personal circumstances, but there is lower culpability because none of the factors indicating higher culpability – such as significant premeditation or use of a weapon – are present. The starting point when sentencing such an offence is a medium level community order with a range between a fine and a high level community order.

Before sentencing, we also have to take into account several aggravating factors such as the assault being domestic in nature, taking place at night in the family home, and in front of two young children. The only mitigating factors are Stephen's previous good character and the fact that the assault consisted of a single blow.

Stephen is prepared to plead guilty to assaulting her, but only on a basis of plea. In other words, he accepts that he has committed a crime but in circumstances different to those alleged by the prosecution, and he puts forward his own version of what happened on the night in question.

He accepts that an assault took place, but it only constituted a push, and he denies that he slapped her or that she fell to the floor and hurt her back. If we accept his account, then the assault would be in the lowest category of seriousness, punishable only by a fine or conditional discharge.

The prosecutor is not prepared to accept a guilty plea on the basis put forward by Stephen and we also decide that if the defendant's version of the facts is accepted, it will make a fundamental difference to the sentence he will actually receive for the crime as, in our view, it crosses the community penalty threshold.

There will, therefore, need to be another hearing, called a Newton hearing, in which a new bench will solely decide which version of the facts is correct – the prosecution's or Stephen's – and then sentence him accordingly.

We fill in a case management form, arrange a trial date, and grant Stephen conditional bail, excluding him from the family home and from contacting his partner except through lawyers or social services to arrange for him to see his children.

We break early for an extended lunch as there is a team meeting for all the legal advisers to discuss the soon-to-be-introduced case management system, Common Platform, which, when introduced later this year, will replace the current DMU resulting and LIBRA systems.

At present, around 40 magistrates' courts are already using Common Platform and, by the end of the eventual roll-out, all cases will be handled on the new system, and the Court Store will no longer be used. Its aim is to provide a comprehensive end-to-end service, which will improve the number of trials that are dealt with on the day they are originally listed, and reduce the administration needed by all parties to progress a case to trial. With any luck, this will make life much easier for our harassed and overworked legal advisers.

Normally, an appraisal only lasts for a morning. After a brief chat, however, Dawn and I agree to continue it into the afternoon as we have not been as busy as expected and, given the circumstances, I have not yet had the opportunity to demonstrate many of the required competences.

*

We start the afternoon by considering an application for a search warrant to seize a dangerous dog that has been terrorising the local area and attacking humans and animals alike. In addition, the dog's walker also threatened the owner of another far smaller dog that had been mauled. There is clear evidence of an offence under the Dangerous Dogs Act that enables us to grant the warrant, which will allow for the seizure of the dog on private premises. Hopefully, it can be taken off the streets as soon as possible – and perhaps the owner too.

Why is it that dangerous dogs almost invariably seem to have names like Psycho, Attila, Satan, and Killer? These were the names of the first four dogs dealt with in court by a colleague of mine. Where are the dogs called Coco, Buddy, Mr Puffles, or Charlie? I think it says far more about their owners than it does about the dogs.

And what about Fifi? Surely a dog with such a cute and innocent name could never be a danger to others? My former colleague, Janice, proved otherwise to me when she recounted her favourite story regarding dangerous dogs – a real shaggy dog story, in fact.

She is sitting in the retiring room one summer morning, with two colleagues, waiting to start the day's business. Robert, the legal adviser, normally a po-faced and very serious young man, comes into the retiring room, clutching a large pile of case files, and sniggering gently. This was very out of character for someone who normally barely cracked his face.

Janice asks him what is so funny. He said, "You'll see", and when pressed, he remarked that it was a Dangerous Dogs case, but would say no more.

These matters are always difficult and problematic as you are dealing with someone's pet, very often a child substitute, and these cases can be extremely emotional. Owning a prohibited species of dog, or a dog dangerously out of control in a public place, also carries – potentially – the last death sentence available in the English courts.

These cases are almost always prosecuted by the RSPCA, who are understandably zealous in their efforts. If a dog has been so out of control, and has caused such serious harm, that the advice from experts is that nothing can be done to prevent this happening again, the bench can make a Destruction Order, which means that the dog is put to death. If, after discussions with the RSPCA, it is considered that the dog can safely be allowed to live, the bench can make a Contingent Destruction Order (CDO) – effectively a suspended death sentence.

This usually involves the dog's owner bearing considerable expense, having the dog neutered, chipped, a registration number tattooed in its ear, and allowing the dog out in public only while muzzled and leashed. Would that we could sometimes make a similar muzzling order on the owner too! The owner must also buy public liability insurance.

When they arrive in court that morning, Janice and her colleagues soon discover what the sniggering had been about. This was a breach of a CDO. The dog concerned was called Fifi – a Chihuahua with a taste for taking chunks out of her neighbour's ankles. Fifi's Daddy, for this was how her owner, Ian, described himself to Janice in court, was a middle-aged punk, with a large orange Mohican hairdo, dressed soberly and appropriately for court in black patent hot pants and knee boots, with a black string vest and black fishnet tights. Fifi had been made subject to a Contingent Destruction Order the year before, when she simply went too far in attacking her neighbour, and Fifi's Daddy seems to have been reluctant to prevent her from repeating her attacks.

On the day in question, Fifi and Ian were in the park where they encountered the neighbour. Fifi, who was not muzzled, in direct contravention of the CDO, had yet again attacked the neighbour, who then called the police.

Janice asked Fifi's Daddy whether he had received and read the CDO. He told her that he had. She then asked him why Fifi had not been muzzled. With a straight face, Ian told her that Fifi needed to pee.

By this point, the entire bench, the legal adviser, the list caller, and even the RSPCA prosecutor, were all having a really hard time keeping a straight face. When asked why this had necessitated taking off her muzzle, Ian then replied, in open court, "Well, could you do a pee while you are wearing a muzzle?" Struggling to keep a straight face, and maintain her judicial dignity, Janice told him that she thought she could! At this point, the defendant burst into tears, dropped to his knees, and begged the court not to kill his Fifi.

The prosecutor, also struggling to remain calm and professional, asked for a brief moment to discuss the matter with the bench. The court was cleared with all solemnity, and the prosecutor told us that if we gave Fifi's Daddy a really strong warning about the consequences of any further breach of the CDO, he was prepared to withdraw the case.

Ian was called back into court and was told that, on this

occasion, no action would be taken. Janice then warned him that if there was any further breach of the order, the CDO would be activated and that he would then be personally responsible for the death of his beloved Fifi.

Ian prostrated himself in front of the bench, thanking them between sobs for "sparing Fifi's life". He was then sent away, and the entire court had to take a five-minute break just to allow everyone to recover!

*

There seems to be a common theme as the next case, a triple-hander, also involves a dog. Three defendants are accused of harassing a neighbour; two of them – Angie and Sara – are sisters who plead not guilty, but the third – Mike – who is Angie's partner, pleads guilty.

Mike's dog apparently attacks two neighbours and is then taken away from him by the police. Mike then threatens the neighbours, a lesbian couple, using some disparaging and upsetting homophobic epithets as well as also threatening to kill *their* dog.

The incident has badly affected the couple, and a victim impact statement states that they both have PTSD and now feel too scared to leave their house.

We examine the facts of the offence in more detail: there is the targeting of an individual or individuals by a group, the homophobic abuse, it was a sustained incident, and the victims suffered serious distress. This means that we place it in the highest category, with a starting point of a high level community order, and a sentencing range of between a low level community order to 26 weeks' custody.

Mike also has two previous convictions, but they were several years ago for completely unrelated offences.

Given that it has crossed the community threshold, we ask the probation services to provide us with an "all options open" fast delivery oral report, which means that they will interview Mike about the offence, what lies behind it, his personal situation, issues and circumstances, assess the likelihood of his offending again, and provide us with a sentencing recommendation. This, however, is not necessarily an indication of the sentence he will be given, as the court can impose any sentence that the law allows, including a custodial sentence. This is why it is called an "all options open" report.

Given that we have now finished all our other business, the list caller checks to see if we can assist any other courts that are overworked or if there are any warrants that we can deal with.

Five minutes later, we learn that there is nothing that we can do to help out, and return to the retiring room. We have to wait for the probation report to be prepared and, to kill time, I examine the shelves of our new book swap service. I am amused to see a worryingly well-thumbed copy of "The History of Torture" which helps me while away a few idle minutes.

About an hour later, we are informed that the probation report is ready, which is really speedy and excellent work on their behalf. The report is short, sharp, and to the point.

Mike is really sorry for what he did and describes his own behaviour as "disgusting". He was drunk at the time of the offence and does not remember too much of what happened, but fully accepts his guilt. He works long hours, at a couple of driving jobs. His mother died recently, which has caused him great distress, and he has a partner and a young child. Probation recommends the imposition of a community order with unpaid work.

After listening to Mike's lawyer speak on his behalf, we go outside the court to discuss the report and decide upon his sentence. It doesn't take too long as the probation report was clear, sensible, and well thought through and we agree to follow its recommendations.

We sentence Mike to a one-year community order with 160 hours (about 23 days' worth) of unpaid work. We increased his sentence because of the homophobic nature of the offence, which makes it more serious, and we inform Mike that we would otherwise have sentenced him to 100 hours of unpaid work, but it has been increased to 160 hours because of the required uplift. He also has to be supervised by probation for up to 20 days of Rehabilitation Activity Requirement (RAR) where, hopefully, he will address his problems and develop new skills. We also order him to pay compensation of £100 to each of the victims and make no order for costs or victim surcharge because of the compensation order, which takes precedence. I also speak very firmly to him and make it crystal clear just how appalling and unacceptable his behaviour was, and the serious impact it has had on both of his victims.

*

Finally, after a post-court review, the day is over and Dawn and I can go off and discuss my appraisal. We fill in the form together and thankfully we are in agreement about what has, and hasn't, been observed throughout the day.

I take photos of each page for reference purposes, and also as a failsafe before the completed and signed report form disappears into the black hole that is the internal mail system. Hopefully, at some point soon, it will arrive safely at Bench

Support, who will then send it off to the JTAAAC for consideration.

So how did I do?

Well, I am still sitting as a Presiding Justice so I must have done something right!

7. MAKING THE GRADE

I am looking forward to today as I am sitting with my mentee, Mandy, for her fifth mentored sitting. She is quick on the uptake, listens well, is always prepared, has strong opinions and sound judgement, contributes thoughtfully to all discussions and is eager to learn. With the experience that only sitting regularly can bring, she is going to be an extremely competent magistrate – not that I can really claim any credit for her progress!

The aim of the mentoring scheme is to provide new magistrates with all the guidance and support needed over their first 12 to 18 months to ensure that they achieve the necessary level of competence.

The recruitment of new magistrates is now a massive priority given that our number has continued to fall, decreasing 43% from 25,170 as of the 1st of April 2012 to 14,348 on the 1st of April 2019. Why has this happened? Mainly because of decreasing workloads in magistrates' courts as well as natural wastage caused by consistent annual levels of retirements. In turn, resignations – sometimes caused by concerns about our working conditions and the impact of court closures – have reduced numbers further, and the system has not been able to replace departees quickly or adequately enough.

Breaking these numbers down further, 56% of magistrates are women, rising from 51% in 2012, and as of April 2019, 12% of magistrates declared themselves as BAME, a rise of four percent since 2012. London showed the most diversity, with 29% of all magistrates identifying as BAME.

The traditional, if now totally outdated, perception of

magistrates is of crusty, reactionary, and out-of-touch Colonel Blimp figures, and the twin set and pearls brigade, with monocles, spats, hats and gloves to the fore. Local rules and customs prevailed at one time, but with the introduction of standardised Sentencing Guidelines, those days, thankfully, are long gone – certainly from my experience of the magistracy.

What cannot be ignored, however, is the age profile of magistrates. The latest Ministry of Justice figures do not make happy reading, with over 80% aged between 50-70 years, and 52% aged 60 and above. Only 5% of magistrates are aged under 40, with a small but growing number aged between 18-30 years. Retired or semi-retired people, but still active, obviously have more time on their hands whereas those building a career or with family commitments cannot so easily spare the time required to become, and remain, a magistrate.

It is extremely concerning that many of our younger and most promising magistrates are minimum sitters in court because of this very problem. In order for them to develop the skills and experience necessary to become presiding justices, mentors, and appraisers in their own right – picking up the baton from the older and more established magistrates – they need their employers to play their part too. Companies need to allow people the necessary time off, either paid or unpaid, and should receive an incentive or subsidy for doing so; they should be encouraged to recognise that, by releasing their staff from time to time, they are also making an important contribution to their local community as well demonstrating enlightened self-interest by providing their employees with an opportunity to develop skills and experience that will help them – and their employers – in their work life.

Becoming a magistrate has always been seen as a way of making a contribution to society; helping to administer justice and putting something back into the local community. Long may that public-spirited attitude remain, and ideally the growing number of self-employed and people with a portfolio of jobs – as well as an ongoing media and marketing campaign aimed at demonstrating the relevance and importance of the magistracy to people of all ages – will help to provide a regular influx of younger, more diverse, and socially mobile candidates.

As with everything associated with law and order, money is in short supply, but what funds are available – and more is surely needed – must be spent wisely with the development of a well-thought-through, cogent strategy, and with targeted activity created and planned by people with a clear knowledge and understanding of how to reach and influence a younger and more diverse generation.

I have sat with magistrates of all ages, colours, and creeds, and from all walks of life – captains of industry, builders, and bus drivers alike – and whilst I accept that it is important that magistrates are seen to be both representative of, and in tune with, the community they serve, it is all about their approach, competence, common sense, life experience, and open-mindedness rather than a label.

The recently published *Senior Judiciary Strategy for the Magistracy 2019-2022* recommends that, "A comprehensive and sustainable plan for recruitment will be created, to increase the number and diversity of applicants, while maintaining high standards of competence."

*

The responsibility for recruiting magistrates lies with 24

regional Advisory Committees, which are composed of approximately two-thirds magistrates and one-third non-magistrate members. They are each charged with creating and executing a local strategy to attract a growing number of younger and more diverse applicants from under-represented groups of society, with far more use of social media as a recruitment tool; last year, a full-page editorial was tested in the Metro newspaper. The current target is to equal or better the 1,000 new magistrates who were appointed last year.

The Advisory Committees interview and recommend to the Senior Presiding Judge, and the Lord Chancellor, suitable candidates for appointment to the magistracy.

There is a vocal minority in the media who make disparaging comments about the need for magistrates' courts at all. They cite the fact that magistrates do not require any legal qualifications to be appointed and are apparently "let loose" on the unsuspecting public without much or sufficient training and guidance. I would simply refer them to the wise words of Howard Riddle, the former Senior District Judge (Chief Magistrate) for England and Wales, and Judge Robert Zara, who stated in their recent book *Essential Magistrates' Courts Law*, "We are unashamed apologists for the quality of summary justice. Simple speedy justice, following the new rules and modern-day practices, is quality justice." The principle of justice by peers has been established for many centuries and is surely as valid today as it ever was.

Whilst it is true that you do not require any formal qualifications or legal training to apply to become a magistrate, the recruitment and interview process is pretty gruelling, and I understand that, on average, only just over one out of every four interviewed is recommended for appointment.

Anyone can apply to become a magistrate, but not everyone will be accepted. Applicants, who can be aged between 18 and 65 years, are required to complete an extremely comprehensive application form, which if not quite the application form from Hell, asks them, and three supporting referees to provide demonstrable written evidence of the six key qualities required for the role: Good character; Understanding and communication; Social awareness; Maturity and sound temperament; Sound judgement; Commitment and reliability.

Magistrates need to assimilate detailed information quickly and communicate effectively, so I see no real workable method of replacing this form with something simpler and less taxing.

Magistrates require intelligence, common sense, integrity, and the capacity to act fairly. Each applicant is carefully assessed for judicial potential and aptitude, as it is essential that a magistrate can identify relevant issues and deal with them even-handedly, understand documents, follow evidence, and communicate effectively. They must accept the need for the rule of law in society, and have a good understanding and knowledge of the social issues in the local area in which they wish to serve. Magistrates must be objective and be able to recognise and set aside their prejudices, think logically, weigh up arguments, and relate to and work with the other members of the bench, so they can reach a fair and balanced decision.

Surely that's not too much to ask for, from any one individual?

This is all very dry and theoretical, so let me illustrate it from my own example. My mother had been a magistrate and was a chair in a busy town centre court for many years. She was a beautiful, intelligent, and vivacious woman with a well-developed sense of the ridiculous, which was hidden and disguised beneath a stern exterior whenever she was in court. Whilst I never saw her in action on the bench, she had a massive respect for the rule of law and I can well believe that some defendants would have felt the rough edge of her tongue in a way that is perhaps not encouraged nowadays. She loved and was inordinately proud of her time on the bench as it gave her a sense of purpose and self-expression at a time when strong women did not always easily find opportunities in society to demonstrate their capabilities. Whenever we met, she used to regale me with highly edited and uproarious versions of her exploits on the bench and I suspect that some of it stuck with me and – to a large degree – my sitting on the bench now is a homage to her. I just hope that she is proud of me.

I had always had an interest in the law but was far too lazy to embark upon the law degree course that I was offered, and instead embarked upon a career in business after university. I finally decided to apply for the magistracy once I had eventually sold my company and had some time on my hands whilst I tried to reinvent myself, put something back, and adopt a portfolio approach to work – something that I am still trying vainly to achieve. I spoke to some magistrate acquaintances of mine and picked their brains about what was entailed, and eventually found the courage necessary to fill in that daunting application form and find three referees prepared to take the time and trouble to provide an independent viewpoint on me.

Currently, pretty much everyone who applies gets an

interview; although a sifting process is being introduced which will eliminate applications that obviously fail to demonstrate evidence of the required qualities.

Candidates are interviewed by a panel of three from a local advisory committee, comprising two magistrates and an independent member, who themselves go through a thorough and rigorous interviewing process and also, ideally, have previous experience of interviewing candidates either for employment or for other public appointments and voluntary roles, or have worked with disciplinary and investigatory procedures. They also have to attend a two-day training course in interviewing techniques before being allowed to interview prospective candidates for the magistracy.

It is imperative that the panels do not simply recruit candidates who are mirror images of themselves; they are always looking to eradicate any sign of unconscious bias and keep an open mind about every candidate. They need to look far more broadly, and recognize and recommend candidates that possess the key qualities required for the job. The independent panel member should play a crucial role in this process.

The purpose of the initial 45-minute interview is to establish the candidate's personal suitability for becoming a magistrate, find out their reasons for applying, discuss their required observation of proceedings at a magistrates' court, and see if they possess all the necessary key qualities, or have demonstrated sufficient potential. If they are felt to have done so, then they are put through to a second and final interview. A detailed form is filled in which also highlights areas that need to be further probed or clarified in the second interview.

For the first, and hopefully last, time in this book, I am

pulling my punches, as it really would not be right or fair for me to reveal exactly what is asked at magistrate interviews. But, I clearly remember that my first interview was probably the hardest and most challenging interview I have ever experienced. Questions were probing and seemed to come from left field. I had to think on my feet and demonstrate my integrity and appreciation for the rule of law when asked how I would respond in several hypothetical scenarios, as well as being queried in depth about my motivation to become a magistrate. I stumbled, mumbled, and stuttered my way through what seemed an interminable 45 minutes.

I didn't feel that I had done myself anything like justice and was gratified – but very surprised – to be asked back for the second interview in which the first question was manna from heaven, "Is there anything you said last time that you would like to express differently or expand upon?"

Where did I begin? I had been kicking myself for what I thought had been a lost opportunity and had rehashed and rehearsed what I should have said first time around. I eagerly seized the liferaft offered to me, and must have done just well enough to sneak through and be accepted.

The second and final interview is totally different in structure and format to the first, and is intended to assess the candidate's potential judicial aptitude. It is totally scenario-related, apart from the second stage panel also having the opportunity to explore any issues identified during the initial interview. Ideally, one of the panel members should also have been present at the first stage interview.

*

One of the main problems in terms of filling the gaps and increasing the number of magistrates is the time currently taken to conclude the entire recruitment process. Of course, proper due diligence must take place, but potential candidates often have to wait several months for their initial interview owing to the shortage of advisory committee members and the need to ensure that there is an independent non-magistrate member present on interview panels. This problem should be rectified, in due course, as there is currently a sustained recruitment drive to attract more advisory committee members across the country.

Candidates are informed within ten days if they have been successful in their second stage interview and recommended for appointment. That is all well and good, but matters then proceed at a snail's pace, and it generally takes around six months for the appointment process to be concluded given the need for DBS checks, and for the appointment to go through the final approval and rubber-stamping process, including a sign-off by the Lord Chancellor's office.

I appreciate that the Lord Chancellor has a lot more important things to do in his busy work schedule than scrutinising and approving the latest lists of potential magistrate appointees, but it is really frustrating and demotivating for new magistrates to wait so long when they are champing at the bit to get started.

After the swearing-in ceremony, which is generally done in front of a High Court judge, the hard work begins for a new magistrate. They learn the basic skills on an intense three-day – soon to be three-and–half-day – induction training course, and are then allocated a mentor by the court in which he or she is going to sit.

The mentor is an experienced magistrate responsible for figuratively holding their hand, and putting the mentee at ease both in the retiring room and on the bench. The mentor will accompany them on three court observations, one before the training and two after, before they sit for the first time. At that point, they can start sitting in court as part of a bench of three.

The mentor is available to answer all their questions and provide ongoing guidance and support. They also hold six formal mentored sittings with the new magistrate in their first year, or so, after being appointed.

The mentor holds regular feedback sessions with the mentee, ensures they fulfil all their training obligations, and submits two formal reports after both three and six mentored sittings for consideration by the JTAAAC before they have their initial threshold appraisal, and once they have demonstrated that they are competent to proceed.

As a mentor, you are a sounding board for your mentee and are hopefully their first port of call whenever they have a question or potential issue. It is also important to nip things in the bud before they can develop into a real problem. Very occasionally, your mentee might make it clear to you either directly or by insinuation that they fundamentally disagree with, and are very uncomfortable, applying a specific law. One possible example is prosecuting people for simple possession of a small quantity of Class B drugs.

This is a time when you have to – gently but firmly – remind them that they cannot pick and choose which laws they wish to apply. Our job as justices is to put our personal feelings to one side and administer the laws that Parliament passes – WHETHER WE LIKE THEM OR NOT.

This is not something that is open to negotiation or discussion. If they still feel uneasy, or their conscience or beliefs do not allow them to fulfil their duty and implement every law, then their only alternative must be to resign as a magistrate. Thankfully, I am unaware of any new magistrate who has taken that ultimate step. Later in the book, I will mention, with a shudder, the iniquitous and highly unpopular Criminal Courts Charge, introduced and then hastily repealed in 2015, which did cause widespread concern and dissent amongst the magistracy and was the catalyst for the resignation of many of our members.

New magistrates learn on the job and gain knowledge and experience by sitting regularly, asking questions, observing what is happening around them in court, and watching other magistrates and District Judges in action. And, yes, they also learn by literal trial and error.

My first sittings passed me by in a blur. At first, I really did not know where to look; there was always something going on somewhere in the court. Everything seemed alien and unfamiliar. I really had no idea of what was happening and found it impossible to keep up. Court is as choreographed as a theatre, and only by experience and observation do new magistrates begin to understand the correct order of proceedings.

I was tested immediately by my colleagues and generally asked to give my opinion first, so that I would not be influenced by the views of others. "It really does not matter that you are new on the bench", was the oft-repeated mantra, "everyone is equal and your view is as valid as anyone else's. Anyway, you've been trained more recently than your colleagues, so you are far better prepared than them." Ideally, we should all learn from each other, but looking at it cynically, given that there are three of you on the bench, a rookie really can't do too much damage as the other two more experienced colleagues are there to advise, outvote, and overrule if necessary – as long as everyone is given the opportunity to have their say and venture an opinion.

Slowly, things began to make more sense, and I was fortunate in having a wily and grizzled mentor in David, who had seen everything in his many years on the bench. He was a bit of a martinet, but he was open-minded and his bark was far worse than his bite. Nobody, however – in court or out – took any liberties with him. His approach was never to volunteer any information, but whenever I asked him something he would make time immediately, take me to one side, and patiently explain chapter and verse of what had just happened and why. He inspired me to learn as much as I could, read as widely as possible, take the magistracy enormously seriously, and do everything in my power to become a good and competent magistrate. He also inspired me, when my turn came, to put something back by helping others.

As mentioned, mentees have six mentored sittings over the first year to 18 months of their time as a magistrate. They provide the new magistrate with the opportunity to put into practice what they have learned during the induction training as well as discuss any issues or concerns with their mentor.

At the end of each session, mentor and mentee sit down for a formal post-court review meeting, which provides an opportunity for issues that arose throughout the day to be clarified and discussed. They then jointly complete a form, which details what happened during the sitting, and identifies any training and development needs. This form has recently been amended and updated; it is now based on the appraisal form and has been made far more comprehensive.

The new magistrate is also expected to follow a comprehensive training framework, as follows:

- Observations (one before Induction Training, and two after)
- Attendance at Adult Court Induction Training (Compulsory, currently three days, usually consecutive) before first sitting
- Mentored sittings (six over a period of 12 to 18 months)
- Domestic Abuse training (Essential, one day)
- Equality and Diversity Training (Essential, half day)
- Unconscious Bias online Training (Essential)
- Visits to an Adult prison and a Young Offenders' Institution (usually half-day, Essential)
- Probation Service Induction training (Essential, one day),
- Visit to Attendance Centre (Essential, half day)
- Consolidation Training (Essential, two days)
- Threshold Appraisal

A report by "Transform Justice" in 2015 stated that only £26 was spent per magistrate on their training in 2013/14, a massive decrease from the £110 per magistrate in 2008/9. I have been unable to obtain updated figures, and hopefully there have been economies of scale, but this is a worrying trend. Malcolm Richardson, the former chairman of the Magistrates Association, endorsed this view when he stated in 2016, "Magistrates deal with more than 90% of the criminal cases that come to court and they cost 1% of the HM Courts and Tribunal Service budget."

The law is increasingly complex and sophisticated, and magistrates need to be given the tools and ammunition to develop their skills and competences. Training methods have also developed rapidly over the past few years with more emphasis on distance and digital learning, and it is crucial that sufficient time, effort, energy, ingenuity, and funds are allocated to guide people through their lifespan on the bench. Why not provide a series of themed podcasts that we can listen to on our journey to court?

The mentor also submits two reports on his mentee to the JTAAAC. An interim report is completed approximately six to nine months after the first sitting which – all being well – demonstrates that the mentee is on track to demonstrate competence at the threshold appraisal. The final report is completed after the sixth mentored sitting and focuses on whether the mentee is ready for appraisal.

I remember discussing my final report form with David and then anxiously waiting for his verdict. When I read these words, it was one of the proudest moments of my life. "X has been a model mentee and has gained experience in all types of court. X has fully engaged in all training offered and is a very competent winger."

The mentor's role comes to an end once the sixth mentored sitting has been undertaken and, whilst I often picked David's brain over the years, I was now flying solo.

Mandy is my fifth mentee, and the majority of them still sit as regularly as their business commitments allow, and have done themselves and me proud.

*

I arrive in court to find the retiring room in uproar with a renewed outbreak of "Biscuit-gate" rearing its ugly head.

Shock, horror, as without notice or explanation, the current brand of cheap cardboard-texture biscuits has just been replaced with meagre and even cheaper wrapped mini-packs of three biscuits sneakily placed inside the current biscuit tin. They practically crumble in your hands, are unappetising in the extreme and, given the extra packaging, are not particularly eco-friendly. They are surely a false economy too, as given the current serious health scare, who is going to fancy eating the last biscuit left in the packet when it has probably already been fingered by another magistrate? This is yet more evidence of cost-cutting, but certainly good news for my diet.

Philip, another experienced winger, joins Mandy and me, and we are in a GAP Court where the defendants are expected to plead guilty. There is a long and varied list, and we anticipate a late finish.

Dean pleads guilty of possession of Class B drugs and of driving a motor vehicle without having a licence. His PNC, which details his previous convictions has not been loaded onto the Court Store and we politely decline his extremely kind and, I am sure, well-meant offer to tell us exactly what he has done in the past and have to wait until a copy is eventually found. We decide not to disqualify him from driving and are greeted by a relieved cry of "That's wonderful", from the dock when our verdict is announced. At least we made someone happy today!

*

Next up is Deborah, an accountant with no previous convictions. After drinking too much, she has an argument in a pub, which turns nasty, and is accused of assaulting a staff member who intervened, and of also damaging his hearing aid. She has hired a lawyer who presses us to adjourn matters so that he can make representations to the CPS to review the matter as, if Deborah is convicted, she will risk losing her job.

The prosecutor confirms that the case has already been reviewed and given how serious the alleged assault is, the decision has been made to proceed. Mandy reminds us that we should always take a plea at the first hearing, and we do so. This is not well received by the defence but Deborah eventually pleads not guilty; we case-manage and set a trial date but state that if the CPS does change its mind, and the case is disposed of in some other manner, then the trial will not take place.

We fully understand that good character is to be guarded jealously, and a lawyer should always fight for his or her client, however the alleged facts of this case appear fairly open and shut, and I suspect that Deborah will need to make a return visit to court.

*

Gordon pleads guilty to possession of a small amount of cannabis. He has one previous conviction for similar offences. Since he spent the night in custody, we order the drugs to be forfeited and destroyed and fine him £50, but deem it served, so he is released with nothing to pay.

*

Said, who is of good character, admits assaulting an emergency worker by spitting in the face of a police officer who was trying to calm him down after he was refused entry to a bar in the early hours of the morning owing to his drunkenness. His lawyer states that, as a Muslim, Said's local community is extremely unhappy with his behaviour, and we can see his mother shaking her head and staring balefully at him from the public gallery. We suspect that no punishment that we impose will match the telling off he will shortly be receiving at home.

Spitting is a revolting offence, and we give him a community order with a month's curfew, and order him to pay £100 in compensation to the police officer. Should this offence have been committed after the new guidance issued by the Sentencing Council in mid-April 2020 – which correctly saw spitting as a seriously aggravating factor given the risk of transmission of the Coronavirus virus – then it is quite possible that Said would have received a custodial sentence.

*

Drew is a bus driver who finds a brand new iPhone that a passenger has inadvertently left behind. He does not hand it in, keeps it, and then sends it to a friend abroad intending to sell it. He then has second thoughts and asks for it back before holding onto it for several more months before CCTV eventually and belatedly reveals his theft. He is middle-aged and of good character and quite simply seems to have had a total brain-fade that will have massive consequences for him. We fine him heavily, and he will probably lose his job.

Hopefully, he will be able to pay the fine as ordered. Many can't. As is customary, we make what is called a collection order, which means that if the sum is not paid – as and when directed – then the offender can be brought back to court and the debt passed onto bailiffs. As of the end of September 2019, I have seen that the value of total outstanding financial impositions comprising fines, costs, victim surcharge, and compensation, has reached the boggling sum of £1.18 billion, up by 9% on the previous year! Fines and other ancillary payments should be set according to means, and the ability to pay them within a reasonable amount of time; sometimes, you just cannot get blood out of a stone.

Knife crime is understandably causing massive concern to all right-minded people and recent Ministry of Justice figures indicate how prevalent it is becoming. In the year ending March 2019, there were around 47,000 offences involving a knife or sharp instrument in England and Wales, a 7% rise over the previous year, and a 49% increase since 2011 when comparable records began. The police and courts dealt with the most knife crimes in a decade in the year to September 2019, with 17,724 offences heard in the adult courts, and a further 4,562 cases involving youths. Just over 12,000 offenders received custodial sentences with 7,845 sentenced to immediate custody and 4,320 receiving suspended sentences (which are still custodial sentences).

This means that 5,559 adult offenders received non-custodial sentences – a figure that many will find surprising – although 38% of knife crime offenders received immediate custody, which is up from 23% in 2009, and the average length of prison sentence rose over the same period from six to eight months. The proportion of repeat knife offenders imprisoned also fell slightly last year with more than a third escaping an immediate jail sentence despite the law requiring the imposition of a mandatory six-month prison sentence unless it is unjust to do so.

Magistrates take knife crime enormously seriously, and new Sentencing Guidelines were issued in June 2018, providing an increased tariff on conviction. Possession of a bladed article in a public place when the offence is committed in circumstances where there is a risk of serious disorder has a starting point of 18 months' custody with a range of between one year to two-and-a-half years in prison. Simple possession of a blade in a public place carries a starting point of six months in prison with a range of between three months to one year in custody.

The more serious offence of threatening someone with a blade in a public place, in circumstances where there is a risk of serious disorder, carries a starting point of two years' custody and a range of between 18 months to three years in prison. These cases are invariably heard in the Crown Court, whereas many cases of simple possession remain in a magistrates' court.

*

It is easy to say, categorically, that anyone found in possession of a bladed article should go straight to prison, but sometimes things are not that simple, as the specific circumstances of the offence and the offender have to be taken into consideration before passing sentence.

We have such a difficult case today when Rodrigo, a 19-year-old student, pleads guilty to possession of a bladed article in a public place.

Rodrigo has no previous convictions or obvious gang affiliations and is a first-year student at university. Police are called at night to break up a street melee in which he was not directly involved. He is seen loitering nearby and is stopped and searched, and a knife is found secreted in his possession. It is a particularly dangerous-looking five-inch-long lock knife.

Rodrigo pleads guilty but claims that he had just found the knife, which he thinks must have been dropped by somebody else involved in the street fight. It did not belong to him, and he was apparently "excited" by it and had not had the time or opportunity to dispose of it safely. He had no real knowledge or understanding of the peril he now finds himself in, until he spoke to the duty solicitor earlier today.

We find that this is a Category 2A offence of simple possession of a blade in a public place, with a starting point of six months' custody, and ask probation services to provide us with a fast delivery pre-sentence report with all sentencing options open, including custody and committal to the Crown Court for sentencing.

They come back just after lunch and confirm that Rodrigo deeply regrets what he has done, has never been in any form of trouble before, comes from a stable home background – although he has yet to tell his parents about his situation – and is a model student and keen sportsman with an exceptionally bright future. Most importantly, despite the seriousness of this charge, they feel that he is unlikely to offend again.

The duty solicitor echoes these comments in his mitigation and tries to persuade us that this was an isolated and totally out of character incident, and that – in these circumstances – it would be unjust to sentence Rodrigo to immediate custody. Given his youth, I then attempt to engage with Rodrigo; however, the enormity of his predicament has now well and truly sunk in and, understandably, he is tongue-tied and struggles for words and looks truly scared.

The bench now has an exceedingly difficult sentencing decision as the guidelines state that the court must impose a custodial sentence for this offence. Mandy, Philip, and I leave court to discuss our options. If we felt that this offence was aggravated by factors such as being part of a group activity, or committed when under the influence of either alcohol or drugs, we could even commit Rodrigo for sentence to the Crown Court as the maximum sentence would be one year's custody which is a greater punishment than we can give.

The starting point for this category of offence is six months' custody less the one-third discount he will receive for pleading guilty at the first opportunity, or a total of four months in prison. We could, however, actually sentence Rodrigo to six months' custody with his discount being that we do not commit him to the Crown Court.

We, therefore, have to go through a lengthy and structured sentencing process, and answer the following questions:

1. Has the custody threshold been passed?

We all agree that this is quite clearly the case, given the nature of the offence and the specific Sentencing Guidelines we need to follow – which state that the starting point is six months' custody.

2. Is it unavoidable that a sentence of imprisonment be imposed?

Passing the custody threshold does not necessarily mean that a custodial sentence is inevitable.

We discuss if a community order could provide sufficient restriction on Rodrigo's liberty whilst also addressing his rehabilitation. We also consider whether he has dependants who would be seriously impacted if he were to go to prison.

Rodrigo has no dependants, lives in student accommodation, and we also agree that the offence is so serious that only a custodial sentence can be justified. There has to be a deterrent element in our sentence given the current knife crime epidemic.

3. What is the shortest term commensurate with the seriousness of the offence?

Given the circumstances, we all agree that a six-month prison sentence reduced to four months would be appropriate.

4. Can the sentence be suspended?

We remind ourselves that a suspended sentence is a custodial sentence. We have to consider, on the one hand, if Rodrigo represents a danger to the public or if he has a poor record of complying with court orders. We do not believe the former as we have been told that he presents a low risk of reoffending, and the latter does not apply as he was previously of good character. We are concerned, though, by his description of being "excited" by the prospect of being in possession of a knife.

On the other hand, we have to discuss if Rodrigo has a realistic prospect of rehabilitation, if there was strong personal mitigation, or if immediate custody would result in significant harmful impact upon others.

The key here is the personal mitigation we have heard in court. This is a very serious crime, but it is also his first offence, so should we deprive him of his opportunity to complete his university course and make a successful career for himself? Or should we give him a second chance?

On balance, we decide that in this instance it would be appropriate for us to suspend the custodial sentence and – after a discussion that has taken around 20 minutes – we go back into court and inform a now tearful Rodrigo that he will receive a four-month prison sentence suspended for 12 months. In addition, he will have to complete 150 hours of unpaid work and attend up to 15 days of rehabilitation activity with the probation services. The fearsome-looking lock knife is to be forfeited and destroyed.

I speak long and hard to Rodrigo on behalf of the entire bench and make it patently clear just how close he was to going to prison today, how stupid and dangerous his actions were on the night of the offence, how people who are in possession of knives are just as likely to end up getting stabbed themselves, why we decided to suspend the sentence, and what would inevitably happen if he reoffends within the next 12 months.

There is an eerie silence throughout the court as Rodrigo leaves the dock a very relieved young man who, hopefully, will not trouble the Criminal Justice System again. Time will tell if we made the correct decision.

*

John is the next defendant. He appears on the video link from prison after previously pleading not guilty to harassing his ex-partner, Angela, and subjecting her to a deluge of highly-threatening calls and texts over a short period of time. The previous bench remanded him in custody, and he is now making a second bail application.

John's lawyer states that he has recently learned that Angela now wishes to resume her relationship with John, is no longer supporting the prosecution, and even tried to visit him (without success) in prison. He proposes that bail – with conditions of non-contact with her, and an exclusion from the areas where she both lives and works – now be granted. He advocates that they would be sufficient to ensure that he does not commit offences on bail or engage in conduct that may cause someone who is legally defined as an "associated person", in his ex-partner, to fear physical or mental injury.

Having heard in detail about the threats that he allegedly made to her, we go outside to conduct our own risk assessment and decide whether it is safe to give John his liberty before his trial takes place.

Irrespective of what we have just heard, John is still accused of very serious offences and if we do grant him bail, we believe that given Angela's efforts to visit him in prison, there is every chance that he will breach his bail conditions and that the two of them will meet up. We therefore refuse him bail; he has to remain on remand and await his trial. Like most magistrates, I am sure, I have the constant nightmare of releasing somebody on bail who then goes on to maim or kill his partner.

*

The afternoon is rapidly drawing to a close, but still the cases keep coming. Josh pleads not guilty to assaulting his wife, Becca, and damaging her iPhone. She has also made a withdrawal statement and we bail him with conditions of non-contact with Becca and not to go to her address.

This is a classic "He said, She said" type of offence with no corroborating witnesses or additional evidence, and it remains to be seen if Becca changes her mind and decides to give evidence; without her doing so, the case will almost inevitably collapse.

*

Then comes something truly ridiculous. Grant is accused of having stolen an expired batch of cooking oil outside a restaurant almost six years ago.

Six. Years. Ago.

He was stopped by the police yesterday for another matter and was amazed to find an outstanding warrant against him from so long ago. There is no time limit for Either Way or Indictable only offences.

Grant claims that he had permission from the restaurant management to take the oil, and it is doubtful if there is anyone still there after so many years that will remember one way or the other. Grant has already spent a night in custody, which I am sure he is not happy about, and we certainly share his anger and concern. We adjourn the case for 14 days in the hope that somebody will see sense and dismiss it.

*

Our final case moves us greatly. Fergal is an elderly but frail career burglar with a chronic addiction to drugs and alcohol. He admits breaking into an office building and stealing £50. He is no stranger to custody and the obvious sentence is to send him back to prison – but, as is so often the case, things are not quite what they seem on the surface.

Fergal is pale, thin, and infirm. His lawyer explains that he gave into temptation when committing the offence but he now lives in a shelter with his terminally ill wife. He is her sole carer, and if he is imprisoned, they will both lose their accommodation and she will be thrown out into the streets. He also shows us documentation that verifies these facts.

We retire to consider the sentence and apply the same considerations as we did when dealing with Rodrigo.

Whilst the custody threshold has been crossed, and Fergal knew exactly what he was doing when he committed the burglary, the implications of sending him back to prison will be horrendous, if not fatal, for his wife. We are being asked to act as social workers again, and not follow our guidelines, and we decide to give him a suspended prison sentence together with 20 rehabilitation days so that he can get some help for his addictions. We are quite certain that we are doing the right thing.

Sometimes, you go home with a sense of satisfaction and achievement that you have done something in court that is helpful to somebody, and which might actually have a beneficial effect upon their life; this is one such occasion. Conversely, I get no pleasure or a kick out of sending somebody to prison. We are not avenging angels or vigilantes, I don't keep score of how many people I have been responsible (along with my colleagues) for sending to prison, but if it has to be done – and you have carefully considered and then rejected all other options – then you simply have to get on with your job. That is not to say that I don't sometimes have sleepless nights about something that has deeply upset, angered, or moved me in court that day.

As soon as I became a magistrate, I was really worried about the prospect of sending somebody to prison and knew that one day, fairly soon, I would be faced with that situation. It really was not one that I relished. I did not have long to wait, as in only my third sitting we had to sentence a prolific thief and shoplifter who had targeted and followed an old lady around a supermarket before stealing her purse containing her pension money. It ticked all the boxes, and given the circumstances – the thief's previous record, the pre-planning, and the vulnerability of the victim – custody was the correct sentence, and I had no qualms in agreeing with my colleagues.

I immediately felt a great sense of relief that the first such sentence I was involved with was so clear-cut, and one that I was not unhappy about. I would have been worried if I had been the sole dissenter, and it might well have affected my decision-making in the future. Hopefully, I will never get *blasé* about imposing custodial sentences and always think through the consequences for all parties with my colleagues; it is part of our job and must not be shied away from when necessary.

I am also concerned that after you have spent a number of

years in court, watching the criminal fraternity pass in endless procession before you, that you run the risk of becoming "case-hardened" – that is to say, becoming so used and inured to hearing about the awful acts that people perpetrate, that you stop being affected by them.

And then, perhaps mercifully, you are suddenly jolted out of your complacency and brought back to the grim reality of crime and human life by something particularly awful or gruesome. It is somehow a genuine relief to know that the depths of human behaviour can still shock you.

One day in the Remand Court, this happened to a colleague of mine in the space of one grim half-hour. A perfectly ordinary-looking man in his late thirties was called to the dock. He faced ten charges of anally raping an under-age girl, and it emerged that the alleged victim was this man's ten-year-old daughter. All three magistrates struggled to maintain their judicial calm and dignity as further, awful details emerged. The accused was sent to the Crown Court for trial. The bench then had to retire for a few minutes to regain their equilibrium, helped by a hot drink and, in one case, a cigarette.

If that was not awful enough for one day, a few minutes later, another perfectly ordinary-looking man was brought up from the cells, this time charged with rape. He had visited his cousin in a local hospital. She had suffered a life-threatening stroke and was unable to speak or move. He was shown into her room and left unattended. About 15 minutes later, ward staff went to her room, just to check on her. They discovered the defendant in her bed, raping her. He was caught *in flagrante,* and the magistrates also sent his case to the Crown Court.

Again, the unfortunate magistrates were so profoundly

shocked and affected by this catalogue of horrors that they had to retire for a few minutes to recover. One of them even rushed to the toilet and was violently sick.

Both of these cases were truly dreadful, and yet, in a perverse way, the magistrates all felt that it was good to discover that they really weren't as inured and oblivious to these awful events as they feared they were.

*

After a post-court review with our legal adviser, it is time for Mandy and me to discuss the day and fill in the mentored sitting form. She states that some of the more convoluted and difficult sentencing issues that we had to deal with today were entirely new to her and she has learned a lot.

Mandy has performed very well, and now only has one more mentored sitting to endure with me. She and Philip really helped make the day go smoothly and efficiently.

We have dealt with a great many difficult cases today and done our best to deal fairly, justly, and sensibly with people who, for many reasons, cannot cope well with life and who really needed our assistance.

It strikes me just how hard a magistrate's job can be. As a renowned judge recently told me, for them their choices are fairly straightforward, simply a case of how long they send an offender to prison for. For us magistrates, almost every day we face a sentencing dilemma – should it be prison or not – and sometimes the choice is not at all clear-cut.

Justice, though, is not just about meting out punishment and today, in particular, I hope we fulfilled our magistrates' Oath of Allegiance by doing, "right to all manner of people after the laws and usages of the Realm without fear or favour, affection or ill will."

8. MIND THE GAP

Court One on a Monday morning is full of hustle and bustle, and bursting at the seams as we enter court. There is a huge list for us to deal with in what is a GAP remand court where we expect to hear guilty pleas, so we had better get started as quickly as we can.

Helen and Maureen, my fellow magistrates, and I have all been frenetically busy for the past half hour reading through what is a massive 12-page long list of cases that we will be dealing with across the day. We then find the relevant sentencing guidelines and bookmark them on our iPads, so that we are as ready and prepped for action as we can be.

There is a buzz of anticipation in the packed courtroom as we warm up for the long day ahead with a simple case of possession of a small quantity of cannabis. Nathan has eight similar convictions for us to take into consideration, but none for the previous 18 months, so we fine him £80 and order the drugs to be forfeited and destroyed.

*

Next comes a textbook case of road rage when James – exasperated at being stuck behind a slow-moving bus – takes the law into his own hands and, after cutting in front of the bus, stops when there is a further traffic delay, gets onboard the bus and hurls abuse at the driver who has suffered from sleepless nights since this incident. Fortunately, James is restrained before the situation can get more serious and out of hand, and having considered the option of disqualifying James from driving, we order him to pay £300 in compensation to the bus driver.

*

Jane pleads guilty to assaulting her friend, Kerry, and damaging her wardrobe. The backstory behind what – on the face of it – seems a straightforward assault is, in fact, far more complex and sad. The two women had been best friends for over 30 years, since childhood, and when Jane goes over to help Kerry move house, she certainly does not expect the bombshell that occurs when Kerry lets slip that she is having a relationship with Jane's father, who has also lent her the money to buy the newly-delivered furniture that Jane is helping her to arrange. The cat is well and truly out of the bag, and particularly given that her mother has cancer, Jane unsurprisingly finds this news hard to take. She attacks her friend, punching her on the neck and grabbing her by the throat, and demolishes a new wardrobe.

Jane is previously of good character, but the assault is serious enough for us to ask for a pre-sentence report from the probation services. This confirms that Jane is suffering from depression and schizophrenia, and her daughter also needs surgery for a foot injury. Given her issues, and the problems she is facing, Jane is not considered suitable for either unpaid work or a curfew, and we sentence her to a community order with 30 days of rehabilitation activity.

Compensation is clearly not a good idea given the current hostility between the two women, as it seems more sensible, in our view, for them to have some breathing space with no contact for the time being.

*

Our next customer, Declan, is accused of not turning up for his probation appointments. Indeed, he is apparently too busy to join us today as we are told he is running a car wash on the Isle of Wight where the local police will shortly be delivering (hopefully in a clean car) a warrant for his arrest without bail so that he can learn that court orders are not to be disregarded.

*

We generally get a lot of drink drivers, and today is no exception. Ivor has registered 57 microgrammes of alcohol in 100 millilitres of breath when the legal limit is 35, although the police do not generally prosecute when the level is under 40. Unfortunately for him, this is his second conviction for driving with excess alcohol within the last ten years, as he committed an identical offence in 2016. This means he faces an automatic ban of at least three years.

Matters are further aggravated by the fact that he collides with another vehicle before being stopped by the police. We disqualify him from driving for three years and fine him £120, and we also offer Ivor the chance to reduce his period of disqualification by a quarter by taking and successfully completing a drink-drive rehabilitation course at a cost to him of around £250; given his lack of means, he declines the opportunity.

I ask him how he got to court today and, thankfully, he doesn't say that he drove here. Finally, I warn him not to even think of driving whilst disqualified, as this is a likely route to immediate custody, particularly if he is caught driving shortly after the start of the disqualification period.

I always ask convicted drink drivers that same question – whether they drove to court that day – ever since Kirsty, one of our best legal advisers, told me a corker of a story. Apparently, John, a long-serving magistrate, was having his final sitting before his compulsory retirement on reaching the age of 70, as is the fate – like it or not – that befalls all magistrates good, bad, or indifferent.

He had been talking to Kirsty that very morning and bemoaned the fact that despite having enjoyed a long and respected career on the bench, nothing particularly out of the ordinary had ever happened to him – and given that this was his last day, it certainly would not now.

How wrong could he be!

Towards the end of a quiet and sleepy morning, Jason appeared, and grudgingly, and with bad grace, pleaded guilty to driving with excess alcohol. The bench disqualified him from driving for two years, and John gave Jason the customary warning against driving any motor vehicle on a road or public place for the duration of his ban.

Jason, who represented himself, had not made a good impression in court, paying little or no attention to what was going on, with a lot of sneering, hand-waving, eye-rolling, glancing down to where his mobile phone was probably secreted, and making a bored and highly dismissive uttering of "yeah, yeah" when John, the chair, made his pronouncement. He was a seething vortex of arrogance, boredom, disinterest, and dumb insolence.

He slouched out of the court without a backward glance, and Kirsty had a sudden brainwave. She asked the bench to retire and, as they did so, with bemused looks on their faces, she scurried to the back of the courthouse to an unused office, which overlooked the car park.

Sure enough, a couple of minutes later, out walked a familiar figure. It was Jason who sauntered without an apparent care in the world towards a parked BMW, opened the driver's door, got in, and a moment later disappeared in a cloud of dust and exhaust smoke. But not before Kirsty had taken a video on her mobile phone of him entering and driving the car.

She immediately called the police, gave them the name of the driver and his registration number, and told them she had just witnessed a disqualified driver at the wheel of his car, driving in contravention of the law.

Unsurprisingly, the police could not find any record of Jason's disqualification, but she told them that she was the legal adviser in the case where he had just been banned, and she had not yet had the time to enter the result onto the system.

The police sent officers to wait outside Jason's home, a few miles away, and, sure enough – half an hour later – he drove straight into their clutches.

He was immediately arrested for driving whilst disqualified, and no more than a couple of hours after he had left the magistrates' court, he was back there before the same bench that had convicted him earlier in the day.

John blinked twice as if not quite believing what he was seeing, and he and his colleagues accepted another guilty plea from Jason, this time made with quite a bit more humility than the last one. Jason was sentenced to six months' custody on account of the negligible or indeed, minuscule, amount of time that had elapsed since his disqualification before he drove again, and the fact that he had driven a significant distance home. Incorrectly, (but perhaps understandably), he also received no discount for his early guilty plea, given that he had totally ignored and flouted the warning given to him in court – that very day – not to drive whilst banned from doing so. John could now retire from the bench knowing that, better late than never, he finally had a story to dine out on for the rest of his life.

Now, you can hopefully understand why I ask the question that I invariably do!

According to the latest published figures, 8,500 offenders did not listen to similar warnings and were convicted of this serious offence in 2018, 50% of whom received custodial sentences, either immediate or suspended.

*

Michael is accused of the same offence as Ivor, with a reading this time of 84 microgrammes of alcohol in 100 millilitres of breath, but, representing himself, he claims that his drinks were spiked and that he is not guilty of the offence. I confirm the situation with the legal adviser before replying and tell Michael that what he is saying is not a defence at all, but instead what is called a special reason and we need to arrange a hearing to decide the issue.

Unsurprisingly, there are no reliable figures for how many people have had their drinks spiked, as many cases go unreported. Independent newspaper, The Tab, recently published a survey that claimed that just over half of the 1,100 female respondents interviewed said that they had been spiked.

What Michael is claiming is that despite admitting to driving a vehicle whilst over the legal alcohol limit, he only did so because of additional alcohol consumed by him – without his knowledge – after his drinks were spiked. If he manages to prove his case, then he will still be convicted of the offence, but he will avoid disqualification; however, he has a high bar to clamber over if he is to succeed in a special reason claim of spiked drinks. He will need to prove all of the following three elements to the court's satisfaction:

1. That he consumed alco...
   someone else had, withou...
   additional alcohol in h...
   alcoholic drink instead of...

2. That, but for the ad...
   consumed, he would r...
   limit.

3. That Michael was unawa... ...
   or, in other words, that he would not have ~~been~~
   aware that something was wrong. The higher the
   alcohol reading, the more difficult it will be for him
   to prove that he was unaware that he was over the
   limit, and therefore should not drive.

Given the above, you can see that it is extremely difficult to successfully demonstrate that your drinks have been spiked. An expert witness will need to confirm that, but for the additional amount of alcohol, Michael would have been under the drink-driving limit. Ideally, he can also provide witness statements from people who were with him on the night in question, to confirm how much alcohol he knowingly consumed. Sometimes, friends even confess to spiking the drinks themselves, which will certainly help Michael but also leave them open to prosecution.

We set a date for the hearing and give Michael a highly *précised* version of the above directions and strongly recommend that he takes legal advice beforehand, but what is worrying is that despite everything that we tell him – and now, tell him again – he says that he does not intend to call any witnesses on his own behalf, and gives no real indication that he has either heard or understood much of what he has been told.

will consult a lawyer who will advise him that
testimony, his case is doomed.

reasons are not to be confused with exceptional
. As we have seen, the former is concerned with the
ce and a potential mitigating or extenuating circumstance
ating to its commission, which can be taken into
consideration by the sentencing court. A defendant can also
only use the same special reason once when prosecuted.

Exceptional hardship is different, and is related to the
offender and his personal circumstances, and how he or
others might be affected by the punishment should he lose his
driving license after he has accumulated 12 or more penalty
points. It cannot be used as a way of avoiding disqualification
following a conviction for an offence such as drink driving
where disqualification is automatic.

*

We see such a case today when Adam pleads guilty to
having no valid insurance, and the six points awarded to him
makes him a totter; in other words, he now has (totted up) 12
points on his licence, and should be subject to an automatic
six-month driving ban.

His lawyer attempts to make a case for exceptional
hardship stating that Adam is a delivery driver and will
certainly lose his job if he is disqualified from driving.

There is no strict legal definition for exceptional hardship,
and magistrates need to consider each case on its individual
merits, but also be clear and robust in their thinking and
decision-making. By its very nature, a driving ban is almost
certain to cause some kind of hardship, which – quite frankly
– is its aim, as it is a punishment. "Hardship" then, on its
own, is not enough and, to have a realistic chance of success,

a claim of exceptional hardship must be something really out of the ordinary. This distinction is crucial.

We listen carefully to his argument but decide that it won't wash as, in our view, it does not reach the required standard. Adam depends upon keeping his licence to remain in his present employment, and yet has still committed three driving offences in the last year. In our view, he really should have been more careful, and not having insurance is something that could easily have been rectified by him, particularly as he is in employment and can presumably afford to pay for his car insurance. We decide to reject his application and ban him from driving for six months.

If, hypothetically, Adam needs to use his car to take his wife to regular hospital or occupational therapy appointments for treatment and she has no other way of getting there, or if he could prove that others close to him would suffer significantly if he should lose his licence, then the claim of exceptional hardship might have more chance of succeeding... depending upon the view of the bench. That being said, the use of public transport or even a taxi is an option that should always be explored by the magistrates, as is actually selling the car in order to fund alternative methods of transport.

Apparently, not all magistrates appear to be as robust as we are today in deciding upon exceptional hardship, as the Daily Mail recently obtained figures that showed that, over the last year, 10,589 motorists have kept their driving licences and stayed on the road despite amassing 12 or more points. This includes three men who each have 60 or more points! Again, I do not know the specific circumstances of all these cases, but it would appear that there are a lot of sick grandmothers around!

Magistrates are also asked, from time to time, to amend a curfew requirement to allow the offender to go on holiday, attend a music festival, or even – in one case I read about – watch his favourite football team play. (I did once have a supporter of a very unsuccessful team almost beg me to impose a football banning order on him, so fed up was he with watching his team lose!) The reason given for an amended curfew request is generally that the holiday or other activity has been pre-booked and paid for. Very often, a bench of magistrates allows such a request if evidence is provided confirming the actual booking. Again, it is wrong to generalise without being in possession of all the relevant facts, but my starting point would be that I am not inclined to allow such a request without very good reason.

If you commit a crime, you should be prepared to suffer the consequences and any reasonable hardship that accompanies it. To me, the relevant question to be asked is not just if the holiday or tickets were pre-booked, but when they were obtained. Was it before the actual crime was committed, and not simply the date of conviction?

There is also a defence of reasonable excuse that can be used, say, for an accusation of possession of a bladed article in a public place if the knife is a tool of your trade – such as a chef's knife or a Stanley knife – or even a Sikh kirpan carried for religious reasons.

I sat on a case, recently, where a builder found with a Stanley knife on his person after being involved in a nightclub fight, claimed that he was only carrying it as it was a tool of his trade. The problem was that it was a Saturday night when he was arrested, he had not worked that day at all, and the knife was discovered in the pocket of a smart jacket that he never wore for work. We, therefore, convicted him of the offence and sent him to prison.

*

Back in court, Terry has failed to comply with the requirements of his community order by twice failing to report for his unpaid work, but both breaches occurred back in 2018, and his original order has now expired, with Terry having only completed 40 out of the 200 hours of unpaid work that he was ordered to complete, demonstrating only minimal compliance with his order.

He admits the breach but states that, over the years, he has lost contact with probation and it was up to them to keep in touch with him. That excuse won't wash. It might well be that he fell through the cracks in the system – not an uncommon occurrence – however, he knows full well that he has nowhere near completed the original requirements of his community order, and should have made efforts to contact probation off his own bat.

Given that his order expired in May 2018, we resentence him for his original offence of assaulting a police officer, and he now has a new community order with 200 hours of unpaid work to complete over the next 12 months. Terry makes it quite clear that he is unhappy with our decision and leaves without speaking to the probation officer who is trying to arrange a new appointment for him. I suspect that we shall be seeing him again, fairly soon.

*

Martin pleads not guilty to making threats to kill, aimed at his brother, Ethan. They have not got on for a long time, and since Martin returned home, recently, there has been serious tension between them, resulting in him allegedly arguing with Ethan and then brandishing a kitchen knife and threatening to stab him in the heart saying that he will "shank the cunt". According to Martin, he was simply defending himself after his brother threatened him. Ethan has recently made a withdrawal statement and no longer supports the prosecution.

We have to deal with allocation and decide where the case will be heard. Given the alleged facts that we have heard, with the presence of a visible weapon, the threats of significant violence, as well as the family history between them, and the level of harm and impact on Ethan, there is a starting point of two years' custody and a range of between one to four years in prison; there is certainly an argument for us to send it to the Crown Court.

We huddle together for a brief chat and decide that the case seems straightforward, there are no complex legal points that will need deciding and, most importantly, we can always commit Martin to the Crown Court for sentencing should he be found guilty. We, therefore, decide to keep the case in a magistrates' court, but – as is his right – Martin elects to have his trial before a judge and jury. He is now staying in a hotel, and we bail him with conditions not to contact his brother or return to the family home.

*

We can probably fit in one more case before lunch, and Robert strides into court wearing a massive woolly hat that almost covers his entire face. He explains that he was recently sprayed with acid, and he needs the hat to hide his scars. He pleads guilty to fraud by false representation, and two charges of assault by beating of an emergency worker. Robert is caught on CCTV using a stolen debit card in a supermarket and, when arrested, he becomes aggressive and punches two police officers who are forced to use CS gas to restrain him.

Robert is well known to probation who inform us that he is unable to do unpaid work and has no fixed address (NFA) so is unsuitable for a curfew; so, we order him to pay £100 each in compensation to the two police officers, as well as to the owner of the debit card that we are told he found lying in the street.

As an aside, when a defence lawyer says to us, "I am instructed to say", before giving us some particularly improbable or outlandish explanation, this is generally a coded message and what he is really saying is, "I have been instructed to tell you this by my client, so I am doing so, but please take it with a pinch of salt." Whilst a lawyer is there to represent and defend the interests of his client, he also has a responsibility to act with reason and common sense, as he is an officer of the court and must not knowingly mislead it.

*

After lunch, we deal quickly with Darren. He is just passing through on his way to be sentenced at the Crown Court for again breaching the terms of his Sexual Harm Prevention Order (SHPO) by making indecent photographs of children after downloading images from the internet and then deleting the browsing history on his computer. Through his solicitor, who makes no application for bail, Darren makes it clear that he wants to go back to prison. He is likely to be sentenced to a substantial period of imprisonment given his previous convictions for making and possessing indecent images of children and the fact that, despite the imposition of an SHPO, he continues to download indecent images. We treat Darren as courteously as any other defendant, but it is noticeable how little eye contact he receives from other court users.

*

Wasim is already in custody and refuses to leave his cell to answer the charge of possession with intent to supply Class B drugs. This is a situation that is occurring more and more frequently, and we cannot order him to be produced by force. There was a time, though, if the defendant was not willing to come to us, then we would go to him; I remember the thrilling, if somewhat chilling and macabre, experience of descending deep into the bowels of the courthouse to take a plea from the holding cells. Things have changed thanks to health and safety concerns; so today we adjourn Wasim's case for seven days for him to be produced via the video link.

*

The cases are still coming thick and fast, and we allow Graham to remain on bail despite him breaching his bail condition by arriving home 15 minutes late for his tagged curfew. Breach of bail is not a crime in itself, and the only options that are open to us are to remand Graham in custody, or return him to bail with the same, or revised conditions. This is his first breach of bail, and he explains it by claiming – in an extremely matter of fact manner – to have been attacked when on his way home.

*

Liam does not receive the same positive outcome. He seems to have totally disregarded and ignored his bail conditions, and since being restored to bail two weeks ago, after an initial breach, he fails to report daily (as required) to sign on at his local police station. Indeed, he fails on no fewer than ten separate occasions, as well as being late for his curfew four times. His only comment is that he, "didn't see it as necessary" to report to the police station. His lawyer finds it hard to find anything positive to say about him apart from highlighting his youth and evident lack of maturity and thinking skills. Liam cannot be at all surprised when we revoke his bail and remand him in custody until his trial.

I wish we could get inside his head, as his behaviour seems totally perplexing; surely he would prefer to be on bail rather than behind bars? Obviously not, and his lawyer can also offer no explanation. We see that the officer in the case is also present in court, whispering to the prosecutor; evidence that the police see this matter as particularly serious, but this plays no part in our decision, which is pretty straightforward.

*

We are seeing more and more arrests lately for assaulting an emergency worker, which implies that a zero-tolerance policy is being adopted, and that is to be welcomed. They all deserve the full protection of the law when they are going about their difficult and sometimes dangerous jobs.

Gary's is a fairly typical case. Stopped and searched after a police officer could smell cannabis on him, he is found to have drugs in his pocket. He resists arrest and bites the arresting officer on his left hand, before elbowing him in the face. He has 14 previous convictions for possession of drugs and obstructing police officers, but has been out of trouble for the past three years.

Gary pleads guilty and says – by way of explanation – that he did not hear the police officer identify himself, and thought he was being mugged. We place the assault in the second highest category because of the sustained and repeated nature of the incident.

Under the 2018 *Assault on Emergency Workers Act*, this

offence now carries a maximum sentence of 12 months' imprisonment. We decide to follow the recommendation of probation and impose a one-year community order with 80 hours of unpaid work, ten days of rehabilitation activity, and also order Gary to pay compensation of £200 to the police officer. There is no separate penalty for possession of the drugs, which are to be forfeited and destroyed.

My personal view is that it is only right and proper to award compensation when emergency workers are attacked. Just because they are wearing a uniform does not give anyone licence to abuse or assault them.

*

We then adjourn the case of Andy, who has not turned up in court to answer an allegation of theft. His lawyer states that Andy was taken ill yesterday and is now receiving hospital treatment. We, therefore, adjourn matters for 14 days and remind his lawyer that Andy must bring a doctor's note or proof of his illness on the next occasion.

*

Last on is Richard, who has been waiting patiently – all day – downstairs in the cells for failing to report to probation for post-sentence supervision (PSS), a requirement which is applied to all offenders who receive a sentence of less than two years imprisonment. PSS provides a second supervision period – for a period of two years – to assist in the rehabilitation of the offender, following on from them completing their licence period. It is moot how successful it is, given that 64% of adults released from a custodial sentence of fewer than 12 months will reoffend, while one in four will be recalled to prison. This leads to the discussion of the efficacy and effectiveness of short terms of imprisonment... an ongoing debate.

Richard has failed to report to probation on two occasions since his release from prison, and we have the options of taking no action, sending him to prison for up to seven days, fining him, giving him a curfew, or making a supervision default order with unpaid work. We check with probation, and Richard has since re-engaged with them and his levels of compliance are now satisfactory.

We therefore fine him £50 but deem it served given that he has now been in custody for the best part of two days and has also been brought up from the cells on a wasted journey on no less than three occasions today, only to find problems each time with his paperwork necessitating further delays.

*

That ends our list; it is nearly 5.30pm, and we cannot assist any other court. Has it been a good day? Well, yes and no. We talk together after the sitting and are happy with how, as a bench, we worked together to deal with both the variety and volume of cases that were thrown at us in what was a really busy day. But what did cause a problem was my lack of empathy with the legal adviser and *vice versa*.

Legal advisers play an absolutely crucial role in court, and the relationship between the presiding justice and legal adviser is fundamental to the successful running of the court; we need to work together in partnership and ideally become a well-oiled machine. It is the bench which is nominally in charge and runs proceedings – after all, it is called a "magistrates' court" – but you won't get very far unless you are working hand in glove with your legal adviser and listen hard to what he or she says to you. Normally, this is no problem; we agree our roles beforehand and do our utmost to trust each other and share responsibilities – and invariably succeed in doing so. It is their job to guide and remind the bench on all relevant aspects of the law, and ensure that all our decisions are lawful. It is the bench's responsibility to come to a verdict, a bail and sentencing decision, or consider an application or point of law from the lawyers, and it is for the legal adviser to keep us on the straight and narrow.

I work hard to develop a good working relationship with all our legal advisers; you cannot hope to survive as a presiding justice without one. It is a partnership, and ideally I have got their back and they have got mine.

Unfortunately, this has never been the case with Jonathan, today's legal adviser. We have never gelled, bonded, or hit it off in any way, shape or form, and seem to find it really difficult to work together. Everything is hard work and stressful rather than seamless and automatic. We just seem to rub each other up the wrong way; there appears to be a personality clash, and today is no exception.

I blame myself totally for this situation, and for letting it fester. By now, I should have developed sufficient people skills to ensure that I can work well in a team with anybody. Generally, I do, but something is definitely not working here.

The only answer is for us both to try harder, or agree not to sit together in the future. Hopefully, it will be the former.

Incidentally, I spoke to a few of our more experienced legal advisers and quizzed them on their main gripes and complaints about magistrates. Thankfully, they were all pretty complimentary about our work, but they did mention the following concerns:

- Not always concentrating on the main issues at hand or keeping to the point

- Going on wild goose chases and focusing attention on irrelevant matters
- Not listening carefully to the legal adviser or what is being said in court
- Not giving detailed reasons or explanations for their decisions
- Agreeing with their colleagues too easily without providing much of their own thought and input
- Having preconceived attitudes
- Being in a rush to leave

I know that I am as guilty as the rest of my colleagues of falling short in some, if hopefully, not all, of these areas. Perhaps I need to award myself 100 lines – "I must not…"

9. SERVING THE COMMUNITY

We see a vast number of people appearing in court, before us, who are suffering from severe mental health and related problems. These are not the common or garden "worried well", with their imaginary or mild complaints that take up so much of our overworked and overstretched National Health Service's time.

No, these are the real deal. A huge diversity of people with chaotic and disordered lives who simply cannot cope. They have a range of highly complex needs, encompassing mental health issues, learning difficulties, addictions, and disabilities.

Mental health problems, addiction, and crime go together hand-in-hand and are natural bedfellows. It is estimated that more than 70% of the prison population has some sort of mental health problem. The Prison Reform Trust states that up to 32% of adult prisoners have an IQ under 80, 60% of prisoners have problems with communication, and around 10% have a learning disability. Around 70% of all crime is drug or alcohol-related and the cost of drug-related acquisitive crime is around £5.8 billion each year. The latest figures from the Crime Survey for England and Wales indicate that, last year, 39% of all perpetrators of violent crime were under the influence of alcohol. According to the Institute of Alcohol Studies, drink is an aggravating factor in around one million crimes per year in the UK, at an annual cost to the taxpayer of £11 billion. What is equally disturbing is the fact that, in 2018, there were 240 deaths following drink-driving accidents, a 20% rise since 2015.

It is good to learn that the Ministry of Justice is now running various pilot schemes under which offenders with mental health needs are diverted from prison and instead receive support to address their underlying needs within the community; the Criminal Justice System is plainly ill-suited to provide people with the mental health support that they need. Prison is surely not the right place for people with such problems.

I well remember when I was contemplating becoming a magistrate – doing my due diligence – and a long-serving magistrate told me to prepare myself for seeing an avalanche of the mad, sad and bad in court (and far, far more of the first two categories than the latter). I dismissed her comment as being both cynical and jaundiced, but now, several years on, I realise that she was spot on in her analysis of the defendants that we see in court every day.

Here, at the coalface in a magistrates' court, we still see so many – and, indeed, far, far too many – defendants who suffer from serious mental disorders. For those appearing in custody, the police should already have arranged appropriate support and help, and the worst afflicted will ideally already have been diverted to hospital.

We are fortunate in having the skilled and patient services of the Together Mental Health liaison and diversion team, which is generally available in court to assess the needs of vulnerable individuals and help ensure that they receive access to the optimum health and social care services. They provide us with invaluable written reports, which give us some of the information we need when making bail and sentencing decisions.

If it is deemed necessary, then defendants can be admitted

to hospital under the *Mental Health Act 1983* and not appear in court, with a new date fixed for their next appearance.

If a defendant appears before us, and we still have great concerns about their mental health, then we can ask for a psychiatric report, otherwise we proceed as best we can and muddle our way through. Not ideal for anyone.

We do have the option to make a mental health treatment requirement (MHTR) as part of a community order or suspended sentence where offenders receive treatment from a doctor or psychologist, but I understand that this is rarely exercised given the uncertainty as to who should receive such a MHTR, how breaches of the order are managed, and the need for a formal psychiatric report.

*

Our first defendant today, Mary, is unkempt and haggard and looks twice her real age. She appears to have problems in following the proceedings but insists that she is OK. She has a long history of both mental health problems and substance abuse, and is a prolific offender. She returns to a bookmaker three times within a short period of time, tries to smoke her crack pipe in the toilet, swears at a staff member who objects to her presence and behaviour, spits on the Perspex protective screen separating staff from the public, and shouts, "I am going to set you on fire." She then keeps her word and attempts to set fire to the Perspex with her lighter, causing some damage to the screen. A staff member presses the panic button, and the police are called.

We order a pre-sentence report and probation services inform us that Mary is evasive and lacking in focus. Her main concerns are her on-going mental health issues and depression, which she feels cause her to offend. In her opinion, however, she has no major addiction problems and she does not want any help.

As we feared and suspected, Mary falls through all the cracks in the system and is not deemed suitable for any defined programme. Unpaid work and a curfew are also totally out of the question. Probation's recommendation is for a one-year community order with 30 days of rehabilitation activity where they will give her whatever help they can.

Mary's lawyer stands up to mitigate on her behalf, and it truly is not his finest hour. He has obviously not listened to what probation have said in court, neither can he have read their report, nor has he done his homework. His opening gambit is to recommend, with a flourish, that we give his client a suspended prison sentence.

Leaving aside that this is a far more severe punishment than probation have proposed (although, of course, it is the bench's decision what sentence to impose, not probation's), Mary has received several custodial sentences before – both immediate and suspended – which do not seem to have either helped her or stopped her offending.

The most important problem with his proposal is that Mary's offences – as serious, potentially dangerous, worrying and unpleasant as they are – do not cross the custody threshold by quite a wide margin, even when taking into account the aggravating factor of her previous record. We are therefore unable to send her to prison (a suspended sentence is a prison sentence) even if we wanted to do so, which we most certainly do not.

Her public order offence is in the lowest category, with a sentencing range of between a conditional discharge and a medium level community order. The arson offence is committed on impulse, Mary's responsibility is substantially reduced by her mental disorder, and the damage caused is of low value (£500). The sentencing range for this offence is, therefore, from a conditional discharge to a high level community order.

We retire to talk through the options, as well as Mary's situation. We have to consider the damage she caused to the bookmaker and the fear she must have instilled in their staff, as protection of the public is paramount. Mary is ill and vulnerable, and there is also her wellbeing to take into account. We decide to follow the recommendation from probation and add a £50 compensation payment for the staff member who was targeted and verbally abused by Mary.

Mary's offences were serious, and she knew what she was doing, although her judgement was surely clouded by her issues. We have to do our job and sentence according to the law and then follow our guidelines, unless we can give good reasons not to do so. We are also bound by our oath (the aforementioned need to "do right to all manner of people after the laws and usages of the Realm without fear or favour, affection or ill will"). Sometimes, it is a real balancing act.

*

The next defendant also has addiction problems, this time with both alcohol and drugs. The police are called because Andy is causing a nuisance in a supermarket. Officers arrive, he is clearly drunk, and they try to calm him down and search him for drugs. Andy is aggressive and resists. Eventually, a Taser is drawn but not used. In the struggle with three officers, he threatens to stab them, spits at one of them, and calls a black officer both the "W" and the "N" words. One of the officers ends up with a cut thumb before Andy is restrained.

Andy has previously pleaded guilty to all offences and is in court today to be sentenced. He presents a far calmer figure in the dock than on the night in question, and his mother is in the public gallery to support him.

He has several previous convictions, but there are significant gaps in his offending history, which occur when he is clean, and off the drink and drugs.

Andy accepts that he was "off my head" at the time of the offences, and that he is now motivated to seek help and would welcome both a drug rehabilitation requirement (DRR) and an alcohol treatment requirement (ATR) to help him overcome his problems. Probation services support his request but feel that his alcohol issues are currently more acute than his drug problems and should be prioritised.

The main aims of DRR programmes are to:

- Help offenders to follow a personal action plan designed to help them self-manage drug use and criminal activity
- Explain to offenders the links between drug use and offending and also how drugs affect health
- Help offenders to change their lifestyle

A DRR is a very demanding treatment order that can run for between six months and three years. The objective is to keep the offender free from drugs and associated crime.

Drug testing is central to DRR. Participants provide regular urine samples in order to allow the sentencing court to review progress; a positive test will indicate that the person has not reduced their drug habit.

Drug users are estimated to be responsible for between a third and a half of acquisitive crime, and treatment can cut the level of crime they commit by about half.

The latest figures available show that 56% of DRRs were successfully completed in 2010/11. What is success though? A reduction in substance abuse that does not involve complete abstinence could still be viewed as a successful outcome, especially if it results in a reduction of offending behaviour.

Alcohol is a factor in about half of all violent crime, and an alcohol treatment requirement (ATR) can also be added to either a community order, or suspended sentence, if the offender is dependent on alcohol and expresses willingness to comply with its requirements. Treatment delivered under an ATR may include psychosocial therapies and support, interventions for assisted alcohol withdrawal, detoxification, and cognitive-based treatment to address alcohol misuse.

There is a new sentencing option for dealing with offenders who commit offences whilst under the influence of drink. An alcohol abstinence and monitoring requirement can now be added to either a community or suspended sentence order.

This can require total abstinence from drink, or specify the maximum amount that can be consumed. Compliance with the order is electronically monitored by a tag, which analyses sweat to determine whether alcohol has been consumed. Trials have been successful, and this is a more than welcome addition to our armoury although it is prevention rather than cure.

Andy's mother has also written us a letter stating that he desperately needs help, and that she will give him all the support she can.

We grant him his wish, and – including the sentencing uplift required for the racially-aggravated comments he made – give him a one-year community order with a six-month

ATR and 25 rehabilitation days where some work will be done to address his drug addiction. We also order him to pay £100 in compensation to each of the three officers he physically and verbally assaulted.

"Listen to your Mother", is the last comment I make as he leaves court. But will he, or even can he?

*

Sometimes, though, there are no apparent drug or alcohol addiction issues for us to deal with; simply a total lack of common sense. Such is the case of a man who, unhappy at the poor service he has received at a nearby shop, posts the store manager a chocolate box packed full of excrement not realising that DNA testing (surely, in this instance, a thankless task) clearly identifies him as the culprit, as he uses his own. Not a criminal mastermind, then!

You also come across cases that are totally boggling and almost defy explanation. Gareth, a young man of previous good character from a stable family background became friends with a woman but was evidently infatuated with her. He persuaded her to accompany him to a tanning salon where he had hidden a camera under a towel so that he could secretly take pictures of her, naked, through a spy hole he had ripped into the material.

When he later tried to retrieve his camera it was missing so, incredibly, he spoke to the manager about it and was told that it had been found and the police called.

When Gareth's home was searched, an indecent image of her was found and in his interview he also admitted placing a hidden camera in his bathroom. Indeed, the victim recounted that Gareth had repeatedly tried to persuade her to take a shower when she last visited his address.

Gareth's unhealthy obsession led to him receiving a one-month prison sentence for voyeurism owing to the premeditated nature of his offences, the total breach of trust, and the psychologically damaging effect they had on his victim. He was dubbed "The Sunbed Pervert" in the national press.

*

Fasil is not legally represented when he comes into court and pleads guilty to drink driving, but there matters grind to a halt, as it is clear that he is unable to follow much, if any, of what is going on. The duty solicitor tries to help and sees if he can take clear instructions from Fasil, but he comes back to court a few minutes later, shrugs his shoulders, and we have to adjourn matters for a week so that a Farsi interpreter can be booked.

*

Roger faces a charge of possessing an offensive weapon and using threatening, abusive, and insulting words with intent to cause fear of unlawful violence. Refused entry to a nightclub, he allegedly pulls out a kitchen knife and threatens to stab the doorman who quite sensibly shuts and bolts the door in his face. Roger states that he never had a knife. We decide that the case can be heard in a magistrates' court given that we can always commit to the Crown Court for sentencing if necessary, but Roger elects to have his trial in the Crown Court.

We give him bail with conditions of residence, in that he must live and sleep at his home address every night, not contact the doorman – who is not known to him – and not go to the nightclub in question. We are asked to ban Roger from the entire road in which the nightclub is situated, but it is a major thoroughfare, more than a mile in length, and we feel that is both excessive and unnecessary.

*

The childlike and diminutive Eileen is next in court. Elegantly dressed and perfectly coiffed, she beams beatifically at us from the dock. She is charged with possession of a self-loading pistol, and we send her case to the Crown Court as it is an Indictable only offence.

*

We are trying to make up for lost time now as we start the morning extremely late, owing to what has become the almost customary series of delays. In fact, at 10.15 am, a quarter of an hour after all courts should have opened for business, I count no fewer than 14 magistrates sitting around in the retiring room champing at the bit for action and for something productive to do. The biscuits take a real pounding.

Roseanne, a carer, is accused of pushing and shoving the elderly lady she looks after, and we therefore amend the charge to assault by beating rather than common assault. She pleads not guilty, and we set a trial date.

*

Jermaine admits assaulting two police officers who are called to his father's house after an argument between the two of them got out of hand. Jermaine was extremely drunk and kicks out at both officers, striking them on the leg and thigh, thankfully without doing any damage. Normally, kicking somebody with a "shod foot" places the offence in a higher category of culpability because of the use of a weapon but, fortunately for him, Jermaine is only wearing a sock rather than a shoe, which therefore reduces his level of culpability!

Jermaine's lawyer tells us that he is very apologetic and has no memory of his actions. He is now getting help for his alcohol addiction, so we order him to pay £75 in compensation to each police officer.

*

A few weeks ago, I tried to deal with a case of a 16-year-old youth who was charged with the robbery of an iPhone from a fast food restaurant along with his adult co-defendant. The youth was in court on that date, but we adjourned matters until today in the hope that the adult, who did not appear, could be traced, as ideally they should be tried together.

Well, today, nothing has changed; the youth is back in court and the adult still nowhere to be found. What is particularly annoying and frustrating is that despite our instructions last time, absolutely no effort seems to have been made to locate the adult.

This situation cannot be allowed to continue, particularly with a youth of good character who faces a serious allegation. Justice needs to take its course as quickly as possible, particularly for someone of his age. We speak together, as well as to the legal adviser, and decide to split the two defendants and issue a warrant with no bail for the adult, which means that the police will finally seek him out, and send the youth for trial to the youth court.

Even that seems to take forever as the Libra technology used to set trial dates appears to be on a self-imposed go-slow. From our desk, we can see the legal adviser's computer, and watch, not the wheel of death, but instead, the crown of death, as the court logo spins round and round without the system spluttering into life. This seems an apt metaphor for this case, which so far has gone nowhere very, very slowly.

*

Richard is in court today for sentencing after being found

guilty, after trial, of assaulting his 26-year-old daughter, Nora. It is a depressing but all too familiar story of a deteriorating relationship between a controlling, authoritarian father with his own issues, and a young woman seeking her own independence. Nora tries to leave the family home after arguing yet again with her father, he attempts to stop her, pulls her hair, and then pushes her down onto the sofa. A previous bench does not accept his claim of self-defence.

Victims of crime are fully entitled to say how they have been affected by an offence against them, and can have their victim personal statement (VPS) read out in court before sentencing. The bench must pass the appropriate sentence for the offence but can also take into account the consequences and effect it has had on the victim. We must ignore any comments or opinions from the victim as to the nature of the sentence they would like to see meted out.

Nora declines the opportunity to read her VPS. Instead, the prosecutor recites her long, carefully-drafted, and excoriating statement that highlights – in excruciating detail – her father's on-going and long-established pattern of abusive behaviour towards her and how seriously it has affected her.

She now has a large bald patch and suffers from anxiety, depression, and sleepless nights after this assault by him. Over the years, he has manipulated her, and his actions have torn the family apart. Whilst she wants nothing more to do with him, she does not ask the court to impose a restraining order, which would forbid him from contacting her.

It is a devastating document but Richard stares straight ahead, expressionless and shows no emotion – not even a blink of an eye – during his daughter's character assassination of him.

The probation report states that he has a problem with alcohol, which has clouded his judgement, he does not accept that he has done anything wrong, and that he also shows a total lack of empathy about his behaviour. Despite that, they feel that he is a low risk to reoffend.

His assault has not crossed the custody threshold, and he is previously of good character, so after a discussion, we decide to sentence Richard to a 12-month community order with 15 days of rehabilitation activity and 90 hours of unpaid work. We order him to pay a victim surcharge of £90 and costs of £200, since the case went to trial. There is no order for compensation, as there needs to be some breathing space between the two of them.

It is a desperately sad case, but as we sentence him I watch him closely and get the impression that Richard is still not really listening, hearing, or understanding; he has not taken much, if anything, on board of what was revealed in court today about either his actions and their impact, or how his daughter feels about him. We make sure that the two of them leave the court separately.

Family members are sometimes in total denial, and today brings back painful memories of a disturbing case from a couple of years ago when Pat – who had a long history of viciously abusing his wife and causing her significant injuries – was being sentenced for yet another assault, this time an ABH, on her. We watched in stunned and horrified amazement as the wife's father – yes, *the father of the victim* – came into court as a character witness for the son-in-law. I have never seen or heard anything quite like it as the poor, vulnerable, hapless, and abused wife was accused of bringing everything down upon herself and causing her own problems because of her lack of obedience to her husband's every command and whim. I will never forget how angry I felt at the words horrifically and erroneously used to describe her, "The female is the deadlier of the species." Despite the character reference, we committed Pat to the Crown Court for sentence as his actions demanded greater punishment than we could give.

*

I fall foul of the victim surcharge in the next case when Sharon admits to snapping off the wing mirror of her ex-partner's car in a fit of jealous pique. She describes Danny as a "controlling narcissist", and we do not detect too much remorse for her behaviour. We fine her £140, order her to pay compensation of £70, and I then add £32 in victim surcharge, not noticing from my register that the offence takes place well before the 28th of June 2019, when the rate of victim surcharge increased. The correct figure should – in fact – be £30, and thankfully, Joanne, the legal adviser is alert to the situation and corrects me before any damage is done.

The victim surcharge is a fairly amorphous, if not mysterious, ancillary payment that has to be added to every sentence. First introduced in 2007, the sums actually paid (and I would not like to hazard a guess of exactly what proportion remains unpaid) are used to help fund victim services through the Victim and Witness General Fund.

It is hard to find up-to-date information on how the money is disbursed, but between 2011 and 2014, there were 277 applications for funding from 256 voluntary sector organisations. One hundred and fourteen of these applications were successful and the areas supported include a variety of organisations assisting victims of domestic violence (as it was termed at the time), hate crime, robbery and burglary, sexual violence, antisocial behaviour, and road traffic crime.

Adding the victim surcharge becomes second nature to every magistrate, particularly when sitting in the remand court and having to deal with a high volume of cases; every sentence must be accompanied by the appropriate level of surcharge.

That is all very well until the amounts increase, as was the case on the 28th of June 2019.

The sum to be added when sentencing an adult to a conditional discharge has now risen from £20 to £21. Even more confusing is the levy on a fine, which is now 10% of the value of the fine, ranging from a minimum surcharge of £32 to £181.

In other words, if you are fined any sum up to £320, you will now have to pay £32 in victim surcharge, and then 10% of the value of the fine thereafter up to a maximum payment of £181. Before the 28th of June, it was 10% of the value, with a payment range of between £30 and £170.

The victim surcharge on a community order has increased from £85 to £90, and the surcharge on either a suspended sentence or an actual custodial sentence has risen from £115 to £122.

Is all this change fiddly in the extreme, and almost impossible to remember? Yes, without doubt. Confused? We magistrates certainly are. We had just about got used to the old figures, which had remained in place for over three years. Now, we struggle to both come to terms with, and also remember, the new ones – although there is often a crib sheet attached to our desk in the courtroom. Most offences that we deal with take place after the 28th of June 2019 but every so often – when we are faced with an older one – we can easily be caught out, as I was today.

We can also award compensation to victims when appropriate, in cases where loss, damage, and injury has resulted from the offence. This takes priority over all other payments such as victim surcharge, fines, and costs, and if the offender cannot afford to pay both compensation and the relevant victim surcharge, then the surcharge may be reduced, if necessary, to nil.

We have a suggested tariff of compensation payments to be awarded, which range from £75 for a graze and £100 for a bruise to £125 for a black eye and £1,000 for a fractured nose, going up to £2,400 for a dislocated wrist. Mental injury is also covered with a suggested payment of £500 for temporary mental anxiety.

Similar to fines, we set compensation levels at a rate that is affordable to the defendant, and just because someone is wearing a uniform – such as a police officer or ambulance staff – that should not preclude them from receiving compensation.

We set fines according to the level of seriousness of the offence. We also have to take into account the financial circumstances of the offender. Fines should be payable within 12 months and cause some level of hardship, but should also not force the offender into desperate straits.

There are five levels of fines from A-E. Band D and Band E fines are only used in the most serious cases as a direct alternative to a community order or a custodial sentence and are not that common.

A Band A fine is set at a starting point of 50% of an offender's relevant weekly income, with a Band B fine being

100%, and a Band C fine being 150% of relevant weekly income.

So what is relevant weekly income? Every offender fills in a means form which provides us with a brief snapshot of their financial circumstances, income, expenditure, and whether or not they are working or on benefits.

We cast a fairly world-weary and cynical eye over them given that the offender himself provides the information, and they often seem to suffer from amnesia when it comes to remembering and noting down all their sources of income. Sometimes, we need to read between the lines and query the initial figures that we are provided with.

Where an offender is in receipt of income from employment or is self-employed, and that income is over £120 per week after deduction of tax and national insurance, then that figure is the relevant weekly income.

If the offender is unemployed, on benefits, or a student, then their relevant weekly income is deemed to be £120.

If we have no reliable information about the financial situation, as might be the case if the defendant has not turned up to court, then we assume a relevant weekly income of £440. That is another reason always to appear in court when required, and not run the risk of being convicted and sentenced in absence.

If somebody pleads guilty at the first opportunity, then they receive a one-third discount off their sentence. This reduces to a discount of 25% if the guilty plea is made before the trial date, and then 10%, if the guilty plea is made on the day of trial.

So, here is a quick example to break up the mind-numbing boredom of this section. Please take notes; I might well be setting a test later on.

Let's say Mike pleads guilty to possession of cannabis at the first opportunity and is on benefits; then we might well sentence him to a Band B fine, which would be £120 (his relevant weekly income) less a one-third discount for his early guilty plea (£40), making a total of £80. A victim surcharge of £32 would be added, as well as perhaps prosecution costs of £85 plus an order for forfeiture and destruction of the drugs. Mike will, therefore, walk out of court £197 poorer – quite an expensive joint!

Fines are due to be paid in full on the day of sentencing. However, that almost never happens, and some element of horse-trading goes on as we attempt to fix a realistic payment structure that the offender can adhere to. Ideally, fines should be payable in full within one year and can also be deducted directly from benefits if no other payments are already being taken from them. Apocryphal stories still abound from the bad old days of defendants being ordered to turn their pockets out in court to prove their assertion that they were unable to make any immediate payment.

The prosecutor will generally ask the bench to make an order that the offender pay costs of around £85 for a guilty plea at the first opportunity or around £625 if an offender is found guilty after going to trial. The sums are meant to cover the costs for preparing the case and we decide how much, if any, to award given the offender's means – or lack of them – and whether other payments, such as compensation should be prioritised.

We always try to remember to make what is called a collection order when imposing a fine or any other payment. This provides for greater enforcement of fines and allows defaulters to be brought back to court or for their case to be passed to bailiffs who will chase up overdue sums.

Magistrates, therefore, have more than enough to think about with all these ancillary charges to sort out and add when necessary. However, a few years ago magistrates were suddenly put on the spot and – in addition – had to deal with the ill-fated and totally unlamented Criminal Courts charge. This was introduced on the 13th of April 2015 by the then-Justice Secretary, Chris Grayling, and very soon became almost as hated and reviled as the Poll Tax to many people.

This was a dark day for the courts and Criminal Justice System alike, which are rightly expected to provide justice for all; the Criminal Courts Charge was certainly not justice.

Grayling introduced it as a way of saving money, attempting to get offenders to "pay their way". On conviction, all adult offenders had to pay something towards the cost of running the criminal courts in which they had just appeared.

The explanatory words were couched in highly duplicitous language that was aimed at appealing to the masses, as all the revenue raised would be used to "reduce the burden on taxpayers", but people soon saw beyond the verbiage.

The Criminal Courts Charge was a *further* fixed payment, which had to be applied whenever a defendant either pleaded or was found guilty in either a magistrates' or Crown Court, and was imposed irrespective of their means.

It certainly did not come cheap, as if someone pleaded guilty to a Summary charge then the Criminal Courts Charge imposed would be £150. This rose to £180 if a guilty plea was made to an Either Way offence.

Somebody quite evidently forgot, or more likely, ignored, that fines should always be linked to both means and the ability to pay.

Things got even worse if defendants decided to take up their inalienable right to go to trial, and were then unfortunate enough to be found guilty. In that case, a Criminal Courts Charge of £520 would be imposed for a Summary offence, which rose to an eye-watering £1,000 if someone was convicted after trial of an Either Way offence.

And if that was not enough, on top of this would still be added any fine, victim surcharge, prosecution costs, and compensation ordered by the court!

The potential imposition of the top rate of the Criminal Courts Charge surely provided a perverse incentive to plead guilty, and quite understandably many defendants who either knew or believed that they were innocent of the crime they were accused of, decided to plead guilty, often against the advice of their solicitors. Why risk the Russian roulette of being found guilty after trial, and then having to face a bill of an additional £520 or £1,000 on top of every other payment ordered?

This was no more and no less than a tax on justice, which was not in accordance with the principles of either fairness or justice, and one that penalised all offenders. Of course, it was imposed mainly on those who could least afford it.

Most acquisitive crime is motivated by poverty in the first place, and it seemed incongruous at best – and deeply immoral at worst – to make those defendants who already had little (or nothing) suffer extra financial hardship. Why should those with the least pay the most? Is that justice?

Sentencing became totally disproportionate. When reviewing the impact of the Criminal Courts Charge, the Howard League for Penal Reform gave the example of the case of a 32-year-old woman who admitted stealing a four-pack of Mars Bars worth 75p. She said she stole the item because she "had not eaten in days" after her benefits were sanctioned. She was fined £73, ordered to pay a £150 Criminal Courts Charge, £85 costs, £20 for victim surcharge, and 75p compensation.

In other words a total penalty of £328.75p for stealing something worth under one pound!

Where is the justice in that? No wonder there was a general outcry.

Perhaps she should have been transported to Australia instead?

Many defendants who fell foul of the courts were unable and certainly unwilling to pay the vast sums ordered and, according to the government's own figures, only a small proportion of the sums owed was collected. The Ministry of Justice revealed, in 2016, that it had struggled to recoup any more than 10% of the £68.6m imposed through the Criminal Courts charge.

Of the £5.7m levied in the second quarter of 2015, the first period after the charge was introduced, just over £1m was paid within six months. Only £2.9m of the £22m imposed in the third quarter was paid, and in the final three months of 2015, just £2m of the £40.9m imposed was paid within a month.

I wonder whether this was worth the opprobrium that the government deservedly received as they were lambasted from every direction.

Magistrates working on the shop floor were put in an appalling and invidious position, having to impose this pernicious tax. Our job is to uphold the law as it stands; we cannot pick and choose only those with which we agree.

We had to impose the Criminal Courts Charge even though it was patently a bad law and one that was also totally unfair. Faced with an impossible situation, and struggling with their consciences, many magistrates resigned. The Magistrates Association, our trade body, puts the number of resignations over the imposition of the charge at over 50 and they, like others, lobbied furiously for the Criminal Courts Charge to be scrapped.

Like almost all of my colleagues on the bench, I hated the Criminal Courts Charge with a vengeance, and I felt embarrassed and angry at having to impose it. The legal advisers watched us like hawks to ensure that we did not try to play games, as we were forbidden from taking into account the Criminal Courts Charge when deciding how to deal with an offence, and were unable to reduce fines or costs and other ancillary payments to make up for, and offset, the extra sums demanded by the Criminal Courts Charge.

I heard of a magistrate who gave an offender an absolute discharge (or in other words, no punishment) for possession of a small amount of cannabis, as the imposition of an absolute discharge meant that there was no Criminal Courts Charge attached to it.

I fully understand what he did, and why he did it, but that is no solution and makes a mockery out of sentencing.

We were warned not to comment publicly on the Criminal Courts Charge – a sure sign that the powers that be were well aware of how iniquitous it was – and I was just pleased that I did not have to try to justify it and defend the indefensible.

Finally, and not before time, on the 24th of December 2015, Michael Gove, the new justice secretary, bit the bullet and scrapped the ill-fated and unjust Criminal Courts Charge, but not before it had caused broadscale and unnecessary suffering and hardship, and placed the Criminal Justice System into disrepute.

It was a blessing for everyone when it was abolished. It was totally misconceived and has not been missed. Let us end with the marvellously apposite quote by Ben Summerskill, director of the Criminal Justice Alliance, who was one of the overwhelming majority of right-minded people who welcomed the demise of the Criminal Courts Charge. He memorably dismissed it as "nonsense on stilts."

10. KEEPING A STRAIGHT LINE

The British Transport Police (BTP) is a national special police force that helps to keep order on the railways and light-rail systems in England, Scotland, and Wales. Every Monday, we hold a court session for people alleged to have committed offences either on trains or at railway stations.

In terms of crime, the railway systems are a microcosm of the rest of society with 68,313 notifiable crimes committed in 2018/19, an increase of 12% over the previous 12 months. Knife crime is as much a problem on the railways as it is on the streets, and incidents involving knives and other offensive weapons have increased by nearly half in the last three years. Indeed, over 5,000 such cases have been recorded since 2017, with 1,840 in 2019.

Knife arches, and the use of stop and search, have ensured that half of the recorded knife crime on the railway was as a result of proactive action by officers seizing weapons before they could be used.

BTP courts are always interesting and varied as they deal with a plethora of offences ranging from fare avoidance, drunks blithely strolling onto the tracks (causing massive delays as well as risking their own lives), and serious assaults on the concourse.

*

I am sitting with Peter and Jane today; a real contrast as the former is a newly-appointed winger, and Jane is highly experienced, having sat on the bench far, far longer than myself.

I often wonder why experienced wingers like Jane have never taken the next step and become a presiding justice. In her case, she is happy to remain as a winger and simply has never wanted the extra responsibility of chairing a bench.

Purely for the purpose of researching this book, I asked several other wingers the same question, and their replies have included:

- I haven't got round to it yet
- I have just applied and am waiting for my interview
- I don't have the time for all the extra training required to become a presiding justice
- There is too much work involved
- I am not interested and am quite happy as I am as a winger
- I am unable to sit often enough to keep up my competences as a presiding justice
- I don't want the extra responsibility
- Why are you asking me this question

There are so many truly excellent wingers on our bench and always a desperate shortage of presiding justices – particularly younger ones. Currently, there are 30 vacancies in the London area with a new recruitment programme in full swing, so – hopefully – some of them will change their mind. If I can do it, then I am sure they can too!

As a presiding justice, you are not 'in charge', all three magistrates are equal in standing and you are simply the person in the middle who happens to have a speaking and co-ordinating role. Very often, wingers have far more experience than the presiding justice or have been trained far more recently, and ideally the team of three works in unison and shares all responsibilities. The wingers also act as the eyes and ears of the chair concerning what is happening in and around the court and public gallery. No one person on his or her own can possibly see everything that is going on. The chair (and I will continue to use both terms for the role) is only as good – or sometimes as bad – as the wingers allow him/her to be. Good wingers can really help the chair, and the entire bench, perform to their optimum.

As a winger, it was my job to support the chair, and I could always tell within a couple of minutes of entering the court if my chair knew what he or she was doing, and whether or not he or she had the manner, knowledge, personality, communication skills, perception, and presence to command the attention and respect of all court users and defendants alike. I am sure – and would expect – that every winger I sit with makes a similar judgment about me.

The rota tells me which court I am going to sit in, so when I arrive in court – unless things change at the last minute – I generally know what I will be doing that day, whether it be remands, trials, prison video links, breaches, youth, DVLA, single justice, applications or, as it is today – BTP.

I will not know with whom I will be sitting, or the identity of the legal adviser, until I see the list that is posted first thing each morning in the retiring room. I am far better with faces than with names and whilst I quite often do not recognise all the names of the other members of my bench, I generally spot at least one familiar and welcome face when they arrive.

Quite honestly, I would be hard put to name more than a couple of magistrates with whom I am not that happy to sit; people who I have to force a smile for (whilst inwardly groaning) when we greet each other. A few need help to log into and decipher their iPads, some have shorter attention and concentration spans than others, some have their own little idiosyncrasies and peccadillos, but – for the most part – I take great pleasure from sitting with pretty much everyone on our bench. We are there to help do justice, but – ideally – we should also enjoy and take fulfilment from what we do.

Being the anorak and perfectionist that I am, I also try to pick the brains of other presiding justices who I admire and respect. It is also eye-opening to sneak off and watch a District Judge (DJ) in action. They are lawyers and experienced, full-time, professional judges who run magistrates' court proceedings on their own, assisted only by a legal adviser or court associate. They follow the Venne criteria and hear cases that are expected to last over two days or which involve more complex points of law, evidence, or procedure. High profile or sensitive cases, or those involving terrorism, extradition, and state security are reserved for District Judges as well, who also handle their fair share of common or garden cases that we see every day in a magistrates' court.

Working on their own, they invariably work far quicker than magistrates, as they are judge and jury (if not executioner) all in one, with no need to consult with any colleagues before reaching a decision. Back in 2001, in his report on the criminal justice system, Sir Robin Auld stated that, "District Judges because of their legal knowledge and experience and because they sit alone, are significantly faster and otherwise more efficient than magistrates."

I did read a Ministry of Justice report from 2013 on *The Strengths and Skills of the Judiciary in the Magistrates' Courts* in which in-depth interviews and discussion groups were held with 355 members of the judiciary, court staff, and professional and lay court users. The report highlighted the perceived closeness of magistrates to their local community and that they were also seen as being more "in touch" and "down to earth" than DJs and possessing a broader "experience of life" without becoming "case hardened". Sitting as a "mini-jury" in a bench of three was also thought by some to be "fairer" for defendants than facing a sole judge.

In the same report, District Judges were praised for their speed and efficiency in dealing with matters and, given their legal training and experience, for not needing to seek advice from legal advisers as often as magistrates. DJs were also seen as more "assertive" and "robust" although concern was expressed that "speedy" justice was not necessarily "better" justice.

Some comments were made by people with little experience of the courts rather than those who worked in them, who generally feel more confident in the professional judiciary rather than magistrates, and it is perhaps invidious to compare the strengths and weaknesses of the magistracy and District Judges as we are not in competition with each other. We work in parallel in the courts, and the current system needs both. Maybe there will come a time when magistrates are replaced either entirely by District Judges or relegated to a supporting and subsidiary role, but I cannot see that happening for quite a while yet. That is for two reasons: firstly, on the basis of cost, given the level of salary that they understandably earn; secondly, because – I believe – there would be uneasiness if all cases in a magistrates' court (which would need to be renamed) were judged by only one individual.

I have nothing but admiration for DJs and have learned a lot from watching them in action and picking their brains, not sometimes – it has to be said – without a slight pang of jealousy when a particularly juicy case is allocated to a DJ rather than to an experienced bench of magistrates who would be perfectly capable of handling it. It is also frustrating when we are bumped at the last minute and sent home early because a District Judge is looking for extra work and takes over our court. We have volunteered to give up our day to fulfil our role as magistrates, and it is wrong – in my opinion – for us to be treated in that manner, however politely it is done.

*

Generally, by around 9.30 am, the various court lists will also have been posted, and some (or all) of the background information downloaded onto our iPads.

I have always been a bit anal, as well as terrified of being late, so I am invariably one of the first to arrive. Most magistrates arrive between 9.15 and 9.30 am with a few latecomers straggling in shortly afterwards. If anyone has not turned up by 9.45 am, then a hurried call is made to Bench Support to see if there is news of traffic problems, or a late withdrawal, and if a last-minute replacement can be found.

Sometimes there has to be a juggling of resources to ensure that the available magistrates are deployed to best advantage. This might mean that to ensure a bench of three magistrates covers a trial, only two might be in a remand court.

Before we go into court, we have a brief meeting with the legal adviser where we go through the list, find out who the prosecutor is, talk through anything on our list of cases that looks out of the ordinary, and check for conflicts, or youths being listed erroneously in the adult court. I also ask whether either winger has any preference for where they sit or needs any reasonable adjustments.

I then split tasks between them in terms of one checking the PNC documents which provide details of a defendant's previous convictions, and the other the necessary Sentencing Guidelines in remand courts, or if we are in a trial court, I ask one winger to check the clock to ensure that the cross-examination of witnesses does not go over the allotted time. I always ask the other to keep a roving eye on the defendant, in case he is stressed or misbehaving or trying to communicate with or intimidate the witnesses, as sometimes happens.

One man, accused, and then eventually convicted of a nasty actual bodily harm (ABH) offence, stared at me intensely nonstop throughout his trial, which I found quite off-putting if not intimidating, particularly when I discovered that he worked in a pub less than a quarter of a mile from where I live. I quickly made a mental note to drink elsewhere from then on, although it transpired that he was going to be away from home for a few months.

I remind my colleagues that we are a team and are there to help and support each other. I will consult both of them for their views and opinions before we make any decision. It is my job to manage and structure the out of court discussions that we have before making major decisions, and to ensure that they both feel equally involved and that their views are both solicited, considered, and valued. If either of them has something to say, then they should speak to me quietly on the bench straight away, rather than write me a note, ideally before I do anything particularly stupid in court. The only time I ask them not to interrupt me is if I am in full flow and in the middle of making a sentencing or bail pronouncement, as I know I have to get the wording totally correct and am easily put off and distracted. Similarly, if anyone wants to leave the court for any reason, then I ask them to inform me immediately, and we will all rise.

Typically, it is fine for the three of us to consult together quietly about a decision for no more than a few seconds on the bench – sometimes a raised eyebrow is enough – but if something requires more prolonged thought and discussion, then we must retire to do so. It is totally inappropriate and lacks dignity for everyone in court to see or hear us in deep and prolonged debate, or even worse, disagreement, on the bench. When making a bail decision, we must always rise to talk things through, even if the decision seems to be a forgone conclusion. This is someone's liberty we are talking about.

I agree a working method with the legal adviser. Some want you to tell them – in advance – about every decision you are about to make before announcing it in open court; others, only the key ones. It is a matter of personal preference and trust. I also agree how we are going to handle PET forms between us. Ideally, the legal adviser has a quick, initial glance and then passes it back to the presiding justice who immediately checks the likely length of the trial so that the legal adviser can start looking for a suitable date, whilst the presiding justice continues to go through and fill in the necessary parts of the PET form. I also ask the legal adviser to let me know once he has finished digitally entering up the results of the previous case, as there is nothing that annoys some legal advisers more than calling on the next case before he/she has finished DMU-ing the outcome of the last one.

Just as we are about to go into court, all of our careful pre-planning goes by the board when another chair rushes up and apologetically nabs one of my wingers as her trial court only has two magistrates. If possible, a trial should always go ahead with a full complement of three magistrates which gives some wriggle room if there is any disagreement, and allows for a majority verdict.

So, it is left to Jane and me to sit together and go through what is, in all honesty, a pretty short list.

*

After the customary delay for papers to be downloaded and lawyers to be consulted, our first case involves Pauline, an anxious-looking woman in her mid-thirties with a lengthy history of convictions for public order offences.

On the face of it, nothing has changed, as she pleads guilty to a similar offence after stumbling towards a black station employee in a drunken stupor, before foully and racially abusing him after he simply asks her for her ticket.

Then things take a surprising but gratifying turn. Pauline's lawyer hands us up a smudged and creased handwritten seven-page letter from her client, which we retire to read. Pauline provides us with a harrowing and heart-breaking insight into her troubled past, including a series of foster homes and abusive relationships, which have led to a total lack of self-esteem and alcohol dependency. Since this latest offence, which took place a few months ago, a Women's Group has helped and supported Pauline and provided her with a home, and she has recently attended a training course on diversity and inclusion. She feels deeply ashamed about her behaviour, has finally been able to take back control of her life, managed to stop drinking, and now intends to train as a beautician.

A note from her social worker, who has accompanied

Pauline to court, confirms the massive change in her attitude and circumstances and substantiates the contents of her letter.

We are a cynical bunch who have seen and heard much throughout our time on the bench, and pride ourselves on not being easily taken in or duped. Initially, our antennae are up, and we potentially smell a rat, but Pauline asks to speak to us directly, and it is clear that these are not just empty words. She has faced her demons and the self-destructive path she has been on, and with a lot of help and support has managed to turn things around, and now wants a chance to move on to make something of her life.

Given what we have seen and heard, we decide to give her the opportunity she has asked for, and go outside the Sentencing Guidelines, ensuring that we provide clear reasons why it is in the interests of justice for us to do so. We sentence her to a conditional discharge for nine months, which includes an extra three months as the required sentencing uplift for a racially-aggravated offence. This means that she is not being punished today, but if she commits any further offences in the next nine months, she will be punished for today's offence as well as the new one.

Pauline bursts into tears and falls into the arms of her support worker – we think we have got this one right.

*

Our next customer is a familiar face to me – as apparently is mine to her, as I am greeted with a gap-toothed smile and a friendly wave of a gnarled hand. It is our old friend Ms T, who I last saw in the breach court not so long ago. Today, she is accused of being drunk and disorderly and hurling insults at random passers-by at a nearby station, before racially abusing a black member of staff.

Sober, she has no memory of what happened, but she pleads guilty, and despite the stage-whispered entreaties of her long-suffering lawyer to keep quiet, Ms T does her best to make things worse for herself and add fuel to the fire by blurting out that, "I'm expecting to go to prison."

Probation services say that despite all her issues, vulnerabilities, and addictions, she is complying with the requirements of her Alcohol Treatment Requirement (ATR), and they are pleased with her progress. We are asked to adjourn this matter until later in the month when she is due back in court for trial on another charge. She can then be sentenced for this offence at the conclusion of her trial.

We bail her until that date, and she leaves the court with an almost regal wave and a cheery cry of "bye-bye". She seems to light up and come alive when in court and – subconsciously, perhaps, given the amount of time she spends here – she feels that this is her surrogate home where she is safe and even supported; some semblance of order in what is otherwise a chaotic lifestyle.

*

Christian is a tall and striking-looking Bulgarian man with a tragic recent history. He is accused of a Section 4A public order offence in that he used threatening and abusive and insulting words to cause harassment, alarm, and distress at a mainline station. The name of the complainant has been left off the charge in error, and has to be added before a plea can be taken.

Christian accepts that he was drunk and was late for his train and in a flustered state he told a female member of the station staff to "fuck off", and to "suck my fucking dick". She was understandably disgusted by his words but, in an indictment of the world we live in, stated that such behaviour is now almost an everyday occurrence.

Christian has enjoyed a relatively successful career as an actor both in Bulgaria and the UK, but his life turned upside down a couple of years ago after he was assaulted, and he is now also HIV positive. Given these recent traumas, he is suffering from depression and mental health issues and is desperately trying to get his life back on track. He is apologetic and states that he is getting help both for his excessive drinking and state of mind.

He is planning to start a film studies course and, recognising his situation, we give him a conditional discharge for two years and order him to pay compensation of £50 to the long-suffering station staff member.

*

Marianne slouches into court wearing a baseball cap and a surly expression on her face and hunkers down in the dock. "Is there a reason why you need to wear your cap in court?" is my carefully expressed question to her. "Yeah, religious", she answers. So that's that.

She fidgets, pouts, grimaces, glares, looks everywhere but at the bench and her lawyer, appears to be totally disinterested in the proceedings, and gives off palpable waves of anger and aggression. The mood darkens in the court as she is potential Nitro-glycerine who needs to be handled and managed extremely carefully.

She accepts shouting and swearing at a female member of station staff on three separate occasions, and calling her a "fucking bitch".

Her lawyer then does a good job of explaining what this is all about. Marianne suffers from sciatica and depression, is in constant pain, and often needs a stick to help support her. Her ten-year-old daughter is her life, and her sole family member, and when the ticket inspector queries the daughter about her Oyster card, it acts as a trigger. Marianne immediately comes, as she thinks, to the rescue of her daughter.

This does not excuse her behaviour or her abusing the same member of staff on two subsequent visits to the station.

Marianne is already on a community order for other dissimilar matters and is receiving help from probation, and medication for her anger and depression. She is neither fit for unpaid work nor suitable for a curfew. We retire to talk through the sentencing options remaining to us, which are now extremely limited, and settle on an award of £100 in compensation to the ticket inspector. Expressionless, Marianne leaves court.

*

We see another protective mother in our next case, which involves Kim, a tall, statuesque 19-year-old model. She is late for an interview for a potential modelling job and uses an invalid ticket for her journey. When challenged, she tells the inspector to "fuck off" a couple of times, refuses to engage with him, and then blithely ignores him by putting on her headphones.

He calls ahead and informs the BTP about her actions, and they are waiting for her when she gets off the train. They stop her and rather than pouring oil on troubled water she behaves in the same rude and dismissive manner towards the police officers. They end up handcuffing and searching her and finding small quantities of cannabis and Ketamine in her bag.

Now she really is in trouble, and ends up in court before

us. Just as we are about to deal with her case, a woman stands up in the public gallery and starts shouting at us. It is Kim's mother. We eventually, and with some difficulty, calm her down, and the story emerges that Kim is of good character and her lawyer has been trying for several months – so far without success – to conclude an agreement with the police for an out of court disposal. They are therefore surprised and angered, and indeed, as we can hear, incandescent with rage, to receive the court summons.

Given her lack of previous convictions, the two possible options would be a cannabis warning or a simple caution.

A cannabis warning may be given where the offender is found in possession of a small amount of cannabis consistent with personal use, and the offender admits the elements of the offence. The drug is confiscated, and a record of the warning will be made. The warning is not a conviction and should not be regarded as an aggravating factor when sentencing for subsequent offences.

The other option would be a simple caution which may be issued where there is evidence that the offender has committed an offence, the offender admits to the offence, it is not in the public interest to prosecute, and the offender agrees to being given the caution, which is a warning that stays on your record for six years if you are an adult.

The prosecutor agrees that this case should go back to the police for review, and ideally an out of court disposal, and agrees to help escalate matters. We adjourn the case for three weeks in the anticipation that it will be sorted within that time. If it isn't, then Kim will have to come back to court and enter a plea.

Kim and her mother leave court without a word. I can well

understand their sense of frustration at not being able to sort things out with the police over so long a period, and for still having this matter hanging over Kim. A drugs conviction, and indeed a caution, might well limit her working opportunities abroad, but what sticks in my craw is Kim's absolute sense of entitlement – which has come over loud and clear today – and the total lack of any contrition or acknowledgement, let alone an apology, for her dismal behaviour.

If you are carrying Class B drugs in your bag, surely it is not the most sensible behaviour firstly to use the wrong train ticket, and then to kick off towards ticket inspectors and the police alike. But what do I know?

Maybe words have been exchanged between mother and daughter in private? Let's hope so.

*

Nigel is not in court to answer the charge of possessing a bladed article in a public place; in this instance, a nearby mainline station. He has been properly bailed to appear in court today, and we issue a warrant for his arrest without bail, which means he will now be picked up by police and held in custody to ensure that he does appear in court.

In an idle moment, we read the police report of the incident and note that Nigel's response, when queried by the BTP about the alleged offence, was, "It's a load of bollocks!" We assume that he will be entering a not guilty plea then.

*

We are now down to our last couple of cases.

Hassan pleads guilty to causing an obstruction on the railway by wandering on the tracks perilously close to two electrified rails. The power is switched off, and the railway network goes down for an hour at a total cost to the company of £48,672.15. This alarmingly precise figure is apparently based on departure losses, journey time losses, and fines imposed on the company.

Hassan is totally oblivious and unaware of the chaos he has caused. He is a cleaner at a nearby college, earns very little, and he states that he drank too much and simply wandered off the platform and was totally unaware of doing so.

He has very limited means, and we order him to pay a nominal amount of compensation to the railway company.

*

Lastly, we see Ahmed who is in custody, brought in on a warrant after failing to appear at the police station on three separate occasions for them to administer a caution for possession of Class B drugs. Like Kim, earlier, he is of good character but this time the police act speedily to offer him an out of court disposal that he cavalierly ignores no less than three times.

He states in court that he has indeed received several texts, but he has not yet got around to answering them or sorting things out, but he fully intends to do so. We remind him that it is not for him to decide when to deal with this matter, and tell him extremely firmly that his foolish behaviour has landed him with a highly unpleasant night in custody.

Luckily for him, the BTP are prepared to give him one last opportunity to accept a caution – and this time, he had better turn up when told to do so. We adjourn matters for three weeks for the caution to be administered, and he leaves with a well-deserved flea in his ear.

It has been a stimulating and wide-ranging day but what comes over clearly, and is so very depressing, is the amount of deeply unpleasant and foul abuse and violence that railway workers of all description are subjected to on a daily basis. It is almost a matter of course for them when simply going about their daily work, and almost invariably without the slightest provocation. It is remarkable how patient and uncomplaining they are despite everything that is thrown at them — sometimes literally — and it is our duty, as magistrates, to ensure that they are protected. They have certainly gone up in my estimation.

11. A WASTED DAY

Judging by the court number on my rota, I expected to be sitting in a trial court today. Instead, on arrival, I find I have been allotted to an applications court. Applications are the bread and butter of the magistrates' court system and can take many guises, including applications for search warrants, mental health warrants, utility warrants, statutory declarations, closure orders, and criminal behaviour orders.

Given the nature of the work, we generally only sit in a bench of two for applications courts, and there is no need for a prosecutor either. Today, we have a very short morning list, and when I speak to the legal adviser I am told – to my chagrin – that we have no planned work for the afternoon either, which is likely to make for a very short day. I am sitting with Mary this morning, an eminently sensible woman with a caustic sense of humour. From past experience, I know that we will work well together, assuming that we have much – or even any – work to do.

The surprising news when I check the rota is that a third magistrate will join us after lunch, when William is due to arrive. It is possible that we will be able to assist other courts with their business, but I suspect that we will be struggling to find much to do, particularly as without a prosecutor we are strictly limited in the type of work we can handle.

William has recently moved away and now lives over one hundred miles from our courthouse. He is waiting for a transfer to come through to his local justice area. In the meantime, he stoically travels back and forth, well over two hours each way, for half-day sittings, which is very committed and public-spirited of him. On a day like this, though, it is hardly the best or most sensible use of his time.

I speak to the legal adviser and he agrees that we should try to cancel William, but despite sending an email and making a couple of telephone calls, we are unable to contact him, as he is obviously already *en route*.

We then look at the rota and see that, with a bit of juggling, William can sit in a remand court after lunch, so hopefully he will not have a wasted journey.

When we go into court, Matthew, our legal adviser, informs us – with a wry and resigned expression on his face – that we will not even be handling the two matters on our meagre and paltry list. An application to vary a restraining order is listed erroneously with us (and has been moved to another court as a prosecutor is required to put the case), and an appeal against the granting of a premises licence has been discontinued.

So here we are, at three minutes past ten, with an empty court and absolutely nothing for us to do. John, our list caller is therefore despatched to see if he can find us any work.

An efficient list caller can make all the difference between unmitigated chaos and the court running smoothly and like clockwork. It is their job to check which defendants have arrived in court, inform the bench who hasn't, see who is represented (and by which firm of lawyers), and who is a litigant in person (representing themselves or needing to consult with the duty solicitor).

He or she needs to be a combination of a juggler, an air traffic controller, and a restaurant *maître d'hôtel*, keeping a clear picture in his head of where everybody is at any one time, and making sure that there is some semblance of order and a steady trickle of cases filtering through to the courtroom. He/she needs to greet, sign in, and organise defendants as they arrive in court and be immune to the siren-song entreaties and wheedling of unscrupulous lawyers trying to get their cases called on first. Charm, tact, energy, initiative, strength of character, resilience, and an ability to multitask are all prerequisites for the job.

It is the list caller who needs to be in three places at once, updating the bench on the progress – or lack of – of every case, and chasing up lawyers who have disappeared and are now "on their feet" in the youth court whilst simultaneously being required in the adult court. They also need to tell the bench and legal adviser which case is ready to be called on next, whilst being careful not to do so until given the prearranged signal by the legal adviser.

It is the list caller who erects the screens when special measures are called for, and makes sure that defendants, complainants, and witnesses from the same case do not cross paths. They also ensure that every witness either takes the oath or affirms before giving evidence, locates a probation officer when required, makes certain that the court list is updated and circulated to the bench and legal adviser, and informs defendants how they can pay their fines by credit and debit card.

Have I missed anything out?

Oh yes, they also chase around other courts either to give away or find additional work for their bench depending upon the time of day and their workload. In truth, list callers are the true unsung heroes who oil the wheels and help keep the creaking court system running as efficiently and effectively as possible. It is also rare for their unstinting work to be noticed or remarked upon, let alone for them to be thanked for their unceasing efforts.

Thanks to John's efforts, work starts dribbling in. We deal with a number of applications from the local authority seeking entry to properties in order to make their annual gas safety check. They have already attempted to contact the residents on three separate occasions without success, and we now grant access for these necessary checks to be made.

*

Next, come a couple of applications for a Section 135 Mental Health warrant. This provides the power to remove a person from their home if it is considered they have a mental disorder and that they may be in need of care and assistance. With the agreement of the person, they can either be assessed at home, or removed to a place of safety for the assessment to take place there.

The process is for an approved mental health professional to present us with evidence in order to obtain a warrant, which will authorise them – along with the police, and a doctor – to gain entry to the premises in order for the assessment to take place. Once granted, they can enter the property and make their assessment or remove the service user to the place of safety.

From our point of view, we expect to be presented with a detailed application form that provides us with a history of the case, the problems that have made this application necessary, the current state of mental health of the service user, and evidence of the recent efforts that have been made to assist them.

In both cases, we grant the warrants, as there is clear written evidence that the people concerned are vulnerable, in desperate straits, without family support, are unable to cope with their situation, and present a potential danger to both themselves and others.

Our only concern is that the case worker who is applying for the warrants is not directly involved with either case and is not able to answer any supplementary questions that Mary and I might have. Fortunately, the application forms provide all the necessary information that we need to justify our issuing the warrants.

*

Finally, we are asked to hear an application for a search warrant under Section 23 of the *Misuse of Drugs Act*. This is an application that is heard by one magistrate only, but Mary remains on the bench, although she plays no active part in the proceedings. We also clear the court, as we are about to hear confidential information about an ongoing police operation.

Like any application that is made before you, it is crucial that all search warrant applications are very carefully scrutinised, as you are being asked to give the police permission to enter and then examine somebody's home. Clearly, this is a massive invasion of privacy and a request that should not be granted without it being subject to forensic examination and questioning.

When examining the warrant, I need to ensure that there is sufficient detail provided into the circumstances behind the application, as well as evidence of why a search is justified.

In this case, I am being asked to issue a warrant to search the home of a man suspected of storing and selling Class A drugs in his home and also selling them from his car. He has several recent convictions for both the possession and supply of Class A and Class B drugs. I then look for evidence of his involvement in selling drugs recently and read that, in the last few days, the police have received several tipoffs that drugs are being stored and sold by him. It appears that a number of people come and go at all hours of the day and night, and that the man is also seen selling drugs from his car.

I query the reliability of this information and am told that the majority of it is rated as B2, which means that the source is mostly reliable and knows or has had dealings with the person involved. There are also calls from neighbours complaining about drug-related activity, and comings and goings from the property in question. This is rated as E4; in other words, untested and anonymous information whose accuracy cannot be assessed or verified.

I ask if the police have conducted any checks themselves, and I am told that they have sent some plainclothes officers to the area who confirm that there is illegal activity going on. The officer making the application is part of the investigating team, and is able to put further flesh on the bones of the application.

The building that the police wish to search is a maisonette with a shared front door; the suspect lives in the ground floor apartment, and to the officer's knowledge it has not been searched before. I ask if there are any vulnerable people, children, or dogs living there and am told that the suspect lives there with his mother. Should the warrant be granted, a team of ten police officers with sniffer dogs would enter and search the property tonight, and that female officers would also be present to ensure that his mother is properly looked after and cared for.

The written application, as well as the additional information provided by the police officer, has clearly set out why they believe that drugs will be found on the premises. It has also been signed off by a senior police officer of the required rank of Inspector or above.

Given what I have both read and heard, I grant and sign a warrant authorising a search of the premises on one occasion only – within a month of today's date – as I am satisfied that there are reasonable grounds for suspecting that an offence under Section 23 of the *Misuse of Drugs Act* has been committed and that controlled drugs will be found on the premises.

This was, without doubt, one of the most thorough and well-thought-through applications that the legal adviser and I have seen recently, and I wish that they were all of this quality. Sometimes, however, applications for search warrants do not stand up to scrutiny; I have seen applications that appear to be mere fishing exercises or which have not been adequately completed. I understand that, not before time, a recommendation has been made that formal training should be provided to police officers on how to ensure that applications are properly filled out. If they have not, then they must be rejected without a qualm, even if time is of the essence. Following a rejection, the police are fully entitled to make a further application, taking into account the comments made by either magistrate or legal adviser.

We have had a spurt of activity over the last hour or so, but it is now just gone 11 am, and there is no more work for us to do. John is sent on a final but fruitless circuit of the neighbouring courts, but it appears that most of them are also struggling to fill their day.

Matthew then releases us, and after an extremely short post-court review, mainly spent bemoaning the lack of work and how daft it was to bring us in today in the first place, we put our unused iPads away and go home. We both scamper away like a pair of kids released early from school for an unexpected half-holiday.

I wonder why the legal team even bothered to open our court today given the lack of work, not only in our court but also elsewhere. I do appreciate that it is simply the luck of the draw, and swings and roundabouts, as sometimes we are totally rushed off our feet and crawl out of court both mentally and physically exhausted well after 6 pm, but the planning went completely awry today and this feels like a totally wasted day. I do hope that William gets to enjoy a half-day sitting in the remand court.

It is all right for me, as I sit regularly, but I feel sorry for Mary who has organised a day off work, feels more than a bit short-changed, and now has to decide what to do with the rest of her day. Perhaps I will write up another chapter of my book.

12. PART HEARD

We need to change the composition of the bench first thing this morning. After a quick reshuffling, I am joined by both Amanda and Craig as, ideally, a trial court has a mixed bench of both men and women.

Amanda is gradually getting over the shock and disappointment of recently not making the cut – and being confirmed as a presiding justice – after her sixth and final appraisal, at the conclusion of her lengthy and exhaustive training programme. She has licked her wounds and, undaunted, has decided to try again after receiving feedback from the JTAAAC. She now knows exactly what she has to do if she is to succeed second time around.

Amanda has already taken the first step by attending the two-day presiding justice training course for the second time, and she asks me if I am willing to sit with her soon in a supported sitting and observe her in the chair before her next set of appraisals. I am happy to do so, and offer to let her chair today. She declines, however, as we are due in court in a few minutes and she feels that she doesn't have sufficient time to prepare for the sitting.

Surprisingly enough, it seems that our first trial is going to start on time.

The defendant, Gordon, is accused of an assault by beating on his partner, Rosemary. He is here, as are the three prosecution witnesses who are all 16-year-old schoolgirls. Rosemary is also present, but she has neither made a complaint, nor is she willing to give evidence against her partner.

Because of their ages, the schoolgirls are not going to come to the courtroom to give evidence but instead will do so via a live video link from elsewhere in the building.

Before we start, I remind the advocates of the guidance and ground rules relating to young people giving evidence, especially in terms of using simple, clear language at all times.

Questions must not be aggressive in nature, only open questions are to be asked, and no tagged questions are allowed (in other words, making a statement before immediately following it with a short question). Breaks must also be given whenever the witnesses ask for them.

They nod their understanding and Amanda then digs me in the ribs and reminds me – courtesy of her presiding justice refresher training course just the other week – that the bench should always go and visit young, vulnerable witnesses before they give their evidence. This is in order for us to introduce ourselves and tell them what we do, explain who everybody else is in court, and reassure them about what is going to happen once the trial begins. Anything, in fact, that we can do to put them at their ease and help make their ordeal less scary and stressful, and as palatable as possible.

I thank her for her suggestion, as I was totally unaware of this requirement. Therefore, we all troop out of court and go backstage into the nether regions to look for the witness support room. Eventually, we find it! A cramped, dark, cheerless bolthole tucked away in a hidden alcove, where the three girls and their parents are ensconced.

This is a part of the courthouse that we rarely venture into. The hinterland, which is the province and natural habitat of defendants and witnesses alike, who gawp at us. As three semi-smartly dressed, middle-aged people – who look totally incongruous and out of place – we feel like animals in a zoo but without receiving any of the smiles and attention that they generally do from the public. It strikes me, yet again, just how crucial is the need for more diversity and youth on the bench, so that the people we deal with each day can identify with us – rather than see us as visiting and out-of-touch alien beings.

As I prepare to knock on the door, I pretend not to have heard Craig's *sotto voce* comment that I should lag behind the others as my profile would be enough to terrify the three youngsters, and send them scurrying off home. Undaunted, I lead the way into the room.

The girls all seem relieved to see us, and we explain that they won't be able to see the defendant, nor he them, as they will give their evidence from behind a screen as well as in another room. We smile and laugh and try our best to reassure three anxious and frightened young school children that everything will be OK. We tell them to take as much time as they want, and to ask us if they do not understand anything or want a glass of water or a break in the proceedings. We thank them all for being so brave and for coming to give evidence today. We have done our best, and it's now time to return to court.

We brave the maze and eventually find our way back to the courtroom, and go through the door to see the two lawyers huddled together – deep in conversation – and quite obviously haggling. Gordon, big, bald, burly and brawny, sits patiently and detached with his eyes shut in the witness box, waiting for his future to be decided. It's clear that much has been going on in our absence, and we are asked to retire for another ten minutes in the hope and expectation that their chat, if successfully concluded, might well shorten and expedite matters.

That is legalese shorthand for a defendant changing his mind and making a late guilty plea. There can be many reasons for this, including the lure of the reduced ten percent discount off his sentence that he will now receive, but guilty defendants often wait until the day of the trial in the hope that the complainant or witnesses will not turn up to court and then finally throw in the towel when they see that the prosecution is ready and prepared for trial, with a full complement of witnesses.

We are therefore not surprised when we eventually learn that Gordon is prepared to plead guilty to the charge, but only on a basis – which means that he accepts that he committed the crime, but in different and less serious circumstances to those alleged by the Crown.

With the help of his solicitor, he has put forward his own version of what happened. The prosecutor has since taken advice from the CPS and is prepared to accept a guilty plea on the basis put forward today by Gordon.

It is now our job to decide that, if we agree to the facts as described by Gordon (rather than the prosecution), whether it will make a fundamental difference to the sentence he will receive.

Jane, the legal adviser, hands us Gordon's basis of plea, but before we look at it, and make our decision, I suggest that the prosecutor firstly tells us the facts of the case, which will help us put Gordon's account into context and perspective.

The prosecutor states that three schoolgirls are walking through a park when they come across a couple who are arguing. In full view of them, the male punches the woman, and she falls over. The girls are shocked at his behaviour and two of them follow the man and the other calls the police.

When the police arrive, they arrest him and find that he smells of alcohol.

Gordon's account today is somewhat different. He and his partner have been out for a couple of drinks and, in good spirits, are walking home through the park. They decide, in jest, to have a play fight and she pushes him harder than he expected, so he responds and defends himself by slapping her in the face with an open palm. She loses her balance and falls over. He now accepts that he used excessive force.

The prosecutor states that this is a Category 2 offence with greater harm, because – in her opinion – the victim is automatically vulnerable because she was assaulted in a domestic context.

The *Overarching Principles on Domestic Abuse* state that, "all victims of domestic abuse are potentially vulnerable due to the nature of the abuse, but some victims of domestic abuse may be more vulnerable than others, and not all vulnerabilities are immediately apparent", so we ask for specific details of Rosemary's background or personal circumstances which might help us to decide whether she is indeed vulnerable.

Gordon points to the public gallery where a fit-looking woman in her mid-thirties is sitting. This is Gordon's partner, Rosemary, who is not supporting the prosecution and has declined to give evidence against him. It is clear that the two of them remain a couple. Whilst we cannot, of course, know what is going on inside her head, on first glance, vulnerable she is not and, crucially, we are not given any specific information by the prosecutor about her state of mind that might persuade us to change our view.

Gordon does have previous convictions, but not for violence, and there are no records of police callouts or previous issues between the two of them.

After due consideration, we agree that we do not believe there is a fundamental difference in sentencing between the versions presented by the Crown and Gordon, and we accept his basis of plea.

Before sentencing, we ask the prosecutor to go and tell the three schoolgirls what has happened and to thank them for coming. There is now no need for them to give evidence, as we are not going to have a trial. They are released with our thanks, relieved no doubt that their ordeal is over. They have done their public duty, and we are extremely grateful to them.

Looking at our Sentencing Guidelines, this is an offence at the top end of Category 3 with a starting point of a Band A fine, and a range between a conditional discharge and a Band C fine.

Gordon's means form confirms that he is a self-employed plumber earning £420 per week. The offence is aggravated in three ways:

- It is domestic in nature
- Gordon is under the influence of drink
- It takes place in front of children

Given these factors we decide on a sentence at the top end of the sentencing range – a Band C fine – which means that this is going to be very expensive for him. He is fined £630 (150% of his relevant weekly income of £420) less a 10% discount for his late and belated guilty plea, making a total of £567. There is also a victim surcharge of £56; plus a contribution towards costs of £120. Given the circumstances of the offence, we do not feel it appropriate to award Rosemary any compensation.

Gordon's extremely ill-advised slap (and we expect that

there is some minimisation going on there too) is going to cost him a grand total of £743. He winces and then grimaces visibly when informed of how much he has to pay, and agrees to pay if off in instalments at a rate of £40 per week.

He could well have escaped with a much lighter sentence had he decided to plead guilty at the first opportunity, instead of waiting until the last minute. Then his fine would have been reduced from £630 to £420, as he would have been entitled to a full one-third discount, plus a victim surcharge of £42 and costs of £85, giving a total of £547 rather than today's figure of £743. He would have saved himself £196.

As everyone leaves court, I have my head down filling in the cracked trial form, but both Amanda and Craig point out to me the foul and venomous look that Gordon apparently gives Rosemary as they are reunited (his bail conditions preclude their having any contact before the trial). That is what you have sharp-eyed and observant wingers for – to observe everything that goes on in court, and ideally catch what you miss. Perhaps the situation between Gordon and Rosemary is yet to be resolved and I would like to be a fly on their wall when they return home, if only to ensure that she is safe.

*

We are now looking for work after what was estimated to be a three-hour trial has been concluded in an hour. Our second morning trial has been allocated to another court in the meantime, so we end up considering and then issuing two mental health warrants (plus suggesting to the social worker involved that he gets a new identity card as his photograph has been worn away to a hazy and almost indistinguishable silhouette apart from his beard), and we are released for an early lunch just before midday.

It is quite a rarity to break for lunch so early. Very often, particularly when sitting in a busy remand court, there is so much work, and you want to make up the time lost for the customary delays, that you might well try to sit right up to – and sometimes just beyond – the 1 pm witching hour in order to finish up one more case.

The presiding justice and legal adviser must weigh up the need to finish the list whilst also ensuring that all court staff enjoy a decent lunch break. Also, prisoners cannot be escorted up from the cells or taken back down again between 1 and 2 pm.

I noticed an advocate complaining on Twitter recently about having a shortened lunch hour because of the pressure of work. That's certainly not ideal, but like so many things in court, it's a balancing act and magistrates are also well used to having a truncated lunch hour. Perhaps that partially makes up for all the time spent sitting around in the retiring room waiting to be called back into court.

*

The afternoon's trial is shrouded in mystery. There is no PET form, so we have limited information about what awaits us. All we know is that Wes is accused of driving with excess alcohol and of criminal damage and that the trial is expected to last for three hours.

Jane, our legal adviser, has made it clear that she needs to leave at 5 pm today, so given that we do not start the afternoon session until 2 pm we can see that time is of the essence, and we have to get a move on if we are to have any chance of finishing the trial today.

Going part heard, as it is called when a trial has started but is not concluded on the day, is something to be avoided if at all possible as it means that everybody has to reconvene on another day in order to finish matters off. It is often extremely difficult to find a date, ideally not too far in the future, that is convenient for defendant, witnesses, advocates, and magistrates alike.

The same bench must both start and finish a trial, and given our volunteer status and other commitments, it is very often the bench that finds it hardest to agree on a date that all three of us can make. We also have to remember where we have got to in the trial, who said what, and also keep and then try to make sense out of our (certainly in my case) indecipherable notes.

The time elapsed also gives a further opportunity for memories to become clouded and witnesses to be less willing to come to court to give their evidence.

My priority when we return at 2 pm is to avoid this if at all possible, but it will be a close run thing and everything will need to go smoothly and with a fair wind, particularly as we will also need to spend time considering our verdict and writing our reasons for it.

But this is the Criminal Justice System that we are talking about, and on past experience something is almost certain to go wrong and put us behind the clock. It does not take long for my worst fears to be realised.

Defendants are instructed to arrive at court at 9.30 am for a morning case and 1.30 pm for an afternoon hearing. This is to help ensure that we get off and running, on time, at either 10 am or 2 pm.

The bench, legal adviser, and prosecutor are all in court on the dot at 2 pm and raring to go, but there is no sign of either the defendant or his lawyer, until – at 2.09 pm – Wes strides in, accompanied by his solicitor, Mr Franklin.

Without a hint of an apology or explanation for his tardiness, Mr Franklin says that he now needs some further time to take instructions from his client. This should, of course, have been done, if not before today, then certainly at 1.30 pm. There is not much we can do apart from stare balefully at him and give him a few minutes' grace. Without instructions, he cannot defend his client.

Before he leaves the court, we ascertain that Wes maintains his not guilty plea for both offences. The issue for the drink driving offence, in other words why he says he is innocent, is that he claims not to be the driver of the car. He also denies that there is any damage caused to his neighbour's car (the criminal damage allegation).

But there is more. The prosecution apparently largely relies on a lengthy interview between Wes and a police officer made shortly after the alleged offences took place and captured on body-worn camera (BWC). This lasts for the best part of half an hour and was apparently served on the defence over three weeks previously.

Mr Franklin shrugs his shoulders, says that he was only instructed yesterday as an agent to take this case, and was unable to view the footage last night, as he does not possess a laptop that can play it. Not a reply that endears him to the bench.

Given that there is proof that the BWC footage was correctly served by the CPS we could – and in retrospect, perhaps should – have started the trial as soon as Mr Franklin had taken instructions from Wes, but again, things are not quite so straightforward.

Mr Ali, the prosecutor, states that the interview contains a number of clear admissions by Wes that he both drove when over the limit, and also damaged his neighbour's car.

Wes has also apparently not yet viewed the footage and, given its crucial nature and content, plus the possibility that after watching it he might conceivably change his plea to guilty and save us all the necessity of having a trial, we reluctantly agree that it makes good sense to allow Wes and Mr Franklin time to watch it before we start.

By now, it is almost 2.30 pm and – given the length of the interview – we have to allow them a further 30 minutes to watch it in full.

If Wes does not decide to change his plea, we are now not going to be in a position to start the trial until after 3 pm, making it inevitable that we will have to go part heard.

It is quite clear that Mr Franklin is in absolutely no hurry at all to get started and is pushing us as far as he can. When he comes back at 3 pm, he says that after viewing the interview footage his client still maintains his innocence and there will need to be a trial. But he also has some further issues that he wishes to discuss and clarify with the prosecutor; he has finally exhausted our patience and, not before time too, I say "no", express our deep concern at his tardiness, and tell him that we are going to start the trial immediately.

Given that there will also have to be some toing and froing in order to find a suitable date for the continuation of the trial when we go part heard, we now only have about an hour and three quarters left today.

Normally, we would be working from a PET form, which sets out the timetable for the trial, and specifies exactly how much time has been allotted for each witness to give evidence.

The bench is strict about keeping them to that time, with one of the magistrates tasked with advising the presiding justice when the allotted time is nearly up. This cannot be done today without a PET form, so I simply clarify how long they estimate they will need for each witness and advise both advocates to conduct their questioning as quickly as is realistic.

The Crown will be calling the neighbour and the police officer as well as playing the police BWC interview in its entirety. For the defence, Wes will be giving evidence on his own behalf and his niece, Valerie, who he claims is the actual driver, will also be testifying.

What is strange is that we now learn that Mr Franklin is a court-appointed Section 38 lawyer who is only here to question witnesses on Wes's behalf. We wonder why this is necessary as neither of the Crown's two witnesses are members of Wes's family or close to him. One, in fact, is a police officer; the other, his neighbour, and they should both be quite capable and robust enough to stand up to being cross-examined by Wes. So why is Mr Franklin's presence necessary at all? This is yet another mystery and unanswered question.

We estimate that, this afternoon, we can hear the entire prosecution case as well as Wes's evidence, both in chief and in cross-examination, but we will just have to see how far we can get before we run out of time.

I am now simply going to describe what is said in court this afternoon – a running commentary in fact – without providing any opinions, comment, analysis, or judgment as (at the time of writing) the case is yet to be concluded.

My colleagues and I have not discussed the case between

us, and we will not do so until the trial is over.

Given the way a trial is conducted, with the prosecution calling their witnesses first and also putting forward any other evidence – such as CCTV or body-worn camera footage, as well as the interview held at the time with the defendant – before the defence can also put their own case and present their own evidence, it is hardly surprising that the bench quite often changes its mind several times about guilt or innocence whilst a trial is in progress, depending upon what we see and hear.

Sometimes, we feel certain that the defendant is guilty halfway through the trial but subsequent events, when the defendant and his witnesses take the stand, are often enough to convince us of their innocence, or puts some doubt in our mind.

Conversely, there are occasions when we believe that the prosecution evidence is not strong and that they are some way short of proving their case, but then the defendant's evidence is so unconvincing, patchy, inconsistent, and lacking in credibility that he manages to convict himself out of his own mouth.

The lesson that we must learn is that we need to be open-minded, listen carefully, and suspend all judgment until the *end of the trial*.

The prosecution has to prove guilt to the requisite standard, which is "beyond reasonable doubt". The defence does not have to prove or disprove anything at all, and the bench of three, or occasionally two magistrates, makes the final decision.

I did once read a definition of "beyond reasonable doubt" from a retired solicitor as, "Such doubt as may reasonably be doubted by twelve reasonably doubtful men." That is not particularly helpful, so from our point of view it does not mean that we think someone is guilty, or that he or she could (or might) be guilty.

To find someone guilty "beyond reasonable doubt" quite simply means that you are certain so as you are sure that they are guilty as charged. If there is any doubt at all in our minds, then the verdict has to be not guilty. Sure means sure and defence lawyers are always – quite rightly – quick to remind us of this fact when they sum up their case.

It might also be helpful to consider the words of Scott Turow, a lawyer himself, and the author of many lucid and beautifully written and researched legal thrillers, "A not guilty verdict means, in plain terms, we do not know, not for sure. 'Not guilty' does not mean innocent, not necessarily. It means something a bit different. If you say 'not guilty,' you are saying, we have thought hard about these charges and this evidence, and we do not know for sure."

I read in a barrister's blog about a case in which magistrates convicted the defendant after a trial with the explanation given that, "We find the complainant credible because she's the complainant, so we find the defendant guilty." Unsurprisingly, this conviction was reversed after appeal, but it just goes to show that magistrates must always avoid muddled thinking and give proper reasons that clearly explain their thinking and the rationale behind every verdict.

We do not have the option of a verdict of not proven, which is only permitted in Scotland, and anyway, in law there is there no legal difference between a not guilty and a not proven verdict.

As there are generally three magistrates, we can convict, or indeed acquit, on a majority decision although a unanimous verdict is always preferable. If there are only two magistrates, and we fail to agree, then there has to be a retrial before a different bench.

What goes on behind the scenes as we examine the evidence, in terms of what is said (and sometimes just as importantly, what is not said) must remain confidential. We use an established, tried and tested, structured decision-making process to come to a verdict, and I will never reveal who exactly said what, as that would be totally improper and a breach of confidentiality.

The legal adviser is also not supposed to join us whilst we are deliberating, except at our request to answer any questions we might have about the law (which must then be repeated in open court). We call the legal adviser in to join us when we have arrived at a verdict and written out our draft reasons for doing so.

A good legal adviser is not supposed to influence our decision – and they almost invariably don't, although some have been known to hover around us whilst we are still deliberating. But they are fully entitled to tell us if they believe we have either misconstrued a point of law, or ignored or misinterpreted a crucial piece of evidence.

If that is the case, we would be foolhardy not to listen to what they say, but ultimately it is our decision and not theirs; they should not tell us if they disagree with it.

Our verdict is always delivered as a unanimous one, as to the general public we must always appear to be united and in full agreement, even if the decision was, in fact, made on a majority basis.

I have heard a suggestion that we should, instead, be

obliged to disclose a majority verdict in court. Whilst I am sure that defence lawyers would be happy if that was the case, I feel that it would totally undermine our authority. There is also no need to do so, as there is an unfettered right of appeal from summary trials anyway.

I heard a story – hopefully apocryphal – of a chair standing up to announce to a bemused defendant and an appalled courtroom that, "My two colleagues have found you guilty." I am led to believe that his feet did not touch the ground as the legal adviser literally frogmarched him out of the room into welcome oblivion... and he was never seen in court again!

The closest I have got to that kind of situation was back in my early days as a winger, when we had to acquit a clearly guilty defendant on a technicality. The police had not followed Code D of the *Police and Criminal Evidence Act* (PACE) and had therefore conducted an illegal identity parade.

Their breach was clear and evident and the defence lawyer quite correctly – if not gleefully – applied at halftime for the case against his client to be dismissed.

The bench retired to consider his application, but this was far too much to take for our *hang 'em, flog 'em* old-school chair, who was rendered almost apoplectic at the prospect of letting a plainly guilty defendant walk free from his court on a technicality.

A decision that should have taken us two minutes to discuss and rubber stamp stretched into an interminable delay as he refused to bow to the inevitable.

"What kind of message are we delivering to our police force if we acquit such a guilty scoundrel?" was his oft-repeated refrain.

My fellow winger made the obvious and unanswerable reply, "That they need to do their job properly!"

The legal adviser eventually popped her head around the door as she was concerned about the delay, and found the chair still unable to accept the situation and mumbling incoherently to himself.

He flatly refused to either accept the decision, or deliver it, so it was decided that it was best if he should become indisposed and recuse himself. It was left to the senior winger to take the chair and go back into court to announce that the defendant had been acquitted.

Total madness, ignorance, and pig-headedness! Quite understandably, the misguided chair had to undergo a comprehensive training and re-education process before he was allowed to sit again.

*

This afternoon, as we finally get underway just before 3.10 pm, Mr Ali is well-prepared and works swiftly. After making a brief opening statement where he states what he intends to prove, he calls his first witness, Wes's neighbour, Mr Johnson.

He gives a clear account of being woken up at about 10.30 pm by the sound of his car alarm going off. He looks out of his bedroom window and sees another car trying to manoeuvre into a parking space far too small for it, and making contact two or three times with his own car, which is parked next to it, right outside his front door.

He could not see who the driver was from upstairs, but less than one minute later he went outside where the car was still trying unsuccessfully to wedge itself into the parking space and touching the bumper of his own car.

Mr Johnson taps on the window and although it is dark,

there is good street lighting, and when the driver opens the window he clearly recognises his neighbour, Wes, who lives further down the street, sitting in the driver's seat with the engine still running.

Mr Johnson can smell alcohol on Wes's breath and removes the car key. He accuses Wes of damaging his car. With slurred speech, Wes denies doing so, before exiting the car and staggering down the road towards his home.

Mr Johnson says that he is going to call the police and Wes turns back and replies that he cannot believe that he is calling the police on another black man, and offers to sort things out with him.

Mr Franklin subjects Mr Johnson to a robust cross-examination, suggesting that any damage to his car is minimal or actually occurred on another occasion, and that he does not see Wes in the driver's seat but rather, standing next to the car, on the pavement. Mr Johnson sticks to his story and stands up well to the questioning.

Next up is the arresting officer who responds to the callout and first describes seeing what he discovers to be Wes's car parked at an obscure angle, wedged into a tiny space and touching the rear bumper of another vehicle. He then describes speaking to Mr Johnson and then walking down the road and knocking on Wes's front door, before talking to him on his doorstep. Wes smells badly of drink with his pupils dilated and voice slurred. He fails a roadside breath test.

We then view the body-worn camera interview, which lasts for almost 30 minutes. In it, Wes accepts that "I'm in the wrong", states that drink driving is inexcusable and that, "You are talking about my licence and my livelihood." He admits that he drove home that night from a local pub where he had a few drinks, misjudged the size of the parking space and agrees that, "You're right, I might have touched his car, and I did touch his car but it is not as if I bashed it."

Wes is later arrested and answers "no comment" to every question without putting forward any specific defence to the charges. He does make a prepared statement in which he states that "someone was driving my car", without specifying who, and it was that "other person" who parked his car.

The prosecution rests. It has put forward all the evidence that it wishes to present.

At this point, there is sometimes what is known as a halftime submission when the defence lawyer claims that there is no case to answer, or in other words that the prosecution case is so weak that the court should acquit now on the basis that the prosecution evidence is insufficient for any reasonable tribunal, properly directed, to convict. If the application is successful, then the trial ends there and then, without the need for the defendant to put forward any evidence at all, or mount a defence.

When deciding upon our decision, we follow what is known as the Galbraith test and decide if there is any evidence at all of an actual crime being committed, or any evidence that the defendant actually committed the crime. If there is some evidence, is it of a tenuous nature, inconsistent, or inherently weak or vague?

The defence lawyer makes his representations followed by a response from the prosecutor before we retire to decide whether the case should proceed.

What we have to ask ourselves is that, listening to the prosecution case at its highest, and taking all these criteria into account, on what we have heard so far *could* we – not *would* we

– conceivably convict the defendant? If we feel that on the evidence presented so far we could *not* convict, then that is the end of the case.

If we decide to proceed, we need not announce any reasons for doing so. However, if we stop the trial, we have to explain why we took the decision to do so.

All I will say, at this point, is that Mr Franklin makes no such submission and calls his client to give evidence.

The clock is ticking, but there are still almost 30 minutes left, so we decide to hear Wes's evidence before concluding matters for the day.

Mr Franklin leads Wes through his evidence in chief. Wes is clearly in an excitable state of mind, and the words tumble out in a torrent, as he is keen to set the record straight. I have to slow him down so that we can all take accurate notes.

In court, today, he states that on the afternoon in question he drives to the pub to watch a football match and has a few drinks. His niece, Valerie, comes to the pub and drives him home in his car. She drops him off outside his front door, as he needs to go to the toilet, and then she parks the car whilst he is in the bathroom.

She knocks on his door and tells him that she has parked the car and has to go home now to look after her daughter. She says that she has left the car keys in the ignition, so when he comes out of the bathroom, Wes goes outside to retrieve them and is standing by his car when he is accosted by his neighbour, Mr Johnson, who accuses him of driving into his car.

Wes states that his car is not touching Mr Johnson's and when he takes a video a couple of days later he cannot see any damage to his own front bumper.

He cannot say why he makes all the incriminating comments on the body-worn camera interview about his guilt, but states that as he has drunk a couple of pints, he doesn't really know what he was saying at the time.

He also claims that he is simply protecting his niece.

In cross-examination, Mr Ali focuses upon all the incriminating comments made in the BWC interview and asks Wes why he made them. He claims that his words are being misinterpreted and that he is just protecting his niece.

Wes also denies driving the car or attempting to park it. Mr Johnson is mistaken; he does not see Wes in the driver's seat, there is no damage at all, and he is just looking for a Christmas bonus compensation payment.

Wes also claims that he actually states on camera that he was not driving, which means that we have to run through all the footage again, but we are unable to find that alleged comment. Mr Ali also asks why he does not mention the fact that his niece was the driver in his prepared statement, but Wes says that he was just following his solicitor's advice.

That is the end of his evidence and it is now 4.50pm. Time to end for the day. Jane, the legal adviser, now has to find a new date for the trial to be concluded. There is only one more witness to be heard, Valerie, Wes's niece, so she is called into court so that we can check her availability. We manage to settle on a morning date, a fortnight away, when everybody is available.

Just before we leave the courtroom, Jane speaks to Valerie and gives her a perjury warning. Perjury is committed when a lawfully sworn witness wilfully makes a false statement that he or she knows to be false, or does not believe to be true. Perjury is regarded as an extremely serious Indictable only offence, carrying a maximum penalty of seven years' imprisonment.

Let's wait and see what the conclusion of the trial brings. More importantly, will I be able to remember *who* said *what* to *whom?*

13. ON THE WING

This morning is going to be a big challenge for me, as I will be sitting on the wing supporting Janice, a trainee presiding justice.

Will I be able to restrain myself from telling her what to do? Will I be able to give her the space and freedom to perform and learn on the job? Or will I fall into the trap that so many others have done – and which so infuriated me when I was in the same position as her – and end up breathing down her neck, providing a constant stream of unwanted and unnecessary advice and instructions, and making her task next to impossible?

Let's see. Hopefully, I will be able to control myself but time will tell!

Janice has been a magistrate for many years, and we have sat together several times. Now that she has retired from a demanding job, she finally feels that she has got enough time to dedicate to becoming a presiding justice, and has just started the process.

I take her to one side in the retiring room, and we have a brief conversation about today's sitting. She tells me that she has only had one previous session in the chair, and that was in a trial court, so she is concerned about whether she can cope with the demands and faster pace of the remand court in which we are sitting today.

My first task is to reassure her and remind her that she will have a strong team around her who will provide all the support she wants. Given the need for the legal adviser to result all the cases before moving onto the next one, the pace will also be a lot slower than she fears. Most importantly, I suggest that she tries to take control of the proceedings from the outset and set the pace so that we work as fast, or as slowly, as she needs.

I then ask her exactly what she wants of me today. Janice looks quizzically at me, so I make some suggestions, and we agree the ground rules:

- That she is the presiding justice, and I am just one of her wingers and will act accordingly
- She allocates tasks to both wingers before we go into court
- As presiding justice, she will lead and manage all discussions if we go outside to consider decisions on bail, allocation, or sentencing
- I will write a note to myself which I will place prominently on the desk in front of me telling me to shut up, and just let Janice get on with things in her own way and not to interrupt her
- I will not remind her, in advance, of what she has to do in court before she has the opportunity to do it off her own bat – I know from my own bitter experience as a trainee chair just how frustrating and infuriating that can be
- I will give her any help and advice that she wants – if, and when, she asks me
- I will only make her aware of any mistakes or omissions at the time if they are going to make a fundamental difference to the dignity and proper running of the court (e.g., missing out essential parts of a sentence or pronouncement)

- If she wants to go outside at any time to discuss or clarify anything, then she just has to say so
- I will make careful notes of all the good things that she does, as well as anything that I would have done differently, and we will discuss everything between us at lunchtime
- At her request, I will chair after lunch, although should she change her mind I am happy for her to continue all day

*

Janice, Tom (the other winger), and I go into court and immediately I can see that this could be an interesting morning. We have a trainee chair presiding over her first remand court, a trainee legal adviser assisting her colleague, and a novice prosecutor in Mr Ahmed, who has only just disposed of his L Plates, and up until very recently was working alongside a more senior colleague.

Janice gets off to a confident start as we deal with Maureen who steals chocolate to the value of £120 from a supermarket. Either she has a particularly sweet tooth or, far more likely, she is stealing to sell in order to feed her long-term drug habit. She is well-known to probation services who give us a quick update. Given her previous record, she receives a 12-month community order with unpaid work and ten days of rehabilitation activity.

*

Next up, Janice has to unpick a case involving Kevin, who steals camera equipment worth £5,000 and then sells it on for £1,250 to an unsuspecting buyer. She quickly grasps all the nuances and engages well with Kevin when there is some confusion about his current means – or lack thereof. The camera equipment is recovered and returned to its rightful owner, Kevin is ordered to pay £1,250 in compensation to the person he sold it on to, and given a community order with unpaid work.

*

Next on is Peter, a large and verbose man, who is not perhaps the best listener in the world. He admits to careless driving but claims to be fully insured. He states that he has evidence to prove that he is properly insured at the time when he is stopped, and we ask him to provide it to the prosecutor during a gap in proceedings, as it needs to be properly checked out. Of course, a suitable opportunity does not present itself, so Peter becomes a seething, and near-voluble presence at the back of the court waiting to be dealt with; his patience visibly diminishing by the minute.

*

Paul pleads not guilty to driving with excess alcohol, and we set a trial date. A privately-funded lawyer who specialises in driving matters represents him. He states that the intoximeter is not properly calibrated and he will be bringing an expert witness to try to substantiate this claim at trial. We have to prepare for the trial by filling in the case management (PET) form, and in this instance, this is quite tricky to do as we need to clarify exactly 'what it is' that Paul claims to be the issue in this case. Nothing more, nothing less. He asserts that the evidential breath testing machine was either not working correctly, or that the police officer did not operate it correctly. This will be difficult to prove as there is a presumption in law that the breath testing machine is reliable.

We need to case-manage carefully and ensure that the time allocated is strictly controlled; the trial should only focus on the specific issues in question and it should not be allowed to become a fishing expedition. We also make it clear that if the defence relies upon expert evidence then the witness must appear in court.

*

We then have to deal with a second bail application for Majid who is accused of an assault on his partner. Allegedly, he shoves her and then strikes her across her face, right in front of some police officers who quickly arrest him. He pleads not guilty on the grounds of self-defence and is initially granted conditional bail but, on the very same day, he breaches his non-contact condition by sending her a number of threatening texts, warning her to watch herself and that she is "going to get it".

He is of good character and Alice, his partner, has recently signed a withdrawal statement. We do not know the reason why she has done so, and we must not speculate as we are only concerned with whether or not to restore Majid to bail today.

We go outside to consider our decision. Janice opens the discussion by asking Tom and me straight out, "So are we going to bail him, or not?" I later suggest that it is probably more helpful for her to set the scene briefly, and concisely list all the specific details of what it is we have to decide, plus the key factors we first have to take into consideration.

Janice mentions his good character, the fact that he has had a salutary week in custody in a particularly ghastly prison to reflect upon his behaviour, and the clear remorse that has been expressed on his behalf in court today. He is also fairly unlikely to receive a custodial sentence should he be found guilty after his trial, although that should not become part of our thinking when considering bail.

We are concerned about the safety of his ex-partner, the severity of his threats, their timing (as he made them almost as soon as he was released on bail), the fact that he breached a court order so quickly, and that the alleged offence took place right in front of police officers.

It is a difficult decision, but we finally decide to return him to bail with the same conditions of non-contact and residence.

Janice does an excellent job of making it absolutely clear to Majid just how close a decision this is; he has already had one chance and if he chooses to breach his bail, yet again, he will definitely be spending the time until his trial behind bars. It is a good old-fashioned telling off, and she does it well.

When giving his reasons earlier – as to why he thought we should not grant Majid bail – Mr Ahmed twice refers to Alice as the "victim", and I suggest to Janice that she corrects him, which she now does. Alice is at this stage in the proceedings "the complainant" or "alleged victim" and it is one of my pet hates when people are referred to as "victims" before the facts have been proved. It is both factually incorrect and deeply prejudicial.

We were hoping that in the time we spent deliberating outside, Mr Ahmed, the prosecutor, would have managed to deal with Peter and decide whether or not he is properly insured. No such luck, though; he is submerged and surrounded by lawyers trying to get their cases dealt with first. Peter remains ignored and is obviously simmering and ready to come to the boil at the back of the court.

*

Barry is accused of possession of Class B drugs – but not just a few bags – he is found with 85 bags in a rucksack in his flat together with four mobile phones. Let me repeat that – 85 bags of cannabis. It's obviously a very large rucksack, and he must have quite a cannabis habit.

We listen to the facts with total incredulity. Barry pleads guilty, admits to being an extremely heavy user of drugs, and states that the drugs are all purely for his own personal use. He claims that he most certainly is not a drug dealer despite receiving a conviction for production of a controlled drug a few years ago, as a youth.

Then it all kicks off. Mr Ahmed is asked by Janice what the weight of the drugs is. He replies "250 grams". He then continues breathlessly that their street value is around £2,500.

The words are hardly out of his mouth when Barry's lawyer, Mr D (of Quality Street fame at Christmastime), appears to be on the verge of self-combusting. He claims that the weight and the value of the drugs is only a relevant factor when the charge is one of possession with intent to supply, and not simply possession of drugs. On a roll now, he asks the prosecutor – who has now gone pale and sunk back into his seat – where he obtained his information about the valuation. Mr Ahmed would have been better served by simply withdrawing his initial comments, but instead he pipes up, "Google". This is a red rag to a bull to Mr D who asks him when Google became a legal authority.

Thankfully, before metaphorical blows are struck, Mr Ahmed regains his senses and composure, and apologises for his remarks. Calm is finally restored.

Janice looks dumbstruck at the carnage unfolding in front of her but recovers quickly to order a pre-sentence report for Barry, and it looks as if I shall be in the chair when we deal with him later on this afternoon. It is fair to say that the vast amount of drugs found in his possession will be a seriously aggravating factor when we come to sentence him.

We exchange bemused glances on the bench as we wait for the next case to be called. How on earth can having 85 bags of cannabis, plus a number of mobile phones, be deemed as merely possession of drugs rather than supply? I really cannot provide an answer, particularly as we are told that the case has been formally reviewed.

*

It is now getting close to lunchtime on what has been an eventful morning. Moving on, we have to deal with Martin, who is of no fixed abode and pleads not guilty to assaulting a paramedic and of being in possession of a lock knife.

He is apparently lying unconscious in the public toilet of a fast food restaurant and, when an ambulance is called, grabs the arm of the paramedic who is treating him and then twists it painfully. When searched, the knife is found in his jacket pocket.

Martin claims that he is sleeping deeply and is disturbed by somebody shaking him and – startled and half-awake – thinks he is being mugged, so he simply defends himself. Having nowhere to live, he uses the knife to cut his food.

He has been out of trouble for several years but has a long record of offending, including two previous convictions for possession of a knife. He faces an inevitable custodial sentence if convicted, and is also on bail for another matter.

Mr Ahmed and the defence lawyer put their heads together and are obviously discussing bail conditions. Amidst much nodding of heads, they seem to come to an agreement, but the prosecutor surprises us by asking us to remand Martin in custody because of the fear of his committing further offences and of failing to surrender (because these offences were committed on bail and he has no regular address). Martin's lawyer makes a spirited response and reinforces his client's efforts to keep out of serious trouble, the fact that he never fails to attend court, and the defence that will be put forward at trial.

Janice leads a much more focused and structured bail discussion this time, and points out that Martin has not been convicted of any offences for quite some time, and that he has invariably turned up to court when ordered to do so. We eventually decide to grant Martin bail, as long as he reports three times each week to his local police station, and does not go to the fast food restaurant in question.

*

Just before we retire, Tom points towards Peter who is still waiting to be dealt with. Janice disarms him by apologising and promises Peter, who is the picture of frustration, that he will be the first person dealt with after lunch, and we finally escape.

The legal adviser has her hands full with her trainee, and we have a quick post-court review. After a short break for a sandwich, Janice and I meet up to review the morning.

I start off by asking her how she thinks it went. She looks at me, perhaps slightly shell-shocked, with a rueful smile and says, "There's just so much going on!" That's the remand court for you, and I reassure her that – in time – things will become second nature to her, and she will also grow eyes in the back of her head.

I firstly congratulate Janice for doing a really good job in difficult circumstances. It was not an easy session, with a slightly overmatched prosecutor doing his best to cope with a full and varied list of cases; I felt that she really stuck to her task and took control of the court.

There were things that she will learn to do with more experience, such as managing out of court discussions, communicating more regularly with defendants, explaining delays, and telling them what is going on. I also suggest agreeing roles beforehand with the legal adviser, and ensuring that there is constant communication and exchanges of information between them.

As far as Tom and I are concerned, Janice has sought our opinion and involved us throughout the morning. I also suggest going through the list with the list caller to check who is here and to issue warrants when appropriate. There did not seem to be a suitable opportunity to do so this morning, given how busy we were.

I then mention the shortcut of informing a defence lawyer in a serious case that, having discussed the matter with her colleagues, the bench intends to ask for a pre-sentence report for his client, unless he wishes to convince us otherwise. Assuming there is mutual agreement, this means that the more loquacious lawyers can often be stopped in full flow and a lot of time can be saved with mitigation given *after* hearing or reading the report, and not beforehand as well.

Janice understandably faltered slightly over her pronouncements and did not give the defendants much eye contact when she was making them, but they are very difficult to master at first. There really is no shortcut apart from constant practice and repetition (plus reading them out loud, at home, in front of family members, bemused to learn that they have just been sentenced to immediate custody!).

We talk about the spat between the prosecutor and Barry's

lawyer, Mr D. I advise her not to get in the middle of a slanging match between advocates and, if in doubt, retire and let the legal adviser sort things out.

She handles PET forms very efficiently and asks penetrating questions. I mention that most legal advisers want to know the length of a trial as quickly as possible so they can start searching for the first available date.

I also suggest that she always check with the legal adviser that a prisoner is not in custody for another matter *before* she orders his release from the cells. That is a highly embarrassing mistake, which fortunately I have only ever made once!

All in all, Janice copes extremely well with everything that is thrown at her, and does a sterling job for someone who has only now taken the chair twice.

I congratulate her and ask if she wants to chair this afternoon as well, but she thanks me, and says that enough is enough for one day. She has enjoyed it and feels more confident, but has a lot to ponder on and the job is mine if I want it.

*

Before we go back into court for the afternoon session, I speak to our legal adviser and ask him to have a quiet word with the prosecutor on behalf of the bench.

He has demonstrated his eagerness and lack of experience and composure, by repeatedly jumping up like a jackrabbit throughout the morning and interrupting everyone else whenever he remembers something that he thinks he should have said earlier. His behaviour has clearly annoyed some of the defence lawyers, and he needs very gently and nicely to be reminded of court etiquette and procedure, and to be put back in his box.

It also doesn't make a good impression when he starts to fill in a trial preparation form in clear view of the bench before we have even begun to have a discussion in open court or made a decision about allocation of a trial for racially aggravated common assault. Irrespective of whether the defendant is eventually going to elect for a Summary trial, he should wait until the allocation process has been concluded – or fill in the form out of sight!

*

As soon as we get back into court after lunch, I call on Peter's case. He has pleaded guilty to careless driving, but claims that his insurance is valid and in order.

He finally provides his policy document to Mr Ahmed, and he does indeed possess fully comprehensive insurance – but only when he is driving for pleasure. He is not insured if his scooter is used for business purposes and, unfortunately for him, he is stopped whilst making a food delivery. We, therefore, give him six penalty points on his licence and fine him for not having valid insurance, and endorse his licence with no separate penalty for the careless driving. He has been waiting around for the best part of five hours now, and we just want to deal with him and allow him to leave.

*

Next comes another case that leaves us all shaking our heads in amazement. Jonathan is a 50-year-old man of good character who finds himself in court this afternoon charged with possession of a knife in a public place.

The police stop him for another matter and when they search him, they find an engraved folding lock knife on his key ring.

He states that this is an engagement present from his

girlfriend, purely decorative in nature, and he has no idea that carrying it around in public constitutes an offence.

We ask to see a photo of the knife, and to our amazement, when the knife is opened up, we see that it is massive and quite frightening in nature. This is not what we expect. What on earth was he doing? How could he have imagined that it was OK to carry this weapon around with him? How did it even fit in his pocket?

He is a cleaner with two children and, given the circumstances, we give him a prison sentence of four months, suspended for 12 months, a curfew for the next four weeks, and the knife is forfeited and destroyed. He seems more upset about losing his cherished knife than thinking about the potential consequences of his actions. I make it clear to Jonathan how foolhardy and idiotic his behaviour is, and how close he has come to going to prison today. Hopefully, his fiancée can give him another more appropriate and less deadly engagement present! A nice watch, perhaps?

*

It is time to hear a couple of cases on the prison video link system, which allows us to deal with serving or remand prisoners without them having to be physically produced in court. Sometimes things go like clockwork as we dial into the prison; the telephone is answered promptly and we see that the correct prisoner is already sitting behind the desk, patiently waiting for the hearing to begin, as soon as we are connected. All too often, though, the connection is lost, the prisoner is not on the day's production list and is still in his cell, or nobody answers and the legal adviser or list caller (at our end) sounds just like Terry Wogan or Graham Norton presenting the Eurovision Song Contest. "Come in,

Pentonville!"

We deal with Aria, a young woman who is making her second bail application. She stares balefully at us, without blinking, on the video link from prison. She is accused of assaulting her mother and making serious threats against her. A previous bench gives her conditional bail, but as soon as she leaves court, she returns to her mother's house, spits in her face, and threatens to kill her.

She has been remanded in custody ever since but is now asking us to release her on bail again. Due to a mix-up, she is not legally represented but tells us that she wants to proceed on her own when we give her the option of adjourning her bail application for another week so that she can arrange for a lawyer to assist her.

For an 18-year-old, she has already amassed a long and serious criminal record, including convictions for possession of a knife and a previous assault on her mother. There is also evidence of mental health issues.

We try to find out what her plans will be if she is given bail, and whether we feel that her mother will be safe if Aria is released.

Unfortunately, when we try to speak to her, she appears distant and distracted and presents as being both disturbed and unstable. She proclaims that she can do whatever she wants and will be sleeping on the floor at her local McDonald's. Her whole body stiffens when we try to talk to her about her mother, and she gives us no comfort at all that she will not return to her mother's address. She is vulnerable and we are concerned for her safety, as well as that of her mother, and therefore refuse her application, and further remand her in custody.

Vince pleads not guilty to being in possession of a knife, which is found in his bunk whilst he is in prison. He denies all knowledge of it. If he is found guilty, this will be his second such conviction, and given the likely sentence he would receive, we refuse jurisdiction and send him for trial to the Crown Court.

Our last case today concerns Barry, who we saw this morning when he pleaded guilty to possessing 85 bags of cannabis. Probation are now ready to address us.

It is clear from the outset that the probation officer is distinctly unhappy with Barry's level of engagement throughout his interview. Barry himself sits in the dock yawning and seemingly paying little attention to what is going on around him. The probation officer tells us that when asked about the offence, Barry cannot remember exactly what happened, but he does recall finding the cannabis – which was already bagged up – but cannot remember exactly where. He puts it all into his backpack and takes it home to smoke himself and also share with his friends.

Barry lives with his parents and two sisters, and is unemployed. He is supported by his mother and intends to apply for an unspecified apprenticeship. He does not do much with his life, and whilst he really enjoys smoking dope, he insists that he is not involved in supplying drugs.

He is ranked as having a 70% chance of re-offending given his lack of engagement and refusal to confront his issues.

The probation officer finds him to be both obstructive and unhelpful, feels that his account is totally implausible, and that he also appears to be tailoring his answers in an attempt to obtain a reduced sentence.

He has breached most of his previous court orders, and then our ears prick up, as we hear something that we do not hear very often, if at all, from probation… they recommend a custodial sentence. Given that they are looking at the situation from the offender's perspective, it is rare indeed that they wash their hands entirely of somebody and declare their unwillingness or inability to work with them.

Barry's lawyer rises to his feet to try to undo all the damage that has been done. It is an uphill task, but he does the best he can with very little ammunition.

He points out that Barry has been out of trouble for several months, and this offence took place last year. Barry deserves full credit for his guilty plea. He is a heavy smoker of cannabis. He only has three previous similar convictions, and he has co-operated fully with the police. He accepts that Barry is only 20, and has a lot of growing up to do, but hopes that we can punish him with a community order.

We go outside to deliberate. I remind my colleagues that although the starting point for possession of cannabis is a Band B fine, the range goes from a conditional discharge up to 26 weeks' custody and that we will, of course, have to give reasons for our sentence.

We consider the many aggravating factors in this case. Barry is found in possession of an enormous amount of cannabis, and we have to accept that it is for his own personal use (in other words, we must not sentence him as if he was charged with possession with intent to supply, although he does state his intention to smoke it with his friends).

He also has several relevant and fairly recent previous convictions for possession of drugs and also for production of a controlled drug.

There is no evidence of remorse or a credible explanation for how he has obtained the drugs. Given his apparent lack of means, how has he been able to fund his habit? He has also totally failed to engage with probation services or demonstrate any understanding of, or even interest in, his situation. We do have to give him credit for his guilty plea at the first opportunity, though.

We discuss the range of sentencing options available to us, which are a conditional discharge, a fine, an attendance centre order, a community order, and custody – immediate or suspended.

Given the massive amount of drugs he is found with, his previous convictions for drug-related offences, the contempt he has shown towards probation services and the court, as well as his history of poor compliance with court orders, we decide that the custody threshold has indeed been passed. He has no caring responsibilities at home and demonstrated no realistic prospect of rehabilitation. We are sure that, in this instance, immediate custody is called for rather than a suspended sentence.

We go back into court and sentence him to six months' custody, reduced to four because of his early guilty plea. There is a victim surcharge of £122 and court costs of £85, and we give him eight months to pay the £207 owing to the court. The drugs are to be forfeited and destroyed.

He stares at me impassively whilst sentence is being passed and disappears downstairs to the cells without a flicker of emotion.

I have never previously been part of a bench that has sentenced somebody to immediate custody for possession of

Class B drugs, so today is a first for me, but there are no regrets. Barry's offending behaviour, attitude, and previous record fully justify the sentence he receives.

The most important thing that comes out of the day is that Janice receives some valuable experience of running a court. I trust I helped her, and hopefully set a good example for her to follow in the afternoon. I have little doubt that, in time, she will develop into a fine presiding justice and I hope that everything she saw in court today has encouraged her rather than put her off!

14. OBSERVING COURT

Today is the ultimate busman's holiday for me, as I am not chairing a court, nor am I a winger. In fact, I am not sitting at all, but instead, I am accompanying my new mentee on her first court observation. My job is simply to explain what is going on around her, and answer all her questions.

Anna is pretty much everything that the Advisory Committee is looking for in a new magistrate. She is young, no more than in her early thirties, diverse – in that she was neither born nor brought up in this country – and extremely bright with a fertile and enquiring mind.

Over the past few weeks, we have exchanged several messages, but this is the first time that we have actually met, and I am immediately struck by her warmth and obvious enthusiasm for what awaits her. She is a commercial lawyer and therefore no stranger to court; however, today is the first time that she has set foot in a magistrates' court apart from her obligatory initial observations, which she conducted before her interviews and appointment.

She has just been sworn in and today will be the first of her three post-appointment observations – one before she undergoes her initial three-day induction training, and two afterwards – before she is deemed ready to sit for the first time.

Without an identity pass or a key fob, she has to run the gauntlet of security, and I am in the retiring room waiting for a call asking me to come and fetch her from downstairs, but she manages to charm one of the security guards into providing her with a personal escort upstairs – no mean feat indeed!

The first few minutes are taken up in giving her the grand tour and showing her the cloakroom, dining room, kitchen, and retiring room. Her eyes light up at the sight of the drinks machine and, shortly afterwards, she pronounces that the peppermint tea is of good quality and eminently drinkable.

We next go to the iPad storage room, and I show her the door combination and then how to both sign out an iPad and log in to it. Already, I can see that she is quick on the uptake, grasps everything immediately, and needs no repetition of any instructions. Another good sign.

We then find a quiet meeting room so that we can clarify and discuss the entire mentoring process. I explain to Anna that I am there to help and support her through the next 12 to 18 months until she is ready for her initial threshold appraisal. I will check that she fulfils all the necessary training and related visits to prisons, probation, and an attendance centre that a new magistrate has to complete, but she will need to organise and co-ordinate them herself. I show her how to do so.

We also discuss how to register for her eJudiciary email account and access her online rota. I also introduce her to a fellow magistrate who is an IT guru and can help her if she has any problems setting things up.

I am there for her as a sounding board and a resource, but I will only be as proactive as she wants me to be, and will take my lead from her. I do not want her to feel pressured by my contacting her every few weeks in order to check on her progress, but I confirm that I am more than happy for her to call, text, or email me at any time if she has a specific question or problem, or just wants to have a general chat and update. I tell her that I will only contact her, off my own bat, if there is radio silence for a prolonged period or if it appears that she is not sitting regularly.

As an example, I outline how things work with Mandy, my other mentee, who initially used to call me after every sitting to discuss what had happened in court so I could answer all her questions about what she had just experienced and observed.

As Mandy has become more comfortable and experienced, the calls have tailed off, but we still speak from time to time and – of course – we meet up formally to review her progress whenever it is time for one of her six mentored sittings.

Anna tells me that she will see how things go and speak to me whenever she needs to, which is fine by me.

Today we shall be observing from the well of the court. This means that we will not sit on the bench or in the public gallery, but we will both sit in the body of the court to observe the bench in action from the perspective of a court user.

We can watch how well the bench, the legal adviser and all the other court users communicate and interact with each other, even if we will not be able to hear any of the actual conversations held on the bench unless they employ stage whispers.

Trainee presiding justices used to have one of their six appraisals from the well of the court, and it was always illuminating to hear what the appraiser had to say afterwards about your communication skills, body language, and even facial expressions.

I would not have made a good – or even an indifferent – poker player when I started out, as I made it pretty clear how I felt about any given situation by my facial expression, which – if not quite a gurn – was apparently pretty easy to read. At least I did not pick my nose, and I have since practised and perfected a deadpan expression in front of the mirror, which hopefully means that my face is no longer an open book in court.

Unfortunately, the well of the court appraisal was scrapped by most JTAAACs a couple of years ago as it only allowed some of the required competencies to be observed by the appraiser. That's a shame, I think, as I learned as much from *that* appraisal as I did from any of my others.

I then explain the ground rules with Anna. We can attend the pre- and post-court briefings and review with the bench and the legal adviser, but cannot retire with the bench whilst they are deliberating. We are simply there to observe and obviously will play no part in the judicial process.

I have had a look at the court list and suggest that, today, we visit both a trial and a remand court, so that she can get a feel for how each one is run, and she readily agrees.

I speak to both presiding justices, introduce Anna to them, and they are happy to allow us to sit in.

*

The trial is an allegation of domestic abuse with the wife, this time accused of assaulting her husband.

We are asked to go in first and, bright-eyed and bushy-tailed, Anna almost skips into the courtroom. We sit together in a couple of remarkably uncomfortable seats at the side of the court and listen as a tale of woe unfolds, and reality hits home. It very soon becomes apparent that nothing is going to happen here very quickly.

The defendant, Marta, is here, but we learn that her husband, Ladislav, does not support the prosecution and is now very unwilling to give evidence against her. Apparently, the two of them are seen sitting together outside the court whispering, deep in conversation (if not quite holding hands), and blithely ignoring Marta's bail condition of non-contact with Ladislav. His interpreter also arrives late necessitating an additional delay.

If the case actually proceeds and it becomes apparent that Ladislav's evidence on oath is markedly different from his earlier written statement to the police about the incident – and he is, in fact, hostile to the prosecution that is calling him to give evidence today – then the prosecutor may request that the bench declare the witness hostile. If the request is granted, he may proceed to ask the witness leading questions, something that is normally only allowed in cross-examination.

If the bench feels that he is deliberately avoiding telling the truth today, then they will have to assess the reliability of his original statement against that of the evidence he gives on oath in court, and decide which to believe.

I have previously chaired a bench that has had to face this situation with an unwilling alleged victim prevaricating and dead batting all prosecution questions, despite her earlier statement which provided full details of the alleged assault. These situations can become extremely difficult, stressful, and unpleasant for all parties.

The defence lawyer then claims that he has not received full disclosure from the prosecution in terms of the tape of a call made by Marta to the emergency services, as well as the body-worn camera footage taken by the police officer who attended the scene.

There are a lot of issues to sort out, and the bench is asked to grant a delay of 20 minutes in the hope that the necessary material can be disclosed to the defence, and then assimilated by them, and Ladislav persuaded to give evidence against Marta. Quite a lot to ask for, and hopefully not wishful thinking. Personally, I suspect that they are pushing water uphill.

This is just a microcosm, and a typical example of what can so often go wrong on the morning of a trial. It helps explain why so many trials start late, or become cracked or ineffective.

Anna is full of questions about what has – or more accurately – what has not just happened. I try to answer them as well as I can, although there is still a lot left up in the air.

Given the length of the delay and the likelihood that the trial will not proceed any time soon, we decide to find another court and make our way to a nearby remand court.

Court is in session, so we wait until there is a break in action, and sneak in through the back door. Quietly, we find our seats in the well of the court, which are also hard, unyielding, uncomfortable, and total backbreakers.

The list caller kindly gives us each a copy of today's court list so we can follow proceedings on the iPad and also read all the downloaded information on each case.

The bench rises regularly to discuss bail and sentencing decisions, and it is highly illuminating to hear the discussions that take place in court when the bench is no longer present.

The lawyers speak openly, not seeming to notice that there are two magistrates still in court, albeit *incognito* and half-hidden in the corner.

Talk is mainly about whether they believe that bail will be granted. The general consensus is yes, and they are both correct.

The prosecutor is new, young, keen, and able. My ears prick up, and he immediately goes up in my estimation when he states to the bench that, "When I was preparing this case last night…"

He deserves kudos for doing that. Many of his colleagues, sometimes for reasons beyond their control, do not seem to start looking at what they will be dealing with until the actual morning of the case – or sometimes even until the defendant is sitting in the dock!

There is a constant influx of lawyers coming into court when the bench is absent, buzzing around the prosecutor with some intense discussions and obvious horse-trading about when a case will be called, or possible plea bargains.

We also see Damian make his first court appearance, and he denies engaging in controlling or coercive behaviour in a family relationship. This is a fairly new Either Way offence, and the bench hears a litany of serious and disturbing allegations made against him by his wife.

Given that Damian's behaviour is said to take place over a long period of time, and allegedly causes significant psychological harm to his wife, this is definitely a Category 1A offence with a starting point of two years six months' custody, and a range of between one to four years' in prison. The bench, therefore, declines jurisdiction and the trial will eventually be held in the Crown Court.

Anna and I read through the statements from both Damian and his wife, and they are practically mirror images of each other, with Damian accusing his wife of almost exactly the same type of behaviour as she does of him, ensuring that this is likely to be a particularly unpleasant and difficult trial with both parties blaming and accusing each other.

We join the bench for their post-court review and listen to their rationale for why they dealt with matters as they did.

Anna has more questions about procedure and sentencing, and after we have finished our discussion, I tell her that her training next week will hopefully fill in most of the gaps. If not, I will do my best to help her.

We arrange to meet up for another observation immediately after she has completed her three-day induction training, and just before she sits in court for the first time.

By the look on her face, she can hardly wait and I wish that I still possessed half the passion and enthusiasm that she does.

15. THE CIRCLE
OF LIFE

Today strongly reminds me of the circle of life. I am sitting with my mentee, Mandy, for her sixth and final mentored sitting and the other winger is Martin, my first ever mentee. He, in turn, is accompanied by his own mentee, Jack, who is observing from the well of the court.

Martin is a long-term asthma and bronchitis sufferer, so I am surprised that he has decided to come to court today given the increasing Coronavirus health scares. At his request, I make a brief announcement explaining that his occasional cough is nothing out of the ordinary and that court users should not be concerned about it. This is another indication of the unprecedented times in which we find ourselves.

We are in a remand (GAP) court today, but as is so often the case – and I find myself repeating the same words sitting after sitting – nothing is ready when we go into court at 10 am. Given that only a bare minimum of defendants have arrived at court on time, there is little prospect of that situation changing quickly, and we beat a speedy, if resigned, retreat to the retiring room.

As we have time to kill, we talk about the mentoring process and Jack is full of questions about what awaits him when he starts to sit (once he completes his induction training next week).

Mandy and Martin have sat together before and chat away happily, and both seem to have come through the ordeal of being mentored by me relatively unscathed. Both have developed into good magistrates.

Finally, we are called into court where we see Kelly in the dock. She has been arrested on a warrant, as she has apparently not paid a penny of the £2,438 in fines and costs that were imposed on her way back in 2016.

Her shoulders slump, then she shudders and bursts into tears in the dock with a look of utter hopelessness etched on her face; the sound of her sobs echo through the courtroom. She is a picture of total despair when she is reminded of the massive sum that she is said to owe.

John, our legal adviser, fills in the gaps and provides details of what is outstanding. Apparently, Kelly was convicted of three separate shoplifting offences on the 12th of May 2016 and fined £660 for each one, or a total of £1,980. When victim surcharge and costs are added, that takes it up to the grand total of £2,438 owing, of which nothing has been paid by her in almost four years. On the surface, this is an extremely worrying and disturbing state of affairs.

Now it is time to do some detective work and digging.

I ask her if she is aware of the debt and, if so, why hasn't she paid anything for the last four years. She seems totally bemused by, and ignorant of, the whole situation, and tells us that she had no knowledge that she owed anything at all until she was arrested in front of her daughter two days ago. She has been kept in custody since then, until being brought to court this morning. She is a single parent with a four-year-old daughter, and lives on income support.

We then try and work backwards so that we can try to understand what must have happened in 2016.

Kelly has been given three fines of £660 each. The most likely way that this figure has been reached is if she was given a Band C fine for each offence, which is 150% of an assumed relevant weekly income of £440, which makes £660.

Where an offender has failed to provide the court with any financial information then their relevant weekly income, as mentioned previously, is deemed to be £440. That, in itself, strongly implies that Kelly did not appear in court and was found guilty and then fined in her absence. Had she pleaded guilty then she would also have received a one-third discount off her sentence.

So, if she had come to court, pleaded guilty, and informed the bench that she was on benefits then each fine would have been £120 (£180 reduced to £120) rather than £660. This assumes a relevant weekly income of £120 rather than £440, and an additional one-third reduction for her guilty plea.

Her overall debt would therefore have been reduced to £360 plus victim surcharge and costs rather than the huge sum that she now faces.

We also check and see that Kelly has no convictions since 2016. It is still a mystery as to why she was not aware of the court proceedings and subsequent ruling against her, although she tells us that she has moved addresses several times in the past few years which might well explain things.

Given the circumstances, and the fact that she has had two nights in custody after being arrested in front of her child (who is being looked after by her grandmother), we agree to remit the fines in full as they were imposed in her absence, and had her true financial circumstances been known at the time then the fines imposed would certainly have been far smaller.

Kelly stares at us whilst she tries to process what I have just told her, until the penny finally drops and she realises that she now has nothing to pay, and she then bursts into tears again.

Hopefully, this time, they are tears of relief and joy.

*

With around £1.18 billion in fines, costs, victim surcharge and compensation remaining outstanding, the courts do possess serious powers to attempt to force defaulters to pay when it is appropriate to do so. In other words, there should be a distinction made between those who can't pay and those who won't pay.

As a first stage, magistrates can impose either an attachment of earnings or a deduction from benefits order. If these do not have the desired effect, a warrant of control will enable bailiffs to seize goods to the value of the outstanding amount, and a money payment supervision order appoints a supervisor who is tasked with advising the defaulter on how best to pay the outstanding sums.

The last resort is committal to prison if the non-payment is considered to be due to either culpable neglect – which is a reckless disregard of a court order where the defaulter has *chosen* to use his available income for non-essential items in preference to paying the fine – or wilful refusal, which is deliberate defiance and a refusal to pay the outstanding sums. This is seldom done and is the ultimate sanction.

*

In our next case, Rashan pleads not guilty to using abusive words and then assaulting a ticket officer by swearing at him and then spitting at him when the validity of his ticket is queried. Rashan claims that it is a case of mistaken identity despite being identified through his DNA on the spittle and his image on the CCTV coverage of the incident. We set a trial date for three months hence.

*

Colin has been waiting for a while to be brought up from the cells to enter pleas on two counts of domestic burglary. There is a further delay when the wrong PNC is uploaded. He is caught in the act, in broad daylight, by residents and pleads guilty.

These offences are Indictable only as Colin has now committed three domestic burglaries and is subject to the third strike rule with a mandatory minimum three-year custodial sentence. We commit him to the Crown Court for sentencing and remand him in custody. In passing, I apologise for keeping him hanging around for so long to which he smiles and makes the droll – and accurate – response, "I'm not in any rush." There really is no answer to that.

*

Steve is also in custody, accused of assaulting his former partner, stalking her, and also assaulting the *au pair* who he believes is now in a relationship with his ex-partner.

The case centres on a fairly confused and complex series of events in which Steve is apparently in a relationship with Astrid for over a year before she ends it, but she still continues to make credit payments on Steve's car (in which he now lives) after she asks him to leave her flat.

Steve is infatuated with Astrid and cannot accept that the relationship is over. He calls and texts her around 40 to 80 times every day over a three-month period. Many of these calls threaten her with violence. Eventually, he returns to her home to pick up the car log book but punches her in the chest and pushes her before – later the same day – attacking Vincent, the *au pair* and stamping on his chest in a fit of anger and jealousy.

Steve pleads not guilty to all offences and we send him for

trial at the Crown Court given the overall seriousness of the charges he faces. We now have to make a decision about bail, and, unsurprisingly, both lawyers have plenty to say about the subject.

Steve has been out of trouble since 2014, when he committed two assaults on his partner at the time (not Astrid) and his landlord. There are concerns about his mental health, although the prosecutor accepts that nothing has been formally diagnosed.

Steve has sent Astrid a series of unwanted gifts despite being asked to stop doing so, and also subjected her to a torrent of calls – many of which have threatened her with violence and caused her great distress. There are serious concerns for her safety and welfare if Steve is released on bail.

The stalking involving fear of violence offence is extremely serious and put in a B1 category by the prosecutor. There is high culpability as the conduct was persistent over a prolonged period and intended to maximise fear and distress, plus a high level of harm as Astrid has been caused very serious distress. If convicted, the starting point for this offence is two years six months' custody, with a range of between one to four years' custody.

The prosecutor wants us to deny bail on the grounds of failing to surrender, given that Steve has no fixed abode and is currently living in a car, and also because there are serious concerns that he will commit an offence that will make an associated person – in Astrid – fear physical or mental injury.

Steve's lawyer then stands up in an attempt to allay any concerns that we might have, and convince us to grant bail to his client. There is no evidence of Steve suffering from any mental health problems. He vehemently denies both assault charges and states that he and Astrid lived together for over three years, rather than the far shorter period alleged by the prosecution, and the relationship only ended two weeks ago. He visited Astrid in order to collect his possessions and also to check on the welfare of her autistic son whom he had grown close to. He also brought her flowers, which she accepted. Steve is not a flight risk as he has lived in the area for 16 years and works as a mobile mechanic.

His lawyer proposes that we grant Steve bail with a non-contact condition relating to Astrid, Vincent, and her two children, and that Steve is not allowed to visit the street in which she lives.

There is a lot for us to mull over, and we retire to consider everything that we have heard in court.

We quickly discount the prosecution's claim that Steve will fail to attend court if granted bail. He has never missed a court appearance before, and the fact that he has no fixed abode and sleeps in a car is not enough, on its own, to give us any concerns about his not turning up in the future.

What is far more pertinent is whether Astrid, or indeed Vincent, will be put in real danger of harm if Steve is released on bail prior to his trial.

He has not been convicted of any violent offences since 2014, however the accusations he faces now are extremely serious and we are particularly concerned about the number and nature of his calls and texts to Astrid. In many of them, he threatened to harm her.

We are not convinced that any bail condition is sufficient to ensure her safety, and we are all in full agreement that Steve should be remanded in custody until his trial, and not granted bail.

We come back into court and announce our decision and nobody, including Steve and his lawyer, seems particularly surprised by it.

*

Mario pleads guilty to using a cousin's passport as his has expired. This is an Indictable only offence and the prosecutor and defence lawyer inform the bench that they have just put their heads together and agreed upon a bail package that is acceptable to both parties. We follow their recommendation, which is both practical and well-thought-through, and I remark quietly and flippantly to my colleagues that, "It seems that magistrates' courts function quicker, better and far more efficiently without the magistrates." Heretical words indeed, although I am sure that more than a few members of the legal profession would heartily endorse them!

*

Joel is looking everywhere but at the bench and his lawyer as the charges he faces are read out. He is accused of sexual assault on a female. He appears to be in another world entirely, and pays no attention to what is going on around him. I ask his lawyer if there is something the matter with Joel, and receive the deadpan response that, "He's not too happy about things." Given the circumstances, there is really nothing I can say to that, and eventually Joel deigns to join us in body – if not in spirit – long enough to plead guilty.

We listen to the facts and learn that Joel touched and randomly kissed a 16-year-old schoolgirl as she walked past him in the park. We make a Section 45 reporting restriction to protect her identity, but she is deeply affected by what happened and needs therapy to help relieve her feelings of fear and anxiety.

Joel has 24 previous convictions, but none for any similar offences, although he is currently under investigation for a rape from a year ago.

Through his lawyer, he states that he was drunk at the time and this was just a spur of the moment act that he now deeply regrets.

We ask for a pre-sentence report that confirms his problems with drink and drugs. After some discussion, where we consider all sentencing options including custody, we decide to follow probation's recommendation for a year-long community order with 40 days of rehabilitation activity where his addictions can be addressed, and tracking monitoring for six months, which means that he wears a tag and probation will be able to keep tabs on his whereabouts at all times of the day and night.

We also grant an application for a restraining order for the next two years, preventing Joel from contacting the schoolgirl who lives nearby and he has to sign the sex offenders register for the next five years, which will ensure that the police are also kept aware of his movements.

*

Olly is charged with possession of a knife as well as five wraps of cocaine. He is a 21-year-old student who has never been in trouble before.

He is at the wheel of his car, late at night, and stopped by police who see him driving erratically. He is searched and the drugs and knife are both found in his possession. He pleads guilty and after a quick glance at my colleagues, who nod their agreement, we ask for an all options open pre-sentence report and grant Olly bail until after lunch, by which time he will hopefully have met with probation.

We break for lunch shortly afterwards, and have a brief post-court review. Everyone seems happy with how the morning has gone, and I decide to go out for a quick sandwich.

I am queuing in Pret, and look around, and who do I see standing immediately behind me? It is Olly who I last saw in the dock no more than 15 minutes earlier. I look at him, he looks back at me, and thankfully he does not give any sign that he recognises me.

Perhaps he was simply showing some tact and discretion, but it is more likely that magistrates in mufti just blend in and are invisible outside the courtroom.

That is not the first time that I have almost literally bumped into somebody I had just dealt with in court. I have already written about my memorable – if not unforgettable – encounter with the redoubtable Ms T on the courthouse steps. I have also travelled on the same bus or train as a few recent customers, and can honestly say that none of them have ever recognised me or paid me the slightest attention. Thankfully so, too, as I would really not feel comfortable engaging with them immediately after their court date, at a time when it probably remains an unpleasant memory for them.

This got me to thinking about how widely we publicise the fact we are magistrates. I see nothing wrong in telling family, friends, and acquaintances that I am a magistrate, and that I am extremely proud of being one. I also spend a fair amount of time proselytising and explaining exactly what it is that we do to anyone who asks. Hopefully, I can encourage some of them to follow my example, too.

Magistrates are expected to have personal integrity, be

circumspect and able to maintain confidences, and have nothing in their private or working life – or in the lives of their family or close friends – which could bring them, or the magistracy, into disrepute.

I do my utmost to follow this advice to the letter, and I am extremely careful about what I post or follow on social media, as it is crucial that we are seen to be both objective and impartial. Even "liking" a politically-themed or contentious comment can be fraught with peril.

I keep confidences, and do not reveal or disclose information that is privileged or confidential, in particular the specific individual views expressed in retiring room discussions.

What about the elephant in the room – *this book*? I have simply tried to give an open and honest account of life as a magistrate. What we do, and how and why we do it. Maybe I have accentuated the positives but I have also tried not to gloss over the negatives – or perhaps, realities – that can make our job so much more difficult.

I very much hope that I do not fall foul of the Advisory Committee as I have taken extreme care not to breach confidentiality, write anything that might bring the magistracy into disrepute, or seriously compromise my own sense of impartiality. All names have also been changed and facts slightly blurred where necessary. What I hope people take out of this book is my feeling of pride and good fortune in being a magistrate, and the belief that we are doing a crucial and difficult job exceptionally well. My ultimate desire is that many of my readers take on board what I have written, and decide to follow in my footsteps.

In idle moments, I often find myself flicking through the

disciplinary statements on the Judicial Conduct website, which provide fascinating and cautionary details about judges and magistrates who have fallen foul of the system, and whose behaviour has fallen below the high standards rightly demanded of us.

One of the most common misdemeanours is the incorrect use of the initials "JP". Magistrates are allowed to use the initials as a suffix, or on private and business letterheads. That is all well and good, but the problems arise if you use these initials or your judicial status in an attempt to gain an advantage, influence, or exert pressure on someone.

Personally, I have played it safe and never used the initials "JP" in any capacity. In fact, there are times when I keep the fact that I am a magistrate pretty close to my chest. I was once strongly advised by a retired magistrate never to tell a police officer that you are a JP if you are unfortunate enough to be stopped and questioned for any reason; it's a sure fire certainty to get you into more trouble than you are already in. I think the words he used were that they would, "take a sadistic delight in doing you." In that regard, I have just read about another magistrate who apparently showed his magistrate ID card to a police officer "in circumstances which created the impression that he was attempting to use his judicial status to gain favour with the officer." He resigned from the bench.

I would trust and expect that there is no truth in this warning. However, I do remember being caught in a police clampdown on drink driving just before Christmas one year, when I had just been appointed to the bench but was still waiting to be sworn in. I had been to a family party on the outskirts of town and my whole life flashed before my eyes when I found myself in a queue of cars that were all waved down for a spot check by a phalanx of police officers – torches and breathalysers in hand – at the side of the road.

It was nearly midnight, and I had consumed a glass of champagne on arrival at the party, and nursed a glass of wine throughout the evening, both washed down by a three-course meal.

My whole life seemed to flash before my eyes as I was so looking forward to becoming a magistrate and was terrified at the prospect of my new magisterial career being nipped in the bud before it had even begun. I resisted the temptation to tell the extremely pleasant police officer what I was thinking before I blew into the breathalyser.

Time seemed to stand still whilst I waited for the reading to be revealed, as I had so much to lose. After an interminable delay of what was probably no more than ten seconds or so, my fate was revealed. Thankfully, I blew a mere six, which was well under the limit of 35 microgrammes per 100 millilitres of breath. The lesson was well and truly learned and I do not drink and drive.

*

Back to the courtroom, where we come back from lunch and, shortly afterwards, probation services are ready to give us their oral pre-sentence report on Olly.

Although he has no apparent gang affiliations, some of his friends have been murdered in the last year; whilst he has not been threatened himself, he feels that he needs to carry a knife for his own protection. He is also suffering from PTSD on account of what has happened to his friends.

He bought the knife a year or so ago, and now accepts that carrying it in today's climate is stupid; he knows that his friends are very disappointed in him. He claims that he does not "do drugs" and the cocaine belongs to a mate of his, but he decides to plead guilty anyway to get things over and done with.

He had been at a boxing match with a few friends on the night he is stopped. He lives at home with his mother and brother and is studying PR and marketing at college. He spends much of his spare time coaching football to kids, and would like to do this on a full-time basis once he graduates. He presents a low risk of reoffending and probation feel that he can be managed in the community, and would particularly benefit from participating in the Safer Streets programme.

We retire to consider what we have just heard and it is extremely worrying that this is not the first time that I have seen students of previous good character convicted of carrying a knife in public.

We consider the facts carefully, and agree that whilst the custody threshold has certainly been passed – and a sentence of imprisonment must be imposed – it can be suspended owing to the strong personal mitigation we have heard.

We go back into court, and I tell Olly that his friends are quite correct; it is incredibly stupid and dangerous to carry a knife on his person in public. Hasn't he seen how many young people have been stabbed recently? Saying it was for his own protection only makes matters worse as it implies that he would have used the knife if necessary. I remind him that it is also very often the knife carrier who ends up getting stabbed.

Generally, when giving a verdict or a sentence, I will try to put the defendant out of his or her misery as quickly as possible, and immediately confirm their guilt or otherwise, or what the actual sentence will be. This is by far the fairest and most humane thing to do particularly when there are also family and friends waiting anxiously in the public gallery. However, when sentencing Olly, we all decide to make him sweat for a few moments and await his fate a bit longer, so that the seriousness of his actions and their potential ramifications can hopefully sink into him.

I inform him that he came within a whisker of going to prison today; however, given his remorse, previous good character, and the bright future that can still await him, we have decided – just – to suspend the prison sentence. He receives a four-month prison sentence, reduced from six months owing to his early guilty plea, which is suspended for 18 months. I make it clear that if he offends again within that period, he is almost certain to have his suspended sentence activated. He also has to carry out 20 days of rehabilitation activity and 180 hours of unpaid work. The knife and drugs are to be forfeited and destroyed. Olly hangs his head in the dock, nods at the bench, and disappears into the arms of his friends in the public gallery. With any luck, the message has got through to him loud and clear, and he will be able to finish his studies and have a productive career. I do mention to him, though, that I believe that he will need to undergo a DBS check before he is allowed to coach children.

*

The next defendant is Marcus, who also pleads guilty to possession of a knife, but this time it is a machete. He is 20-years-old and is arrested when he is part of a gang of young men who are attacked by a rival gang using guns and knives. Tragically, one of Marcus's friends is killed. Marcus is seen brandishing the machete and waving it at the rival gang. He was also convicted of a similar offence a few years ago, when he was a youth.

A machete attack takes place on Britain's streets almost every two hours. In the last two months of 2019, police dealt with 664 crimes involving machetes – an average of eleven each day, and they are increasingly becoming the weapon of choice for gang members.

Every case is dealt with in isolation, and the circumstances surrounding this offence are totally different to those in the last knife possession we dealt with. We have to take into account that Marcus has been through a lot in his young life, but what cannot be ignored is that he is a gang member with a previous conviction for possession of a knife and has now been found carrying a deadly weapon in a machete. He, therefore, faces a mandatory six-month "second strike" prison sentence, unless it is unjust to do so, and the starting point for this latest offence is 18 months' custody as it was committed in circumstances where there was a risk of serious disorder. We commit Marcus to the Crown Court for sentencing and remand him in custody.

*

It is crucial that magistrates always try to put their personal feelings to one side, but occasionally we have to deal with a case that moves us and tests our judicial resolve to its limits.

I heard about a distressing case in the Youth Court in which a young man of 17 comes into court, accompanied by his parents. He is waiting to start his university course and finds a summer job working as a waiter at an extremely smart restaurant in the centre of town. The defence lawyer tells the bench that the young man is openly gay, and within days of starting work, two of his fellow waiters subject him to relentless, non-stop homophobic abuse.

The court watches CCTV footage, which shows the defendant waiting to collect his trays of food in the kitchen. His two abusers approach from both sides and start whispering in his ears. He becomes more and more agitated and upset, and finally cracks. The defendant picks up a plate, smashes it on the counter and uses the broken edge to slash the throat of one of his tormenters, causing a gaping wound that needs 64 stitches to staunch the flow of blood. The victim nearly dies.

The young man pleads guilty to Grievous Bodily Harm. Given his age (under 18), the case is heard in the Youth Court where the magistrates can sentence offenders to a maximum of two years' custody, rather than the six months available in the adult court.

Apparently, the two fairly inexperienced wingers spent a considerable amount of time trying to persuade the chair that they could deal with the young man in the Youth Court rather than committing him to the Crown Court.

The chair sympathised with their view but the Sentencing Guidelines show that the starting point, when sentencing this offence in the adult court, is 12 years' custody. Given his age, the defendant is entitled to a ten per cent reduction from this figure, plus a one-third off his sentence for his early guilty plea. There is also the massive provocation he endures that will be taken into account in mitigation.

However, whichever way you look at it, a custodial sentence of at least seven years is inevitable, and it proves impossible to keep the matter in the Youth Court.

Although it is terribly upsetting to do so, because the magistrates understand that seven years in prison means that this young man's life will be changed forever, they all finally agree to commit this case to the Crown Court for sentencing. You also have to consider the terrible injuries suffered by the victim.

The defendant and his parents burst into tears, and it takes the bench a very long time indeed to recover from the trauma of the case, and their sadness at its outcome.

Hard and bitter though it was, they had simply fulfilled their judicial duty without fear or favour. Something that is, at times, terribly hard to do. I can attest to the fact that there are many cases that you take home with you, and replay on a constant tape loop in your mind, as you toss and turn in bed and struggle to find sleep.

*

There are still a few more cases left for us to deal with in what is turning out to be a busy and complicated day.

Nick denies being drunk, rude, and abusive and calling a minicab controller a "black bastard" and a "monkey". Instead, he claims that it was he that was insulted and sworn at, rather than the other way around. Hopefully, the truth will emerge when it comes to trial later this year.

*

Harriet has not had an easy life, and after the death of her son in 2012, she was convicted of drink driving, and she now pleads guilty to failing to provide a specimen for analysis when asked to do so by the police.

She is driving on her own, late at night, when she collides with two parked cars. The police arrive and find her unhurt but unsteady on her feet, with her speech slurred. She is carrying an empty bottle of rum in her bag. The police try to breathalyse her both at the roadside, and at the police station, but on each occasion she refuses to comply.

We hear that she has long-term problems with alcohol and the news of her brother's death a few weeks ago has utterly depressed her and caused this latest episode.

We place this offence in the most serious category in our Sentencing Guidelines, as it was a deliberate refusal and there was a high level of impairment. The starting point is 12 weeks' custody with a range from a high level community order to 26 weeks' custody. Because this is her second such offence within a ten-year period, her driving ban will last for between three and five years.

Given her obvious drink problem, we decide to ask for a pre-sentence report, which will examine whether she is suitable for an alcohol treatment requirement. We bail her for three weeks and impose an interim driving ban. Hopefully, she will be able to get the help she needs.

*

Our final case concerns Renata, who pleads guilty to drink driving. It is her second such offence within a few years so her driving ban is increased to 36 months. We fine her £80, which takes into account her discount for her early guilty plea. We are surprised when her lawyer instead suggests that we apply the one-third discount to the ban instead of the fine. Unfortunately, for Renata, he is incorrect as the discount applies to the ancillary order, which is the fine, rather than the ban, which is the main sentence that we impose for such an offence. Good try though!

*

I have really enjoyed sitting with Mandy and Martin and it has been an enjoyable and productive day. We have worked well together. I hate to use the expression "well-oiled machine" as it is a *cliché* and seems a bit self-serving. But everything flowed, we operated well as a team, and everyone's views were confidently expressed and properly listened to. I tried to be supportive and solicited everyone's opinions. The decisions we came to – and there were indeed some serious cases today – were agreed by all parties, and were made after structured and thorough debate in which everyone had their say. In other words, this was one of the most pleasant days I have had on the bench in recent weeks, and hopefully this was reflected in the standard and quality of our work.

Our legal adviser was also happy with how the day went. Jack, too, joins us for our post-court review, and is full of questions about the day's workload and how we managed it.

There is one more task to complete, and Mandy and I find a quiet corner to fill in her sixth and last mentored sitting form. I also complete her final mentor report, which will be sent for review and, ideally, approval by the JTAAAC.

I remember how proud I felt when I was signed off and deemed ready for my threshold appraisal by my mentor, all those years ago, and I just hope that Mandy feels the same.

I trust that she won't mind me disclosing that she received an exceptional report from me and her progress is entirely due to her own efforts, hard work, and conscientiousness. She will undoubtedly progress further as she gains even more experience.

Given that she no longer has any need for a mentor, I ask Mandy for her thoughts on how the last year or so has gone, and what she has taken out of the mentoring process. Does she have any tips for the likes of Jack and other new magistrates coming through the system?

Here are her thoughts:

"Different people learn in different ways, and so will need

different levels and types of mentor support. For me, the best thing was the high level advice you gave me at the outset, in particular:

- Do as many sittings as you can
- Play as active a role as you can from the outset
- Don't be shy to ask questions of everybody you sit with. The greater the variety of opinions you can take on board, the more it will help you learn the role.
- Reflect on what happened in any court sitting that was out of the ordinary, whether positive or negative. Here I found it useful to keep a notebook, in court, to record things I wanted to follow up on.
- Use the time when your bench has risen to speak to the other magistrates you are sitting with, and get their views.
- Everyone in court has something to offer that you can learn from, from the legal advisers to the list callers to probation.
- Once you have sat for a while, go and sit in the public gallery if you have the time. It will help you consolidate what you have been learning and hopefully you can see both good and bad practice."

This is great advice, which I will shortly be passing onto my new mentee, Anna, and I am sure that she will benefit from it.

As for today, forgive me for my unashamed sentimentality, but I am just bursting with pride and delight at how well both Mandy and Martin have done.

Truly the circle of life, as I am doing my small bit (and best) to encourage and support an influx of new, young, and talented magistrates who have the potential to become exceptional at their job.

16. TRIAL AND ERROR

Today is the conclusion of the trial I began to describe in Chapter 12 that went part-heard as we ran out of time.

Just a brief recap, first. Wes is accused of driving with excess alcohol and of damaging his neighbour's car (belonging to a Mr Johnson) whilst parking. Despite the clear admissions of guilt that he makes on his lengthy body-worn camera (BWC) interview with the police, which takes place shortly after the alleged incident, he says – in court – that it is his niece, Valerie, who is driving the car and that there is no damage at all caused to the neighbour's vehicle. We have heard the prosecution case, and Wes has also given evidence on his own behalf.

Just as we are about to go into court, Jane, the legal adviser, throws us a curveball. We gave everyone clear instructions to be back in court at 9.30 am this morning, but she tells us that – for some unknown reason – the court office has erroneously sent out reminder notices to all parties with a 2 pm start instead! She tried to get the letters stopped, but without success.

This could cause us a real problem, as Craig, one of the wingers, is only able to sit this morning as he has a work appointment after lunch.

We open the courtroom door with our hearts in our mouths. Will anyone be there, or will we be faced with an empty room?

To our relief, the prosecutor, Mr Ali, and the defendant – Wes – are both in court, although there is no sign of his lawyer, Mr Franklin.

We are quickly off and running, and Wes calls his niece,

Valerie, to give evidence. Before she takes the oath and identifies herself, Jane gives her another perjury warning.

She is a confident-looking woman in her mid-40s, and she gives a clear account of walking to her local pub on the night in question to watch the football and finding her uncle there. She buys him a few beers and then offers to drive him home in his car, as he has had too much to drink.

She drops him off at home, as he needs to go to the toilet, and then parks the car right outside.

She carefully manoeuvres the car into a tight space, and the car is slightly sticking out when she finishes parking, but other cars can still get past.

Valerie then receives a phone call from her daughter asking her to come home, so she switches off the engine, leaves the car keys in the ignition and then bangs on his front door and tells Wes, who is still in the bathroom, what she has done.

She then goes home and is totally unaware of what happens afterwards, but she makes it clear that she was the driver, not Wes. She does not touch or cause any damage to the neighbour's car, nor does his car alarm go off.

Mr Ali then conducts his cross-examination and shows her the body-worn camera footage, which confirms that Wes and Mr Johnson's cars are both parked down the road, by Mr Johnson's house, and not directly outside Wes's home as she indicated.

He then asks Valerie why she leaves the keys in the car rather than take them with her to give back to Wes? She initially struggles to answer, and finally replies that she wasn't thinking straight at the time.

Wes has no other witnesses and no further evidence to put forward, and the defence rests.

That is the end of the trial apart from closing statements. Given that Wes is now unrepresented and a litigant in person, Mr Ali is not allowed to say anything, so it is now Wes's turn.

He simply reiterates what he told us previously when giving evidence. That there is no proof that he is the driver, or that he is even in the car when Mr Johnson came downstairs, and that there is no damage to Mr Johnson's car. He also denies making any admissions of guilt and says he is just protecting his niece.

Before retiring to discuss our verdict, I ask for us to see the BWC interview again, in its entirety, in order to refresh our memory, as it is a fortnight since we last viewed it. Mr Ali's laptop then crashes, and it takes a frustrating half hour before we are able to watch it.

Valerie has remained in court and is seeing her uncle's interview for the first time. I am watching her carefully as she does so – as the contents are revealed – and Wes makes his series of admissions. Her face is an absolute picture. Her expression changes from initially one of indifference, to mild interest, to surprise, to confusion, to bemusement, and finally to stunned amazement as she watches the interview unfold.

I tell Wes that we are going outside to consider our verdict and will be back as soon as we can. We find an empty room and start to deliberate.

At first, and even second glance, it seems a pretty obvious, clear-cut, and straightforward decision to us all, but we need to suspend our preconceptions and consider all the evidence carefully, objectively, analytically, and in a totally structured manner. Despite seemingly overwhelming evidence to the contrary, can there possibly be a parallel universe in which Wes and Valerie's accounts can be the truth?

I first restate to my colleagues what it is we have to decide: whether Wes drives a motor vehicle after consuming excess alcohol and, then, if he causes criminal damage to Mr Johnson's car.

The issue that we have to consider is that Wes denies either being the driver or causing any damage to his neighbour's car.

We now examine the evidence given by each witness, starting with the neighbour. Mr Johnson's attention is drawn by the sound of his car alarm, and when he goes downstairs and outside, he identifies his neighbour, Wes, the worse for wear, sitting in the driving seat of his car and touching Mr Johnson's car a few times whilst parking. He also correctly describes the clothes that Wes is wearing that night, in particular, his beanie cap.

Amanda, Craig, and I see no reason to disbelieve him. He gives his evidence clearly, confidently, and in great detail, and he does not change his story even when subjected to strong cross-examination by Wes's lawyer, Mr Franklin. His evidence is credible. We are also told he is of good character, and as such, he is – therefore – more likely than not to be telling the truth. We discount Wes's unsubstantiated assertion that he is simply looking for a compensation payment, and we have also been shown a quotation for carrying out the necessary repairs to his car.

We also accept the arresting officer's evidence of seeing the two cars parked together down the road from Wes's home and "kissing" each other, and also that Wes smells badly of drink with his pupils dilated and voice slurred.

The most compelling prosecution evidence is the BWC interview, which provides a 30-minute long snapshot of Wes's behaviour and demeanour.

In response to questions by the police officer, Wes, over the course of the interview, makes the following comments:

- "I'm parking the car"
- "I've done some damage to the car"
- "I've had a couple of drinks"
- "I've driven from down the road"
- "I'm in the wrong"
- "You're right, you're right, you're right" (when responding to a comment that he was driving)
- "Maybe I touched it"
- "We could have worked it out, but the man did not want to work it out"
- "I'm talking about my livelihood"
- "I might have touched his car"

The police officer is also shown twice telling Wes exactly what he is accused of, and mentioning the specific accusations of drink driving and criminal damage. On neither occasion does Wes, who is listening intently, query what is said, disagree with him, or mention that someone other than him was driving.

To our eyes, this visual evidence is compelling. Wes has made several self-incriminating comments that – at this point – we see no reason to disbelieve.

The comment he made that, "I'm talking about my livelihood" is also particularly telling, as it provides a potential reason for Wes to make every attempt to keep hold of his driving licence.

We also consider his no comment interview on the day after the alleged offences when he did not take the opportunity offered to him to put forward a detailed defence, followed by his short, prepared statement with its vague assertion that "someone was driving my car", and it was that unnamed "other person" who parked his car.

Why did he not identify his niece Valerie as the driver when he had the opportunity to do so? We draw an adverse inference from this as he could have provided a detailed explanation, but he declined to do so.

Next, we have to consider Wes's evidence in which he claims – for the first time – that his niece, Valerie, is driving his car and not him. He only comes back to the scene to retrieve his car keys and is accosted by Mr Johnson. Wes also states that there is no damage to Mr Johnson's car. For us to believe him, he needs to convince us to ignore and disregard all the damaging comments and admissions he makes in the BWC interview.

He struggles to come up with a convincing explanation for them, stating only that – as he has drunk a couple of pints – he does not really know what he is saying, and that he is also protecting his niece.

We also do not understand why he feels any need to protect Valerie. She is not accused of any offence, and according to their evidence, there is no damage to Mr Johnson's car anyway.

We do not believe him.

Valerie's evidence is clear and consistent, and totally backs up her uncle's account. The problem is that *none* of it is credible; we simply do not believe her either. She states that the two cars are parked directly outside her uncle's home when the BWC footage clearly shows that they are both parked further down the road.

We also find that it beggars belief that anyone would

deliberately leave a set of car keys in the ignition of a parked and unlocked car in the middle of the night in an inner city street, when the obvious thing to do is lock the car, take the keys with her, and give them back to her uncle before she goes home to see her daughter.

We are all sure that Valerie is showing a totally misguided loyalty to her uncle and that the two of them have concocted a story together (which they certainly both stuck to in court) to try to help him escape a driving ban. A fortnight ago, we warned them both not to discuss the case together, but it is difficult to find a credible explanation other than that they have colluded with each other.

The look on Valerie's face when she sees and hears Wes's series of damaging and self-incriminating admissions on the BWC footage is revealing, as the scales fall away from her eyes. It is also telling that Wes admits that he is worried about losing his livelihood if he is unable to drive, and later states that he has a drive of an hour and three quarters to work each day, and a two-hour drive home. If he loses his license, then perhaps he will lose his job.

Given that we are sure that Wes is the driver, and that Mr Johnson's car is damaged that night, we also find him guilty of the criminal damage charge.

We take quite a long time to consider our verdict and then write out our reasons. No decision that magistrates come to is ever made lightly or without due consideration given that it is peoples' lives that we are talking about, but this one seems on the surface to be so obvious – with all the evidence pointing to Wes's guilt – that we take extra care to evaluate everything that we have seen and heard. We ensure that we are not missing or misconstruing anything.

We come back into court, and the first thing I notice is that Valerie is no longer sitting at the back of the court, and has left. I wonder how she feels now.

I announce our verdict, and Wes visibly slumps with disappointment etched all over his face.

Mr Ali reveals that Wes has some totally unrelated minor convictions, but has been out of trouble for well over 30 years. He asks for costs of £625 to be levied against Wes because he decided to go to trial, as well as compensation to be awarded to Mr Johnson.

I ask Wes if there is anything that he would like to say to us in mitigation before we decide upon his sentence.

Normally, a defence lawyer will carry out this important task, but Wes is now unrepresented and has to make do on his own. We always ask the defence lawyer to provide us with mitigation before we sentence their client after they have either pleaded or been found guilty; we want to give them the opportunity to try to explain on their client's behalf why the crime was committed, and also provide us with details about the defendant's personal circumstances, state of mind, and background, as well as what was going on with them at the time of the offence. All too often, we will hear about serious issues relating to addiction, homelessness, unemployment, or mental health problems. It is up to the bench to decide how much weight we give to this information, which may or may not go some way towards explaining the offending behaviour.

Most defence lawyers do their utmost to put a favourable spin on what they are instructed to tell us and gild the lily as much as possible. They walk a tightrope without veering from the truth or attempting to pull the wool over our eyes. And why not too, as they are simply trying to do their best for their client?

One exception to this is the redoubtable Ms Y, an experienced defence advocate at our courthouse who is invariably brief, blunt, and brutally to the point. She has been known to tell the bench that her client has behaved like a total idiot and has no excuses except for his lack of common sense and maturity, and fully expects and deserves what is coming to him. She tells it exactly as it is and I wonder if her searingly honest approach results in more lenient sentences for her clients?

Wes asks whether he can appeal, and I tell him that since he pleaded not guilty he has an automatic right of appeal within 21 days against both his conviction and his sentence. Any appeal is heard in the Crown Court before a judge and two magistrates, and the entire case can be reheard, but if he loses then his original sentence might change and he might also be liable for extra costs.

Wes starts to tell us what a huge mistake we have made in convicting him. I acknowledge how disappointed he must now be feeling, but quickly stop him from talking any more about the case. I remind him that he needs to confine his remarks to information about his personal circumstances and how the obligatory driving ban he is about to receive will affect him.

He tells us that he has a responsible job with a building company for whom he has worked for many years, and has a long commute to and from work every day. He now fully expects to lose his job, as he needs to drive to and from building sites. We also ask him to fill in a means form, which he does, but he states that all the figures on it are going to be meaningless given the likelihood of him losing his job given the loss of his driving license.

We now have to consider his sentence. He has a breathalyser reading of 88 microgrammes of alcohol in 100 millilitres of breath (the legal limit is 35), which places him right at the top end of the third most serious category of the sentencing guidelines.

We decide to ban him from driving for 22 months but offer him the opportunity to reduce his ban by a quarter by successfully completing, at his own cost, a drink-drive rehabilitation course.

He currently earns £438 per week and we give him a Band C fine, which is 150% of his relevant weekly income. As there is no discount for a guilty plea, the total fine is £657.

We award Mr Johnson compensation of £650, which is the amount of his insurance excess. There is also a victim surcharge of £65, but we decide not to charge Wes any costs given the circumstances and the other payments – particularly compensation – that he now has to make.

Wes now owes a total of £1,372. We make a collection order and given how much he owes, he will have to talk to the Fines Office to agree a payment schedule within the next 14 days.

Wes still looks devastated, but just as he is about to say something, he is cut short as the door at the rear of the court bursts open, and in rushes a harassed looking Mr Franklin, his Section 38 lawyer. He is huffing and puffing, and very hot and bothered.

The words burst out of him in a torrent. When he arrived at court this morning, he saw a note from the office stating that the trial was not starting until 2 pm. He now finds – to his shock and horror – that we have concluded matters without him.

I firstly state that as a Section 38 lawyer, his job was officially done when he finished cross-examining prosecution witnesses on Wes's behalf and also remind him that, a fortnight ago, he was given a clear instruction by me to return to court today at 9.30 am for a 10 am start; something that everyone else bar him has managed to do. I ask him what time he arrived today, and he says that he got here soon after 9 am.

Why then had he not thought of coming to the actual courtroom when he arrived, and checking to see who was there and what, if anything, was going on? Had he taken the time and trouble to merely walk down the short corridor to the courtroom, then he would have found the prosecutor and Wes waiting for proceedings to commence. He has no answer to this suggestion.

There is really nothing more to say about this matter.

*

After a much-needed break for lunch and some reflection, Amanda and I return to court for our only other case today, which is supposed to be a domestic abuse trial. The defendant turns up, along with the lawyers, but there is no complainant.

We are told that the complainant emailed the court today to tell us that she is self-isolating as she is apparently at risk of contracting Coronavirus.

Given the fact that she has placed herself in voluntary quarantine, we receive no medical confirmation of her situation.

Our antennae are up but, in the circumstances, all we can do is question her commitment to the case. We are told that she supports the prosecution and fully intends to come to court as soon as she can to give evidence against her partner, who is accused of a particularly unpleasant and serious assault against her.

The defence lawyer also sensibly takes matters at face value and makes no objection to the prosecution's application to adjourn the case.

We follow the dictates of the Criminal Practice Directions and agree to the adjournment, and the trial is set for the next available date, which is in three months' time.

This is a sign of the times, and we are certain to be inundated with similar applications. Given human nature, I am sure that amongst all the genuine cases, some defendants and unwilling witnesses will use the virus as an excuse to evade their responsibility to attend court.

It's early days yet, but I wonder how Coronavirus will affect the courts system over the coming months?

Initially, I can see many more benches of two sitting, as magistrates start to catch the virus or fear doing so. There will probably also be circumstances – such as when granting or refusing bail or warrants – when only one magistrate will sit. Non-essential cases will surely also be adjourned for the time being. I also wonder how long it will be before jury trials are suspended, as is already the case in Ontario. The already massive backlog of outstanding trials will undoubtedly increase even more.

There will surely also come a time, perhaps very soon, when magistrates are stood down for their own safety. District Judges might well hear high priority cases. The health of every court user is paramount and has to take precedence over keeping courts open at all costs, and I doubt if defendants and witnesses alike will want to risk the journey to court, particularly on public transport.

Massive efforts will also need to be made to clean the courthouses every day, provide and replenish stocks of hand sanitisers and even PPE, and ensure that an acceptable level of hygiene is maintained. Maintaining social distancing will also be hard to choreograph within a court setting.

We finish early, and I spend the whole journey home thinking about Wes, the situation he got himself into, the implications of what was a most unusual and disturbing trial, and how someone was obviously so desperate to keep his job that he and his niece put forward a spurious defence that just did not stand up to any serious scrutiny.

17. MAKING THE GRADE

Today is my new mentee Anna's last court observation before she is finally deemed ready to sit as a fully-fledged magistrate.

Before her first observation, she received a personal escort from security to the retiring room, but she is unable to work the same magic today, and I have to go down to the front door and vouch for her before the security guards will allow her upstairs.

I take her straight to the administrative offices and, miraculously, the normally elusive and drastically-overworked office manager, Mitchell, is sitting at his desk; even more fortuitously, he has just received a new stock of key cards which are normally as rare as hens' teeth, and Anna will now be able to access the building on her own. He also takes her photograph for her ID card but explains that this could take several months to come through, as there always seems to be a backlog. Mine, in fact, took the best part of 18 months to arrive, which caused me no end of problems whenever I needed to visit a courthouse other than my own.

Anna completed her three-day induction training at the end of last week, and I ask her to give me a brief summary of what topics were covered. Pretty much everything, would seem to be the answer, as she and the other 15 new recruits were given a theoretical introduction to most of the situations they would imminently face in court:

- Trials
- Remands
- Case Management
- Sentencing

- Custody
- Community Orders
- Driving Offences
- Allocation
- Bail

There were also a lot of role-playing and team-building exercises, which she found very useful.

Anna enjoyed the training, which was very thorough and quite intense, although she felt that it could perhaps have been condensed into two-and-a-half days rather than three. She now realises that she has a lot of information to digest and process. The training was well run by several legal advisers, but attendees would perhaps have benefited from talking to some current magistrates who could have shared their own personal and practical experiences of what to expect when sitting in court, and how best to deal with every eventuality.

Whilst Anna is having her first official sitting in a few days' time, as soon as possible after her training and final observation, she was surprised to discover that several of her fellow delegates are not planning to sit for several weeks, or even months, and she feels that – ideally – every newly-trained magistrate should sit for the first time with learned content still fresh in their minds.

She tells me that she was worried and lacking in confidence beforehand, but now feels far better equipped for the task that shortly awaits her, and is really looking forward to her first sitting.

I can sense that she is champing at the bit and sees today as the final hurdle to overcome before she is finally let loose on an unsuspecting public.

*

We go through the court lists and choose what looks likely to be an extremely busy remand court. I approach the presiding justice, Rebecca, and she is more than happy for us to sit in and observe. This will be a good experience for Anna as Rebecca is a chair who controls and manages the court extremely well, always involves her wingers, and will set her a good example.

What's more, the prosecutor, Ms Davies, is also one of the best ones around who does her job efficiently, but is always fair and pragmatic too.

We go into court just before the bench and take a couple of hard and horrendously uncomfortable seats at the side of the court. Now I can understand why advocates like to jump to their feet in court at every opportunity!

There are a few nods of recognition and acknowledgements from advocates, and I exchange pleasantries with Mr C with whom I have had the odd run-in in the past. The first thing I see is the list caller, Antonia, and the duty solicitor, Ms Khan, both sporting a fetching pair of black gloves and looking like a Michael Jackson tribute act.

The Coronavirus threat is growing more serious by the day, and they are wise to take every precaution. It is also having an increasing influence on court proceedings, as Ms Khan immediately makes clear. She informs the bench that a defendant who has asked for her assistance as duty solicitor is coughing ominously and uncontrollably in the cells. Quite understandably, she is not prepared to expose herself to potential infection by taking instructions from him, which means that his case has to be adjourned for three weeks.

Antonia gives us both copies of the court list, and we can also follow most cases on our iPads. The first case involves

Kevin, who is accused of threatening to kill and then actually assaulting his partner, Georgia. He pleads guilty, and we hear the brief facts so that the bench can decide how best to sentence him.

Kevin is in his mid-50s, and previously of good character, although there are reports of some problems between the couple. On this occasion, he is drunk and aggressive and threatens to cut Georgia "into pieces" before throwing an apple at her, which hits her in the face, leaving her with a bruised left eye. Their two children, aged ten and 12 respectively, witness the whole episode.

As the bench retire to consider their decision, I ask Anna, who is looking at the Sentencing Guidelines, how she would deal with Kevin. After some consideration, she says that initially, she would have given him bail but – on further thought – she now feels that these are both extremely serious offences and she would commit him to the Crown Court for sentencing, and remand him in custody in the meantime.

She is quite correct about the threats to kill offence, which is deemed to be in Category 2A, with higher culpability, as the offence was committed in front of children, and some distress was also caused to the victim. The starting point is two years' custody with a range of between one to four years in prison. The assault is also a Category 1 offence because of the use of the weapon (the apple) and, in this case, the vulnerability of the victim.

Anna then asks me what I would do. I suggest that whilst these are indeed serious offences, Kevin was previously of good character and it might, therefore, be helpful to ask probation for a pre-sentence report with all options open. I would also reserve the right to commit him to the Crown

Court for sentencing if the eventual view is that the offences are so serious that Kevin needs greater punishment than the magistrates' court can give. I would also grant him bail in the meantime, but with conditions of non-contact with his wife and children, and a restriction from going to the family home apart from on one occasion – to collect his property when accompanied by a police officer.

There are not many people left in court and the prosecutor, Ms Davies, is listening in to our conversation with interest. We ask her what she thinks the bench will do. She smiles and says that her guess is that they will order a pre-sentence report and give him bail.

The magistrates return a few minutes later and do exactly what Ms Davies predicted they would. Anna looks crestfallen, but I tell her that her initial thoughts about the case were spot on, particularly in where they sat within the Sentencing Guidelines, and that she should always follow her instincts – as long as they are backed up with a sound knowledge of the facts.

There is a gap at the conclusion of this case as there is nothing else ready for the bench to deal with. The magistrates file out for a well-earned cup of coffee, but before we can join them, Ms Davies comes over to where we are sitting and very helpfully gives Anna a brief introduction and insight into the role of the prosecutor. That was extremely kind of her and greatly appreciated by the pair of us.

*

Eventually, the next case is called on and Alan, who is in custody, pleads guilty to two separate charges of possessing cannabis. On the face of it, not perhaps the most serious of offences. Things change though when we learn that this is the fourth time that this case has been called on, since he failed to appear on the previous occasions, and Alan has now been arrested on a warrant.

Anna and I read his PNC, which lists his previous convictions and discover that – despite the fact that he is only 21 – Alan already has a long, ever-growing, and serious criminal record, mainly for drug offences but also for criminal damage and assault.

I also point out to Anna that he disobeys almost every court order that has been made against him. He has breached his previous community orders and doesn't turn up to court when ordered to do so.

Less than a month before these two new offences, Alan pleaded guilty to possession of a quantity of cocaine, and received a community order with unpaid work. Four months on, he has not done a single hour of the unpaid work he was ordered to complete, nor attended any of his appointments with probation, and is likely to be breached for his total non-compliance.

In other words, on the face of it, Alan appears to be a young man with an attitude. He repeatedly offends and then totally disregards court orders.

He does little to help himself in court, lolling and lounging backwards in the dock, and seemingly paying little or no attention to what is being said about him. There's a lot of sighing and eye-rolling. He is the epitome of dumb insolence.

If I was on the bench, I would not be feeling particularly happy with Alan's general demeanour and what has been said about him, and wonder what sentence he will receive.

I ask Anna for her opinion on Alan, and how best to deal with him, and she states firmly that he is only heading in one direction, and that is towards custody.

Rebecca and her colleagues take their time and eventually come back into court. Alan is told to stand and receives an extremely stern talking to from Rebecca, which makes it quite clear how much his behaviour has displeased her and her colleagues. He is told quite firmly that court orders are not to be ignored, or only followed if – and when – he feels like it.

She then revokes his previous community order for possession of Class A drugs and, given his previous record and total lack of compliance with it, resentences him to 12 weeks in prison, suspended for 18 months, along with 20 days of rehabilitation activity with probation. She then reinforces the message by reminding him that if he reoffends within the next 18 months, he can expect to serve this prison sentence. He is fined £100 for each of the two new drug offences, but this sum is deemed served because of the two days he has spent in custody awaiting this hearing, and the drugs are to be... wait for it... forfeited and destroyed.

Alan belatedly stirs into life and visibly recoils when he hears mention of the possibility of going to prison. Finally, something has concentrated his mind, and maybe, one day, the penny will finally drop with him. He slinks back to the cells escorted by a couple of prison officers, and Anna looks at me and nods. She agrees with everything Rebecca and her colleagues just did, as do I. Alan has been dealt with firmly and fairly and given a much-needed shock to his system.

*

After court ends, we meet up with Rebecca and her colleagues and exchange views and opinions about the day.

Anna and I finish the day by talking through what she has observed and whether she now feels ready and prepared to sit as a magistrate for the first time.

She says that she has learned a lot from the cases she saw in court today and, in particular, how a good bench worked together – methodically and as one – to come to a number of good decisions.

I then pass on to her my previous mentee's recent thoughts about the mentoring process and how to get the most out of it.

Anna's first sitting is only a few days away, and she asks me if I have any last-minute advice for her. I think carefully and say that it is quite natural for her to be nervous, but she should remember that she has been trained far more recently than any of her colleagues and will, therefore, be more aware of procedure than them. I tell her to keep her eyes and ears open and not to be afraid to give her opinion, and to ask questions throughout the day.

Lastly, I suggest that she look carefully at, and try to familiarise herself with, the Sentencing Guidelines for the most common offences such as possession of drugs and common assault that she will need to refer to most days in court. She should also have the specific figures for the victim surcharge close to hand, as she will make herself instantly popular with her presiding justice (me) who often struggles to come up with the right amount for each type of sentence.

Most importantly, I remind her that she is an equal member of a team of three, and we will all go out of our way to help and support each other. With any luck, she will sleep well the night before she makes her debut. I was a total bag of nerves before my first sitting, but I am pretty sure that Anna will cope just fine and come through her ordeal with flying colours.

18. FAREWELL FOR NOW

It is my mentee – Anna's – first ever sitting today, and I arrive extra early at court to meet her. I know that she will be bashing the doors down in her eagerness to get started.

She comes into the retiring room with iPad in hand, hot to trot, and bursting with enthusiasm. As soon as she sits down next to me, she produces a spreadsheet from her bag and reminds me that at the end of her last court observation I had suggested that, before her first sitting, she try to learn how much victim surcharge is applied to each different type of sentence, as presiding justices often struggle to come up with the right figure, particularly given how often the sum changes.

She tells me that she sat down last night to do some online research and discovered that – as of the 14th of April 2020 – the victim surcharge figures will increase yet again. This takes me totally by surprise; I was not aware of this forthcoming change, which has yet to be disseminated to magistrates.

I have previously written about the victim surcharge, but this latest increase has motivated me to delve even more deeply into its history. It was introduced in 2007, initially at a flat rate of £15 on every fine. But it has mushroomed since then, and is now applied to all sentences that offenders receive from the courts, irrespective of their type.

Its purpose is to ensure that offenders take some level of responsibility towards the cost of supporting victims and witnesses. The late (unlamented) Criminal Courts Charge, by comparison, was intended to make offenders pay something towards the cost of running the actual criminal courts in which they were convicted.

I also found a recently published Ministry of Justice

announcement about the latest increase in the victim surcharge, which provided some updated information about how the sums raised are actually used (details of which have traditionally been hard to come by). Income from the victim surcharge is pooled and distributed through the Victim and Witness General Fund and contributes towards: local community support services for victims, 94 rape support centres across England and Wales, the court-based witness service, and the national homicide service.

What I find hard to accept is that the victim surcharge has been raised five times in the past eight years: October 2012, September 2014, April 2016, June 2019, and now April 2020. The rise on each occasion has been small, generally about 5%, and rounded to the nearest pound.

From the 14th of April 2020, the surcharge level on a conditional discharge will increase to £22 from the current level of £21. Victim surcharge on a fine remains 10% of the total fine value, but with a minimum charge of £34 and a maximum of £190 (a slight increase on the previous minimum of £32 and maximum of £181). The sum imposed for a community order increases from £90 to £95, and for either a suspended sentence – or immediate custody – of six months or less, the figure rises from £122 to £128.

From the 14th of April 2020, if an offender is sentenced to two separate fines, then he or she will be charged victim surcharge on the aggregate of all fines, rather than solely on the largest one, as was previously the case.

As a writer far more gifted than me once said – much ado about nothing!

Why are the changes made so often and for such minimal amounts? Why make things so much harder for magistrates to remember and administer the charges, despite the crib sheets left so helpfully on our desks? We have already got more than enough on our plates and barely got used to applying the old surcharge before yet another one replaced it.

It is anticipated that this latest increase will bring in an additional one to two million pounds each year to help fund victim support initiatives.

I understand that there is a move eventually to increase the victim surcharge by 25 per cent, which would see an extra seven million pounds raised each year. This will be considered as part of an upcoming consultation on a Victims' Law.

Why not increase victim surcharge every ten years or so, and more meaningfully, perhaps by around ten per cent rather than this sneaky and monotonous drip-feed? Alternatively, why have it at all? Is it not really just another stealth tax?

I understand, but cannot really endorse, the objective of getting court users to pay more towards the cost of the courts themselves as well as for victim support. The Criminal Courts Charge was a disaster, and offenders can already be ordered to pay compensation directly to their victims as restitution for the injuries or loss they suffered. Fines and ancillary payments should also be set at an affordable level rather than at a fixed rate, and a huge proportion goes unpaid.

Anyway, Anna has already won lots of brownie points for being so ahead of the game and for telling me something I did not realise (but probably should have already known).

*

I look at the court list which has been left for us and see that we are in a remand court. Anna and I are sitting with Penny, who is also a presiding justice, and – by reputation – an exceptionally good one, as she is calm, measured, and highly analytical in her approach. Given that I will have my hands full keeping an eye on Anna and making sure that she is OK, I ask if Penny would like to chair today, but she declines, saying that she welcomes the chance to sit as a winger, as she so rarely gets the opportunity to do so. I would have been happy if she had accepted my offer, as I could have observed her in action and maybe picked up some tips and pointers, which I could potentially incorporate into my own chairing.

I look around the retiring room and see that it is far less populated than normal. Those who are there appear to be more subdued and reflective in tone than usual and, of course, doing their best to sit well apart from each other in line with the latest social distancing guidelines. Coronavirus is a frightening, unknown, and ever-increasing threat to us all, and quite frankly I am fully expecting to hear confirmation that – very shortly – it will prove to be impossible and unsafe to keep any magistrates' courts open in their present form. Already, the travel restrictions are taking their toll, and with so many magistrates falling into the vulnerable age brackets, it is hardly surprising that the number reporting for duty is falling.

Today might well, therefore, be my last sitting for a while, so I determine to make the most of it and ensure that Anna has a proper introduction to the magistracy – even in these most unusual of times.

On the way back from the drinks machine, I almost literally bump into Jonathan, the legal adviser I had a falling out with, which I described in Chapter Eight. Our paths have not crossed since that episode, and I suspect that we have both been giving each other a wide berth for the last couple of months, which has provided a helpful cooling off period. I cannot ignore him now, given that we are facing each other directly in the passageway – that would just make things even worse – and I take this opportunity to apologise and tell him that I have done a lot of thinking about what happened. I say that I will do my utmost to develop a better working relationship with him from now on. He agrees to do the same, and we walk off in separate directions. We are never going to be bosom pals – nor, of course, do we either want or need to be – but it is important that we are able to work together professionally and co-operatively in court. I trust this has cleared the air between us for when our paths next cross.

Back in the retiring room, Anna, Penny, and I go through our list and see nothing particularly untoward or out of the ordinary, just your normal, day-to-day ragtag and bobtail of alleged domestic abusers, shoplifters, drug offenders, drink drivers, burglars, scofflaws, and all the other flotsam and jetsam of inner-city crime. Penny agrees to check defendants' PNC records, and I ask Anna to look up the relevant sentencing guidelines whenever necessary.

Anna also agrees to enter court first, with Penny bringing up the rear. As we reach the door, Anna gives it two stentorian knocks that make it abundantly clear that we mean business.

Then, what a letdown. In an act of pure bathos, we enter the room to find *absolutely nobody there* – apart from Robin, the long-suffering legal adviser, who shrugs his shoulders phlegmatically and explains that the prosecutor, Ms Parkinson, has just left the court to take an urgent telephone call but will be back shortly. A few defence lawyers are taking instructions either in the cells or outside. Martha, the list caller, is scouring the corridors looking for errant or absent defendants, and nothing is ready yet anyway.

"Welcome to the wonderful world of the magistrates' court", I whisper to Anna. She could not have had a more apposite and fitting start to her career as a magistrate.

*

We return, in single file, to the retiring room to find practically every other magistrate sitting around socially distancing and waiting to be called into action. Eventually, our turn comes, and it is finally time for Anna to hear her first-ever case in a magistrates' court.

It concerns Joshua who pleads guilty to possession of cannabis. It is his third such conviction, but the last was a couple of years ago. I spoke quietly to Penny whilst we were twiddling our thumbs in the retiring room, and explain that given today is her first sitting, I am going to seek Anna's opinion first – and hopefully she is OK with that. She graciously agrees, so I turn to Anna and ask her how she thinks we should sentence Joshua.

I check to see that she has her iPad open to the correct Sentencing Guideline, and I pass her a copy of his means form. After a brief perusal of both, she looks at Penny and me and confidently rattles off her answer: "Given his previous record I would propose a Band B fine which, as he is receiving benefits, is £120 reduced to £80 to take account of his early guilty plea. The victim surcharge is £32, plus costs of £85, which gives a total of £197. Oh, and don't forget the forfeiture and destruction of the drugs and to make a collection order." I look at Penny, and we exchange a wry and relieved smile. We have nothing to worry about with Anna. Perhaps she should already be sitting in the middle seat! She is totally on the ball, and absolutely spot-on with her analysis, which is word perfect. We both agree with her suggested sentence, and I follow it to the letter. Anna has got off to an excellent start and this initial sentencing exercise will have really boosted her confidence – and our confidence in her.

*

Serhan has been arrested on a warrant for non-payment of a fine of £270 imposed on him over two years ago. His English is poor, and we are waiting for the arrival of a Turkish interpreter. A moment later, the door opens and in walks a smartly-dressed middle-aged woman who asks to speak to him. Assuming she is the interpreter we agree to retire for a couple of minutes so that they can get acquainted, and are embarrassed to learn, on our return, that she is not the interpreter after all, but his partner, who simply wanted to have a quick word with him as he had been kept in the cells overnight. What *chutzpah!* We fell for it hook, line, and sinker. That is a mistake that I will hopefully never repeat.

Once his partner is removed to her rightful place in the public gallery, we have a further wait until the real interpreter eventually arrives and we can finally get on with the matter in hand. Serhan states that he was out of work for many months but started a new job recently and promises to pay his debt in full within the next three months. I exchange glances, raised eyebrows, and nods with my colleagues. We agree to his proposal, and I warn him to pay off his debt as agreed today, or he could well find himself having another overnight stay in custody unless he first comes back to court to explain why he is unable to keep up with his payments.

*

Jim is already in custody and is awaiting sentencing for other serious matters at a nearby Crown Court next month. He appears over the video link and pleads guilty to a particularly nasty, serious, and unpleasant assault on a young woman who was walking towards her parked motorbike – where her girlfriend was waiting for her. Jim follows her, making a series of unprovoked, sordid, and suggestive homophobic and sexual comments towards them both. They include, "You are both my fantasy" and "I wish I had a vibrator with me."

He catches up with them and threatens to kill the two young women, before punching one of them – Mary – in the face, which results in her suffering a chipped front tooth.

Jim is 30 years of age and has many previous convictions for violent offences. We also learn that he has a long-term addiction to both drink and drugs. His lawyer asks us to give his client a short custodial sentence given that he is already in prison and is likely to remain there for quite some time.

We go outside to consider this case, and given the seriousness of the injury incurred by Mary, we are surprised that Jim is accused only of assault by beating rather than assault occasioning actual bodily harm (ABH). We place this offence in the most serious category because it was a sustained assault that was motivated by hostility based on Mary's sexual orientation.

In our opinion, it easily crosses the custody threshold. After a discussion in which Anna and Penny fully participate, we decide to send Jim to prison for six months, reduced to four months, on account of his early guilty plea. That is the most serious punishment we can give him, as common assault is a Summary offence, which must be dealt with in the magistrates' court, with a maximum penalty of six months' custody.

Had Jim been charged with ABH, then we would have had

more sentencing options. We could have either committed him to the Crown Court for sentencing, or even sent him to prison for the full six months available to us, as his early guilty plea discount would have been to sentence him in a magistrates' court (and not to commit him to the Crown Court).

Somebody far more cynical than me might well feel that Jim has been given a "free hit" for this nasty crime as, given the seriousness of the other offences that he will shortly be sentenced for, it is highly likely that the four-month sentence we have just imposed will be swallowed up by – and incorporated within – the longer prison sentence that the Crown Court will probably give him. Our hands are tied – we cannot impose a heavier sentence than we just did. We also order him to pay Mary £500, as compensation for the injury he caused her.

*

Keith is 18, of good character, and this is his first appearance in court. He is small, thin, with a shaven head and looks far younger than his actual age. His eyes dart from side to side as if he is desperately trying to accustom himself to his surroundings and locate the best way to escape the courtroom. He is stopped and searched on the street and found to be in possession of a Rambo knife and a small amount of cannabis. He pleads guilty, and we ask probation services to interview him and provide us with an oral pre-sentence report.

The report is ready immediately after lunch, and we hear that Keith has co-operated fully with the probation officer. He is walking down a busy main road with a friend, late at night, when he is stopped and searched by a police officer who finds the knife and drugs in his jacket pocket. He says that he is not in a gang but knows people who are, and a friend of his was stabbed outside his mother's house a year ago. As a result, since then, Keith has taken to carrying a knife with him for his own protection, particularly when he spends time with those of his friends who are gang members.

He accepts that he needs to change his behaviour and is aware of just how dangerous it is to carry a knife, but insists that he would never have used it and is very sorry for his actions.

He was expelled from school after being caught smoking cannabis but now works with his Dad, who is a painter and decorator, and fully intends to obtain some (unspecified) qualifications.

He has no issues with alcohol or his mental health but regularly smokes cannabis.

Probation services assess him as a medium risk of harm to the public but as a low risk of re-offending.

Keith's lawyer stresses his previous good character and early guilty plea, and, just as pertinently, the fact that Keith has recently moved away from his local area in an effort to separate himself from his friends who are a bad influence on him.

We go outside to consider what we have heard, and I ask Anna which category she puts this offence into. She pores over the Sentencing Guidelines and correctly states that this is Category 2A matter as Keith is in possession of a bladed article. But, given the circumstances in which he was arrested, there was no risk of serious disorder, and the starting point is six months' custody with a range of between three months to one year in custody.

Penny, Anna and I then go through the necessary in-depth structured process to decide exactly how we are going to sentence Keith. In order, we ask and answer the following key questions:

1. Has the custody threshold been passed?

Absolutely, given what Anna has just reminded us about what the Sentencing Guidelines prescribe.

2. Is it unavoidable that a sentence of imprisonment be imposed?

I remind my colleagues that although the custody threshold has been passed, that does not necessarily mean that a custodial sentence is inevitable.

I ask if either believes that a community order would provide sufficient punishment and opportunities for rehabilitation for Keith, and if he has dependants who would be seriously affected and disadvantaged if he were to go to prison.

We answer "no" to both questions and agree that the offence is so serious that only a custodial sentence can be justified. We must also demonstrate our concern about the epidemic of knife crime on our streets.

3. What is the shortest term commensurate with the seriousness of the offence?

We discuss our options and agree that a six-month prison sentence reduced to four months would be appropriate.

4. Can the sentence be suspended?

We discuss Keith, his background, hopes and aspirations, the key fact that he has moved away from the local area and that four family members support him in court; as well, of course, his offending behaviour. After a prolonged discussion, we decide that because of his youth and previous good character, and the steps he has taken to remove himself from bad influences, it would be just to suspend the sentence. However, we agree to add a further punitive element in terms of an unpaid work requirement.

We also discuss how he would benefit from a Rehabilitation Activity Requirement (RAR), which would help him develop better thinking and decision-making skills.

I ask Anna if there is anything else we need to deal with, and she thinks for a minute before shrugging her shoulders. Penny jumps in and reminds her that we also have to sentence Keith for possession of cannabis. Given that the cannabis was found at the same time as the knife – and the fact that we are about to give Keith a suspended prison sentence – in the interests of totality, we decide on no separate penalty for the drug offence, with the cannabis to be forfeited and destroyed.

I ask Anna to summarise the entire sentence, and with only a little bit of faltering, she does.

For the possession of the offensive weapon in a public place:

- Six months' custody reduced to four months, to take account of Keith's early guilty plea, suspended for 12 months
- 25 days of RAR
- 100 hours of unpaid work
- Victim surcharge of £122
- Contribution to costs of £40
- Forfeiture and destruction of the knife

For the possession of Class B drugs

- No separate penalty
- Forfeiture and destruction of the drugs

We go back into court, and I sentence Keith accordingly and explain that it is only his previous good character, youth, remorse, the fact that he has moved away from potential trouble, and some evidence of rehabilitation and increasing maturity, that has kept him out of custody today.

It is up to Keith in which direction his life goes from now on, but it is made quite clear to him that if he does re-offend within the next 12 months, then the suspended sentence will most likely be activated, unless it is unjust to do so.

*

The rest of the day passes without incident, and Anna shows that she has maintained her concentration levels until the end. She notices that the last defendant we see, Sammy, is in breach of a conditional discharge by virtue of his conviction today for possession of cannabis. We fine him and extend the period of his conditional discharge.

After a brief post-court review, I meet up individually with Anna to discuss how she thinks today went. She tells me that she has really enjoyed herself and felt that whilst there is a lot to learn, she got to grips with the basics and was able to contribute and keep up with proceedings. Anna then laughs and tells me that her boning up last night – about the victim surcharge – also came in helpful several times throughout the day!

I ask her how she feels about sending someone to prison on her first day and if she wants to talk about it, as I am well aware of how big a step this is. But she assures me that she feels OK about it, and has no regrets about our decision.

We fill in the new Mentored Sittings form, which goes into great detail about what was both experienced and observed in court today. She has only just embarked upon her long journey but she has made a confident and assured start to her career as a magistrate.

We say our goodbyes and I make my way towards the stairs, but something is bugging me. Fortunately, I see that Robin, our legal adviser today, in still in his office and I ask if he can spare a moment.

He nods and asks me to sit down. We have always got on well together, and I know that I can be open and honest with him, as he will be to me. I tell him that over the past few months, I have chaired several benches where young defendants all pleaded guilty to possession of a bladed article in a public place. I believe that whilst I am certainly not in the *hang 'em and flog 'em* brigade, I have never been afraid to mete out tough sentences when I am certain that they are justified.

I tell Robin that – with only one exception – I (and of course my colleagues) have, over the past few months, invariably given suspended sentences, rather than immediate custody for young men, often students of previous good character, who plead guilty to this offence. I abhor knife crime, and am well aware of its seriousness, and yet I only rarely seem to send someone straight to prison for it. Am I going soft, or am I overthinking things, I ask him?

Robin leans back in his chair and thinks about it for a moment or two before looking me in the eye. He replies that every case is different and there are very often times, like today, when a suspended sentence is absolutely the correct outcome, and, no, in his opinion – which I value – I am certainly not going soft in my old age.

I thank him and leave his office reassured that I have been doing the right thing.

It is dark when I start walking down the main road, and

given what I fear is shortly to come when the Coronavirus takes a firm hold over our way of life, I find myself gazing back wistfully at the courthouse. So many memories of recent cases flash through my mind. With a sinking feeling, and a dawning realisation, I appreciate that it might be quite some time before I find myself back there again.

19. THE VERDICT

Hopefully, after reading the previous 18 chapters of this book, you now have a fairly good idea of how magistrates think, what we do on a daily basis, and the obstacles and issues that we face in trying to do our job.

Of course, there is the odd bad egg and unreconstructed dinosaur within our ranks – as there is in any field – and I do read with bemusement about the occasional ruling by benches which, at first glance, without the benefit of the full facts, seems utterly bizarre. But, ideally, what has come through loud and clear from my descriptions of our court sittings is our passion, dedication, and commitment to the job! Plus, our uncompromising determination to keep to our judicial oath to do "right to all manner of people… without fear or favour, affection or ill will."

The overwhelming majority of magistrates that I have either met or worked alongside are entirely fair, pragmatic, and open-minded, with a thirst for knowledge and improvement. Typically, magistrates have a well-developed sense of teamwork, broad life experiences, and – despite being under a great deal of time pressure – they make sensible and accurate decisions having firstly carefully assimilated and considered all the information thrown at them.

What makes these achievements even more praiseworthy is that they have been accomplished whilst working, at times, with one hand seemingly tied behind our backs. We have had to come to terms with playing our part in a judicial system that is suffering death by a thousand cuts after an estimated overall 25% HMCTS budget decrease over the last decade. Cutting costs does not necessarily result in greater efficiency.

I mentioned, earlier in the book, the high levels of satisfaction expressed by magistrates about their job, but I would suggest that they are perhaps referring far more to their actual core task of 'sitting on the bench' which – if not always fulfilling – is invariably stimulating and empowering, rather than making reference to all the other pinpricks and constant delays (and lack of support both in and out of court) that have both affected and afflicted us behind the scenes. The things that every day get in the way of our enjoyment of the role and our ability to do the best possible job.

It is important to remember that we are unpaid volunteers, so little things mean a lot and go a long way. Poorly maintained buildings, non-functioning toilets and lifts, IT that does not work and – in many courts – the lack of perks such as hot drinks and biscuits (petty though they might seem), do little to boost our flagging morale. They make us feel like we are not really valued, and are taken for granted by the Ministry of Justice and HMCTS.

Magistrates have been in existence for over 650 years, so we must be doing something right, but I totally accept and embrace the need for change, adaptation, and innovation as long as it is change for the better.

I have little sympathy for magistrates who moan, are resistant to change, and who fail to adapt to and master the use of new technology; when it functions correctly, it is effective and efficient. It also seems inevitable that we will see digital courts in the none-too-distant future.

What has affected magistrates, and not for the better, is the knock-on effect of the massive court closure programme, and the resulting move towards centralised administration that diminishes local autonomy and identity. We have been homogenised, and benches have been forced to amalgamate and often travel far further to their home court. Accordingly, the traditional concept of local justice by local people has been fatally undermined and is now a chimera. The effect of court closures and the rationalisation of magistrates' courts on all court users – defendants, complainants, and witnesses alike – has also, in many cases, been drastic.

When considering the worth of the magistracy, it also needs emphasising that every criminal case starts and – more often than not – finishes in a magistrates' court. We dealt with almost 1.4 million cases last year, as well as countless applications for search and mental health warrants. Magistrates are the workhorses and lifeblood of the Criminal Justice System and help the courts function as efficiently and seamlessly as is possible, given the current constraints and decay.

Now it is time to consider all the criticisms of the magistracy made by *The Secret Barrister* and others, and whilst you will by now have perhaps made up your own mind, I will also provide my view, whether it be a passionate defence of our role or perhaps, in some cases, simply mitigation after an admission of guilt.

Let's look at *The Secret Barrister*'s main concerns about us, namely:

- Our age
- Lack of diversity
- Lack of formal legal qualifications
- Being slow to make decisions
- Being unrepresentative of those we judge
- Poorly recruited
- Inadequately trained

- Naïve and out of touch
- Being unable to grasp or interpret much of the evidence presented before us, as well as fundamental legal points, judgments, and principles

Those are damning accusations to make, and whilst I would suspect that there is an element of unwarranted antipathy and condescension on the part of some members of the judiciary towards the magistracy – which might lend to exaggeration – there is, indeed, some truth in many of these assertions.

I have already provided some of the latest statistics confirming the high average age of the magistracy, its gender bias, and its insufficient levels of diversity and social mobility.

What, though, do we mean by the word "diversity?" Who do we expect to see sitting on the bench? In the context of the magistracy, I take it that it should, in totality, be representative of all the different types of people who come before it, who themselves comprise a wide range of ages, characteristics, and ethnicities.

It is easy to highlight the issues and problems, but it is far harder to solve them, particularly when you are making bricks without straw. Serving as a magistrate takes a lot of time and commitment. The minimum annual sitting requirement of 13 days is, in reality, almost doubled when you take into account the need to attend training events and bench meetings. How can you attract an increasing number of younger candidates who are still making their ways in their careers, rather than depending upon those at the other end of the spectrum?

The Advisory Committees do an excellent job – given the constraints under which they work – but the method of recruitment appears to be generally pretty much more of the same, and it brings to mind what Einstein said about doing the same thing and expecting a different result. Whilst I would hardly call the current recruitment efforts "insane", a totally fresh approach and perspective are required. This is simply a strategic marketing conundrum that needs to address how best to persuade employers to release their youngest, brightest, and best, as well as highlighting the advantages and benefits of the magistracy as a career-enhancing move through the valuable skills that they develop. Can employers even be required to release employees for magisterial duties?

It is all very well asking current magistrates to retweet ads concerning current magisterial vacancies and to put up flyers in retiring rooms. That simply means that we are preaching to the converted. We want to attract a new core of 25 to 45-year-olds, particularly from the BAME communities, so the answer is to go to a proven marketing or social media agency that specialises in reaching and influencing our key target markets, and give them the ammunition to do the job. The problem, of course, is money, and I suspect that my words are mere pipedreams which will wither on the vine of the current funding gap.

We also need to make the most of what we already have in terms of community engagement by promoting and publicising, and then further developing, the highly successful Magistrates in the Community programme, which helps improve public awareness and understanding of our role.

As for the magistracy being out of touch, surely the judiciary as a whole is unrepresentative of – and does not reflect – today's society as a whole? It appears to be predominantly comprised of white, independently-educated males. At least most magistrates, like many jurors, have seen and experienced the world.

I cannot dispute that our training and appraisal system requires some overhauling. It is eye-opening as well as eye-watering to discover just how much the overall training budget has been cut for magistrates; this is at a time when the mantra seems to be less is more. Yet, an increasing level of competence and professionalism is required on the part of all court staff. The Ministry of Justice urgently needs to increase funding to HMCTS and the Judicial College to invest in improving the calibre of all magistrates.

The recent introduction of specific IT training for magistrates is to be welcomed, and far more use needs to be made of distance and digital learning and professional trainers.

Why can't we have a regular series of podcasts focusing upon different aspects of the law for us to listen to on our way to court? The gap between new magistrates being appointed and actually being sworn in, trained, and able to sit, is also far too long, and this needs to be addressed.

Cross-bench appraisals are difficult to arrange, but they are the fairest and most open way of ensuring that an impartial and independent judgment is made on every magistrate. Wingers also need to be appraised every two years, rather than the current four, if standards are to be maintained and even raised.

Distinguished former judge Sir Richard Henriques makes it clear, in his recent book, that as criminal law has become increasingly complex and sophisticated, so too have the demands on magistrates.

We all have to deal regularly with applications for adjournments, bad character, bail, disclosure issues, and much else, but our knowledge is often narrow and sometimes confused, and we rely upon the advice of our legal advisers.

There is so much more that we should know and understand about the Police and Criminal Evidence Act (PACE) and the overall Criminal Procedure Rules.

I am not suggesting that we become professional magistrates – we already have District Judges to fulfil that role – but the better informed we are, and the more we know, the more efficient and speedy we will be in our decision-making.

Howard Riddle and Judge Robert Zara recently wrote an invaluable textbook on "Essential Magistrates' Courts Law". Could they not be inveigled to *précis* this and produce a cut-down series of mini pocket guides, each focusing upon a different and relevant aspect of the law which would be of enormous assistance to magistrates in general, and presiding justices in particular?

Ideally, all justices would wish to improve and increase their body of knowledge but I would make it mandatory for all prospective presiding justices to undergo specific training on the main legal issues and points of law that they will face in court. They should even have to pass a formal test before they can be confirmed in post, with annual refreshers as necessary.

Legal advisers, too, have a part to play and should become more proactive and robust in managing their bench and offering firm advice and even censure when necessary. Post-court reviews should be more structured, and used as an opportunity to clarify and discuss issues and reinforce best practice, rather than something to rush through and pay lip service to before making a mad dash home.

Given the above, we would gradually develop a more knowledgeable and better-trained and prepared magistracy that would be entirely fit for purpose. If there was a grudging acceptance from both defence and prosecution lawyers that benches were far better-informed about the basics and nuances of the law, then this would go a long way towards reducing the barrage of criticism that we face.

It is also time to end any veiled hostility on our part towards District Judges. They are highly qualified, trained, and competent and are here to stay; they will only increase in numbers and – for the most part – they do an exceptionally good job. We need to observe and learn from them how to do our job better. Their appointment is not a criticism of the magistracy, merely a recognition that given their qualifications and training, they are far better equipped to handle more serious and complex cases.

Will they eventually replace magistrates? Who knows? But, looking at the maths, I don't think that it will happen for many years. You would need to hire and train a few thousand additional new District Judges if they were to take over all the work currently fulfilled by magistrates. Allowing for an annual salary of around £100,000 per head, plus training and administrative costs, this is realistically never going to happen in the near future. Given the falling crime rates and the lack of reasonable remuneration for legal aid cases, will there even be enough able lawyers interested in this role to meet the growing demand for new District Judges?

There is a perennial discussion about increasing the sentencing powers of magistrates from its current six months, or 12 if dealing with two Either Way matters. There does not seem to be much will on the part of previous or current governments to grant this request, despite it being advocated by a recent Commons Justice Committee report as well as by such experts as Howard Riddle. It might conceivably have occurred if Michael Gove had remained in office longer as

Secretary of State for Justice.

Certainly, an increase to 12 months would mean that many more Either Way offences would be dealt with more speedily in a magistrates' court and allow those people who wish to be tried in magistrates' court the opportunity to do so. Perhaps a defendant's right to elect for a Crown Court trial for an Either Way matter will also come into question given the need to reduce the ever-growing backlog of trials waiting to be heard in the Crown Court.

Very few offences have a maximum penalty of 12 months' custody, so to have much impact, magistrates would need to be granted the power to impose sentences of up to two years in prison – and that is just never going to happen.

Coronavirus has exacerbated the already appalling situation regarding delayed cases. Justice delayed appears to be the *status quo*. The number of outstanding Crown Court cases stood at 43,676 on the 26th of July 2020, and the entire backlog of cases across both magistrates' and Crown Courts has reached more than 560,000. Given the delays, there is also the ticking time bomb of expiring custody time limits which means that many remand prisoners could be released from prison and potentially put the public at risk. Could magistrates help take up the slack? John Bache, Chair of the Magistrates Association, confirmed that magistrates were eager to pull their weight when he commented, "It is important to remember that justice delayed is justice denied."

The idea of two magistrates bookending a Crown Court judge in order to deal with less serious Either Way offences, without the need for a jury, has already been floated by the Lord Chief Justice, Lord Burnett of Maldon, and is currently under discussion. This is something that Sir Robin Auld previously suggested at the turn of the century without anything coming of it. It is a move that would be welcomed by the magistracy, as was overwhelmingly confirmed in a recent Magistrates Association poll, as long as they were invited to participate equally in the entire process – including sentencing – rather than simply acting as a mini-jury with their involvement in the trial ending after the verdict has been given. It is clear that advocates would not be in favour of this proposal nor in the sidelining of jury trials and, quite frankly, neither am I, except in cases of dire emergency. Ideally, the jury system should remain sacrosanct if at all possible.

So, where does the magistracy go from here? It is quite clear that there are still a large number of unresolved issues relating to our entire existence and being, and there is a crying need for a national strategy – something that was called for in the 2016 House of Commons Justice Committee report on the role of the magistracy. This would deal with the topics raised both in this book and elsewhere. Money, too, will have to be found from somewhere to fund whatever reforms are proposed in any new strategy.

The magistracy has survived by being flexible, open-minded, and by adapting its role throughout the past 650 years; today, such agility is required more so than ever before. We must concentrate on our strengths and our USP, which is that in England and Wales nobody can be convicted, or remain convicted, without the agreement of laypeople, whether they be juries or magistrates. By improving their overall competence, magistrates will continue to retain the confidence of the general public and maintain their crucial position within the Criminal Justice System.

GLOSSARY

I have tried to use as little legal jargon as possible throughout the book, and hopefully these definitions will help make some sense out of what I have written.

Appeal A defendant can appeal any magistrates' court sentence or conviction to the Crown Court. A circuit judge, sitting with two magistrates uninvolved with the initial hearing, hears such appeals.

Attendance Centre A place where groups of young offenders aged 18-24 are sent for three hours on alternate weekend afternoons, for a total of between 12 and 36 hours, to learn life skills and discuss and address their offending behaviour.

Caution A caution is an out-of-court disposal administered by the police. It forms part of someone's criminal record and can only be given if the person admits to the offence and agrees to the caution.

Community Order A sentence for mid-level offences. It can last for up to three years and will include one or more requirements including Rehabilitation Activity, an alcohol treatment, a curfew, or unpaid work.

Conditional Discharge (CD) The court makes a conditional discharge if it thinks it is inappropriate to punish given the nature of the offence and the character of the defendant. The defendant must stay out of trouble for the duration of the CD. If they are convicted of another offence during the life of the order, then they may also be sentenced for the original offence.

Cracked trial A case listed for trial which does not proceed, either because the defendant changes his plea to guilty, or pleads to an alternative charge, or because the prosecution offer no evidence.

Criminal Procedure Rules (CPR) The Criminal Procedure Rules determine the way a case is managed and set out the process that must be followed as it progresses through all the criminal courts in England and Wales.

Crown Court Established in 1972, the Crown Court deals with appeals and committals for sentence from magistrates' courts, as well as jury trials and the sentencing of those convicted in the Crown Court.

Crown Prosecution Service (CPS) CPS lawyers advise the police on charging decisions and prosecute at all levels of the criminal justice system.

Curfew A curfew can be imposed as part of a community order or a suspended sentence, is electronically monitored (if available), and can last for up to 12 months for between two and 16 hours in any one day.

Defendant The defendant is the person accused of committing an offence.

Disclosure The prosecution has a duty to disclose, to the defence, material gathered during the investigation of a criminal offence, which is not intended to be used as evidence against the defendant, but which may undermine the prosecution case or assist the defence case.

District Judge A District Judge is a professionally qualified lawyer, who sits in magistrates' courts and has the same decision-making powers as a bench of magistrates.

Duty Solicitor Duty solicitors are paid from the legal aid fund to advise and represent defendants at their first court appearance, but they cannot represent defendants at trial.

Effective trial An effective trial in a magistrates' court is a trial that commences on the day it is scheduled and reaches a verdict (See also: rare as hen's teeth!).

Either Way offences These are mid-range offences that can be heard in either a magistrates' or Crown Court. The defendant retains the right to choose jury trial at the Crown Court, but otherwise magistrates determine the venue for trial.

eJudiciary A service using a Microsoft platform that provides secure e-mail and access to judicial information and training materials.

Indictable only The most serious offences, including murder, manslaughter, rape, and robbery, which must be tried at the Crown Court.

Ineffective trial A trial that is unable to proceed on the scheduled trial date, and is adjourned to a later date.

Lawyers Lawyers tend to be solicitors in a magistrates' court, but occasionally a barrister might take the role. The defence advocate is there to advise the defendant and the prosecutor is there to prove the defendant's guilt.

Legal Adviser Legal advisers are professionally qualified lawyers who assist the magistrates by explaining points of law and helping to manage the cases before the court. All decisions are taken by the magistrates, but with due regard to the professional advice offered by the legal adviser.

List Caller The list caller's job is to bring people in and out of the courtroom and ensure everyone is in the right place at the right time. The list caller also helps the legal adviser with administrative tasks.

Magistrates Magistrates decide if defendants have committed the offence they are accused of, and how to deal with them if they have. They normally sit in benches of three and make their decisions collectively with each magistrate, irrespective of their experience, having the same voice in the decision-making process. The presiding justice sits in the middle and acts as the spokesperson for the whole bench. The magistrates on either side are referred to as wingers.

Newton Hearing A Newton hearing is held when the defendant pleads guilty to varied facts that differ from the specific accusations of the prosecution. The magistrates will listen to both parties and decide which to believe and then sentence accordingly.

Police and Criminal Evidence Act 1984 (PACE) The PACE codes of practice regulate police powers to combat crimes and behaviour while protecting the rights of the public. They cover:

- Stop and search
- Arrest
- Detention
- Investigation
- Identification
- Interviewing detainees

Post-Sentence Supervision (PSS) Post-sentence supervision is a requirement which is applied to all offenders who receive a sentence of less than two years' imprisonment. It provides a second supervision period to assist in the rehabilitation of the offender following on from the offender completing their licence period.

Pre-trial application An application usually made by the prosecution to the court to introduce certain forms of evidence in a trial (e.g., bad character).

Probation Probation officers provide the court with advice on sentencing, rehabilitation of offenders, managing offender behaviour, and also administer most community penalties.

Public Virtually all cases held in a magistrates' court involving an adult defendant are open to the public.

Special measures The provision of special measures enable vulnerable or intimidated witnesses in a criminal trial to give their best evidence. Special measures include giving evidence though a live TV link, screens around the witness box, and intermediaries.

Summary offences Summary offences are heard only by a magistrates' court. They include many motoring offences but also offences such as common assault and criminal damage of up to £5,000.

Suspended Sentence A custodial sentence available to defendants aged 18 and over. The custodial sentence can be suspended for a period of between six months and two years. A defendant who is convicted of any offence during the operational period of the order can expect to have the suspended sentence activated, and serve some or all of the entire original prison sentence, unless it is considered unjust to do so.

Witness The witness gives evidence from the witness box. They answer questions put to them by the prosecution, defence advocates, and the magistrates. They give either an affirmation or oath to tell the truth during their evidence.

BIBLIOGRAPHY

Afzal, Nazir. *The Prosecutor,* Ebury Press, 2020

Atkins, Chris. *A Bit of a Stretch: The Diaries of a Prisoner,* Atlantic Books, 2020

Auld, Sir Robin. *Review of the Criminal Courts of England and Wales,* Stationery Office Books, 2001

Clegg, William. *Under the Wig: A Lawyer's Stories of Murder, Guilt and Innocence,* Quercus, 2019

Gibbs, Penelope. *Fit for purpose: do magistrates get the training and development they need?* Transform Justice, 2014

Grove, Trevor. *The Magistrate's Tale: A Frontline Report from a New JP,* Bloomsbury Publishing, 2003

Henriques, Richard. *From Crime to Crime,* Hodder & Stoughton, 2020

House of Commons Justice Committee. *Follow-up Report on the Role of the Magistracy,* 2019

Langford, Sarah. *In Your Defence,* Black Swan, 2019

Leveson, Sir Brian. *Review of Efficiency in Criminal Proceedings,* 2015

Ministry of Justice. *The strengths and skills of the Judiciary in the Magistrates' Courts,* Ipsos MORI, 2013

Riddle, Howard & Zara, Robert. *Essential Magistrates' Courts Law,* Waterside Press, 2019

Secret Barrister. *The Secret Barrister: Stories of the Law and How It's Broken,* Picador, 2018

Sentencing Council, *Sentencing Guidelines*

Smartt, Ursula. *"Without fear or favour, affection or ill will": the lay magistracy in the 21st century,* Magistrate Magazine, June/July 2020

Sutherland, John. *Crossing the Line,* W&N, 2020

The Criminal Law Review, *Issue 3,* 2020
Turow, Scott. *The Last Trial*, Mantle, 2020

Another book that might interest you…

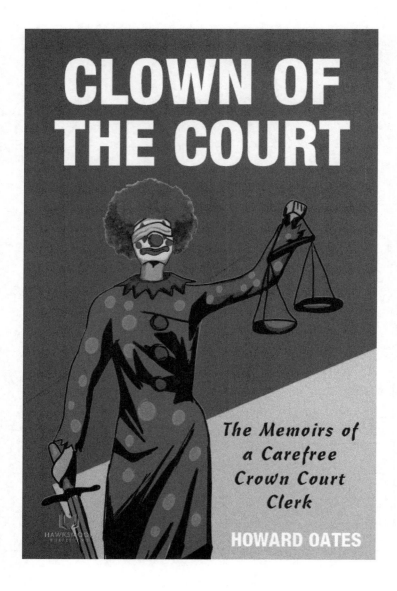

CLOWN OF THE COURT

The Memoirs of a Carefree Crown Court Clerk

HOWARD OATES